HAROLD NICOLSON

was born in Tehran, Persia, in 1887, where
his father, the late Sir Arthur Nicolson, 1st
Baron Carnock, was British *chargé d'affaires*.
Before beginning his education in England,
Mr. Nicolson lived successively in Constantinople, Budapest, and Tangier. From Wel-
lington College he went to Balliol College,
Oxford, then entered the Foreign Office and
the Diplomatic Service, in which he was
alternately engaged in various capitals from
1909 to 1929. He resigned from the Diplomatic Service in 1929 to devote himself to
writing. His main literary concern has been
with biography. The first, a life of Verlaine,
was published in 1921. It was followed by
"Tennyson," "Byron, The Last Journey,"
and "Swinburne". In 1926, he published
"Some People", a delightful composite of
biography, autobiography, and fiction; in
1927, "The Development of English Biography", the most up-to-date and concise
manual of the subject. In 1929 appeared Mr.
Nicolson's "Portrait of a Diplomatist", a
life of Lord Carnock, his father, who was a
prominent figure in pre-war European affairs. This was followed by "Peacemaking:
1919", the author's personal recollections
of the peace Conference with a summary of
its achievements and failures. As the third
part of this political trilogy of the last half
century, "Lord Curzon, The Last Phase
1919-1925" describes the author's chief as
he knew him and studied his life work.

DWIGHT MORROW

Books by Harold Nicolson

SOME PEOPLE

PAUL VERLAINE
TENNYSON
BYRON: THE LAST JOURNEY
SWINBURNE

SWEET WATERS
PUBLIC FACES

DEVELOPMENT OF ENGLISH BIOGRAPHY

PEOPLE AND THINGS

PORTRAIT OF A DIPLOMATIST
PEACEMAKING, 1919
CURZON: THE LAST PHASE
DWIGHT MORROW

DWIGHT WHITNEY MORROW

Dwight Morrow

BY HAROLD NICOLSON

*Our law surely would say that it is best to keep as tran-
quil as possible in misfortune and not to be vexed or
resentful: for we cannot see what good or evil there is
in such things, and impatience does not in any way
help us forwards; also because nothing in human affairs
deserves serious anxiety, and grief stands in the way to
hinder the self-succour that our duty immediately requires of us.*

PLATO: *Republic:* 604 B

HARCOURT, BRACE AND COMPANY
NEW YORK

first edition

PRINTED IN THE UNITED STATES OF AMERICA
BY QUINN & BODEN COMPANY, INC., RAHWAY, N. J.

Typography by Robert Josephy

Author's Apology

I AM well aware that for an Englishman to write a biography of an American may seem a hazardous, and perhaps impertinent, enterprise. With whatever modesty he may approach his task, however scrupulous may be his endeavor to appreciate the American background, there must always occur some gaps in comprehension, some mistaken attribution of values, some errors in perspective.

My disqualifications are to some extent mitigated by the fact that Dwight Morrow, while remaining completely American, was also something more. Others among his compatriots have been able to realize in their careers or characters all that is most valuable in the American idea. The point about Dwight Morrow is that, while representing the perfected type of American, he also became a model for the completely civilized man. It is thus justifiable to approach him from the human, or universal, rather than from the national, or particular, point of view. And whereas I am unqualified accurately to relate him to his national environment, I hope that I have been able to indicate in their real proportions the contributions which he made to international thought.

The influence which he exercised upon those who worked with him in the New World and the Old was both durable and intense. It was not merely that he was able to interpret Europe to America and to give to Europe a fresh conception of the American mind in action; it was also that he created a new pattern for the practice and the theory of diplomacy. He demonstrated that coöperation between the peoples of the world can more effectively be achieved by a meticulous though tolerant investigation of basic facts than by any adjustments of current political or economic theories. He demonstrated also that the hurried imprecisions of democratic diplomacy are but frivolous factors in the stream of progressive evolution, and that effective agreements bearing upon concrete points are more valuable to mankind than any ineffective idealisms however righteous or comprehensive these may seem.

His ideas, his methods, and his technique were not improvised as sudden expedients to meet the needs of the moment. They were patiently evolved from his early ethics and later education, and patiently confirmed by the discipline of study, the lessons of experience, and the processes of trial and error. My task has been to trace the development of this ideology throughout his life.

It would be invidious to mention by name all those who, in the United States, in France, in Mexico, and in England, have assisted me in the compilation of this biography. Certain specific acknowledgments must, however, be made.

To Colonel E. G. Lowry I am grateful for his action, not only in placing at my disposal the rich store of material which he had collected, but also for postponing a study of Dwight Morrow on which he himself had been engaged. To Miss Madelon M. Shiff I am indebted for expert secretarial assistance and for valuable research. To General Jay J. Morrow, to his sisters Mrs. Scandrett, Miss Alice Morrow and Mrs. McIlvaine, as well as to his nephew Richard Scandrett, I must express my thanks for the patience and sympathy with which they have furthered my investigations.

My obligations to Mrs. Dwight Morrow and to her immediate family are apparent in every line of this book. Without her support and encouragement I could not have hoped to achieve an authentic portrait of this most magnanimous man.

H. N.

Cuernavaca, March 1935

CONTENTS

The affairs of the Equitable Office Building Corporation — The affairs of the Utah Power & Light Company — His brief on behalf of the latter.

order to leave the field clear for examination of more important activities — Difficulty of defining what was personal work of an individual and what corporate work of firm as a whole — Early cases, Pere Marquette and New Haven common stock — The Erie Railroad mortgages — The Kennecott Copper Corporation — Other activities — The mutualization of the Equitable — The affairs of Interborough Rapid Transit Company — The rescue of Mr. W. C. Durant — His home atmosphere — Reminiscences and sketches by his two elder daughters.

the Trust Companies banquet — His views on the League of Nations and the ratification controversy — Realism and prescience of his opinion — Reconstruction loans — The debt problem — The saving of Austria — His "statistical survey" of French economic and financial conditions — Nature of his sympathy for France.

Morrow is offered the presidency of Yale — He refuses and thereafter regrets his refusal — Amherst and Alexander Meiklejohn — Causes of the controversy — Reasons why it became an issue of national importance — Morrow's distress at failure to achieve a compromise — His private fortunes — Nassau — Panama — His mother's death — His work in Cuba — American policy towards the Island Republic — The Platt Amendment — Morrow's original interpretation of that Amendment — The Sugar Tariff and Herbert Hoover — The Zayas Administration — Morrow arranges two Cuban loans — The lessons he derived from his Cuban experiences.

Death of President Harding — Morrow's relation towards, and opinion of, Calvin Coolidge — Although new President offers Morrow no immediate employment, fact of their intimacy increases latter's prestige — His refusal to exploit that intimacy — The Reparations question — Morrow hopes to be appointed Agent General but is disappointed — Further reconstruction loans — Morrow on the debt settlements — Appointed to Aircraft Board — Origins of that Board — Its procedure — Its recommendations — Colonel William Mitchell — The Morrow report increases his public reputation — His name mentioned as Secretary of Treasury, Ambassador

ILLUSTRATIONS

DWIGHT MORROW

THE origins of the Morrow family are obscure.

Dwight Morrow, being indifferent to genealogies, remained content with the belief that his forbears had vaguely
immigrated from Ireland. There were occasions, on subsequent transatlantic journeys, when he would watch the
Fastnet light throb out across dark waters and would hum
to himself, gaily but incorrectly, "The Wearing of the
Green." It may be questioned whether there was any firm
foundation for these intermittent Celtic appeals. The sur-
name of Morrow is unfamiliar in southern Ireland, whereas
in Ulster it is common enough. We may assume that the
Morrows were of Lowland Scottish stock, richly improved
by residing for a hundred years or more in northern Ireland.
The stuff of his heredity was akin to the tenacious material
of County Antrim or of County Down.

The first member of the family to assume identifiable
shape is a certain Alexander Morrow who sailed for America
in the early years of the nineteenth century and settled in
the panhandle area of what is now West Virginia. This
Alexander Morrow staked out a farm on the eastern bank
of the Ohio River, in a district which is now called Han-

3

cock County, in a locality which now bears the name of Fairview, and at a point on the river almost exactly opposite the spot where today stands the town of Toronto, Ohio.

A younger son of Alexander Morrow transferred himself and his children across the border to Kentucky, but the elder branch retained the old homestead in Hancock County, and it was there, on March 28, 1837, that James Elmore Morrow, father of Dwight Morrow, was born.

Although the eldest son of a family of seven, James Elmore Morrow displayed no desire to carry on the yeoman traditions of his ancestors, and from his earliest childhood it was realized that his gifts were not agricultural but academic. He was sent to Jefferson College, from which he graduated in 1856, hoping thereafter to enter the profession of the law. The straitened circumstances of his family did not allow him to indulge in the luxury of such an ambition, and he felt obliged to accept immediate employment as teacher in the village school at Fairview. This occupation was interrupted by the Civil War. James Morrow, being a strong abolitionist, joined the Union forces and enlisted in the First Virginia Regiment. He became a corporal; he was wounded; he was promoted captain. His ensuing desire to remain in the army was not encouraged by his superior officers, who felt that the then state of his health did not qualify him for a successful military career. He thus returned to the profession of school teacher, in which capacity he served with credit and integrity until his death in 1904.

During the Civil War, James Morrow had met Clara Johnson, who, with gay efficiency, was winding bandages at Wheeling. In September 1867 they married. Although born in Ohio, Clara Johnson had been reared at Bethany, Virginia. Her mother, Mrs. John Jay Johnson, whose maiden

name had been Rebecca Jeffers, was of the southern type
and possessed some aristocratic tendencies. She was apt, as
her grandson subsequently recorded, to "inquire into family
connections." In the course of this inquiry she evolved the
theory that her own grandfather had been a first cousin of
Chief Justice Marshall. In later years, Dwight Morrow,
under pressure from his relations, caused this legend to be
investigated. It was found to be optimistic. "We shall have,"
Dwight Morrow wrote to his mother, "to get along without
it." Yet a southern flavor did in fact hang about Mrs. John
Jay Johnson, and from this her daughter inherited, not indeed any aristocratic pretensions or symptoms, but a certain warm-hearted gaiety, a sympathetic tolerance, which
blended happily with the more rigid austerities of Hancock
County and of Ohio.

To this union between James Elmore Morrow and Clara
Johnson eight children were born.[1] The problem of rearing
a rapidly expanding family upon the earnings of a school
teacher was one by which James Morrow was continually

[1] Namely: (1) *Agnes*, b. Jan. 27, 1869, married, July 1890, Richard Brown
Scandrett, and had issue (a) Richard B. Scandrett, Jr., b. April 12, 1891, married, October 1930, Mary Emma Landenberger, and had issue, Nancy Day, b.
May 8, 1932, Dwight Morrow, b. June 26, 1933, and Eugenia, b. April 22,
1935; (b) Rebekah Scandrett, b. July 10, 1893, married, September 1921, Lucien
Greathouse; (c) Jay Johnson Morrow Scandrett, b. October 16, 1895, married
firstly, June 1929, Marian Satterthwaite, secondly, July 1933, Ernestine Cooper.
(2) *Jay Johnson*, b. February 20, 1870, married, October 1895, Harriet M. Butler (d. May 1935), entered Engineer Corps of U. S. Army, Brigadier General,
Chief Engineer of 1st U. S. Army in France, Governor of Panama Canal Zone
1919-1924, Chairman Special Commission on Boundaries Tacna-Arica Arbitration.
(3) *Alice*, b. July 23, 1871, Resident Trustee of American College for Girls,
Constantinople. (4) *Dwight Whitney*, b. January 11, 1873, d. October 5, 1931—
the subject of this memoir. (5) *Hilda*, b. October 9, 1874, married, July 1900,
Rev. Edwin Linton McIlvaine, and has issue (a) Ruth McIlvaine, b. November
19, 1901, married, December 1927, Frederic Voorhees; (b) Rebekah McIlvaine,
b. 1903, d. 1905; (c) James Morrow McIlvaine, b. June 10, 1905; (d) Katharine
McIlvaine, b. June 16, 1907, married, May 1931, James Kenric Leighton. (6)
Fred Walton, (7) *Earl Alexander*, (8) *Ralph Benson*, who died in infancy.

oppressed. In the whole course of his career his annual salary never rose above $1800, and during the first twenty years of married life their joint income did not exceed $1500. Nor did the thrift which he was thus obliged to practice and enjoin come readily to a man addicted to impulses of generosity and afflicted with a passion for possessing books. Clara Morrow confronted the situation with humorous, but by no means uncomplaining, efficiency. It was she who did most of the housework in the early days and who sat up at night mending the children's clothes. "Yes," she would answer to some admiring visitor, "far too many books: far too little money." Never did Clara Morrow lose the habits of outspoken economy then acquired. In later years when her son (a partner in J. P. Morgan & Co.) would send her presents, she would temper her gratitude with words of warning. "Dwight," she would say, "you will surely end in the poorhouse," echoing in that cautionary phrase the gay but harassed vigilance of her early motherhood.

In 1871 James Morrow was offered and accepted the post of President of Marshall College at Huntington, West Virginia. The title attached to this position was more lavish than its emoluments, although the latter were supplemented by free lodging within the college building. It was in these small rooms that, on January 11, 1873, Dwight Whitney Morrow was born.[2]

2

More than fifty years later, and six years after his mother's death, Dwight Morrow revisited the place of his birth. In

[2] "My father," he recorded later, "was a great admirer of the late William Dwight Whitney (the Yale grammarian). He named me Dwight Whitney be-

June of 1928 he was accorded an honorary degree at Marshall College, and in replying to the customary allocution he referred with pride to the difficulties which his parents had then surmounted. "Those," he said, "were meagre days in this college," and as a tribute to the faith and endurance of his father and mother he enlarged upon his favorite theme, the "tragedy and glory of a teacher's life."

For James Elmore Morrow, during the early 'seventies, there was in truth but little overt glory. In that same year, 1873, he left Marshall College for the normal school at West Liberty, and in 1875 he was appointed to the Oakdale Academy near Pittsburgh. In 1876 he became teacher of mathematics at the Central High School in Pittsburgh itself, and three years later he received the post of principal of an elementary school, the Fifth Ward School at Allegheny. This appointment he held for ten years.

It was thus around Pittsburgh and Allegheny that Dwight Morrow's earliest memories were condensed; and it was against the heavy atmosphere of an expanding industrial region that the preoccupied benignity of his father, the worldly wisdom of Grandmother Johnson, the gay and sometimes irritable vivacity of his mother, the rock-like devotion of his sisters Agnes and Alice, the calm virility of his brother Jay, the prattle of his younger siblings, assumed definite shapes and outlines in his consciousness.

It would be well to analyze in greater detail the elements of this Allegheny background. Not so much because Dwight Morrow (that extreme individualist) derived many habits of thought from the monochrome of his childhood, but rather because it was almost as a reaction against the rigidities of

cause our family was a large family and the family names, like James, John, and Alexander, were many, many times repeated."

7

his early education that he evolved that tolerant mobility of mind which was the very essence of his intelligence.

It is a temptation, when faced with this contrast between early doctrine and later philosophy, to exaggerate either the certitude of a father's convictions or the narrowness with which these convictions were enforced. James Elmore Morrow was tenacious, precise, and uncompromising; he was agreeable rather than amenable, and his career suffered accordingly; yet it would be a grave mistake to picture him as either bigoted or obtuse. His love of learning was passionate in its sincerity; his culture was both wide and deep; he possessed great pedagogic talent; he was a scholar both in Hebrew and in Latin; and as a mathematician he was endowed with capacities far higher than any provincial circle could either recognize or absorb.

Mrs. James Morrow again—small, stout, bustling, practical, and sharp—was more than shrewd and more than merry; she was frequently witty and acute. There was nothing grim or dark about Dwight Morrow's childhood; it was strenuous, congested, intensive, penurious, happy, competitive, and crude. The rope of Morrow's personality was twisted from many strands, some silken and some of hemp. The subtleties of his nature were delicate and various; yet in and out of these subtleties was entwined a sturdy hempen strand. These strong fibres of insensitiveness contrasted curiously with the delicate antennae of perception which he subsequently developed. The problem, and therefore the fascination, of his personality is to be sought in the strange association of, the even stranger disassociation between, such silken and such hempen materials. The more delicate elements in his nature derived, it may be supposed, from his Johnson and Jeffers forbears, and were enforced by that

8

gentle standard of cultural integrity which is the glory of the American teaching class. The sturdier elements have a more directly pioneer origin and derive from the old homestead in Hancock County and from the banks of the Ohio River.

It would be a mistake again to paint in too sombre colors the smoke and squalor of this Allegheny period. Today the town of Allegheny has been absorbed into the city of Pittsburgh and shares the saddened industrialism of that distressing spot. Yet in the 'eighties Allegheny was still an autonomous township, separated from its adjoining monster not only by the Ohio River, but by its own eponym, the river Allegheny—a word which, in the Indian language, signifies "clear water." There were light green trees, in those days, upon Brunot's Island: the steel bridges did not at that time crush the horizon: and the hills above Sheraden were not, as now, veiled in an almost perpetual shroud of smoke.

The Morrow family, in those early days, lived in a two-storied little house at No. 52 (now 1720) Franklin Street. The whole district has since deteriorated, but in those days it was a pleasant quarter containing many semi-detached and even detached residences. The Morrow home was not detached: it was merely the second in a row of six red brick houses having no pretensions either to social or to architectural elegance.

Franklin Street was in itself a gay and cobbled roadway, tripping down quite happily from Allegheny Avenue, past the Presbyterian Chapel, past a large house and garden on the left, to the muddied flats of the Ohio River, where the towboats chunked and hooted in front of their attendant coal barges. In spring there would be a scent of lilac in the roadway, and in autumn the maple would flame scarlet

9

against the small wooden houses on either hand. Behind No. 52 ran an alley, at that time well adapted to the game of marbles, but today decayed into a dank and cemented passage. The whole atmosphere of the place was suburban, neighborly, and small.

Dwight Morrow's subsequent feelings for Allegheny were dutiful but not affectionate. As a young man in Pittsburgh he would sometimes return to Franklin Street and revisit the haunts of his childhood. The feelings with which these visits inspired him were appropriate rather than warm. A letter to his sister Agnes, dated July 30, 1902, describes a somewhat stilted evocation:

". . . Yesterday evening I went down to the Pattersons to see Mrs. Patterson and Leslie. May was there as was also our old friend Alex Marion. Mamma said, 'Ha! I told you so, I told you so!' We played bridge whist all evening. The place down there has been changed less than any part of Allegheny I know. As I walked from Beaver Avenue down I could see the little old brick house at '52' where we were brought up, and the place where the Lewises lived and where the Caskeys lived on the corner. I wanted to run through that alley back of that row of houses, to see how it would feel. The houses seem horribly crowded and close together and the people did not seem to be as nice as they used to be. And the church up there on Market Street seemed to me much smaller than it used to be. Still I always feel that that church was the last one to which I went regularly. I never got acquainted with the people at our Central Church. If I get home for a Sunday in September you and I will have to go down to that old church, dear. We'll try and sit in the pew where Jay used to fight me for the corner.

"But there! if I write this way maybe I'll make you as blue as I was when I walked down there last night. Still, I think it's a good thing to be thrown up against the people and places we

JAMES ELMORE MORROW   1837-1904

knew when we were little ones. It really oughtn't to make us altogether blue, either. We have to give up the freedom from big troubles and the childish faith in everything when we grow up, but we get a lot of things in their places, things we wouldn't give up even to be free from the suffering that comes with them. . . ."

Even when we discount Morrow's habitual indifference to his physical surroundings, it is evident that Allegheny, as a place, left little impress either upon his memory or his emotions.

3

Yet when the street door was shut on Franklin Street, when the student lamp with the green glass shade was set in the centre of the round table; then indeed would encompass him an atmosphere—intensive, unforgettable, distinct. Night after night the five elder children would be grouped around the green lamp; would tie behind their ears the cardboard eyeshades on which their father insisted; would spread their primers and their copybooks beside them, and, turning slantingly from the table so that the light should fall from the left angle, would concentrate upon the preparation of tomorrow's lesson. There would be McGuffey's "Readers" or Ridpath's "History of the United States," or Eaton's "Common School Arithmetic," or Mitchell's "Geography." The basket chair in the window creaked slightly as their mother, intent upon her sewing, reached forward for another strand of wool. Their grandmother, from time to time, would interrupt them with some passage from a weekly paper. Their father, about to leave them for some night class, would pace the floor restlessly, pausing now and then to lean over the shoulder of one of his children; pointing out some error here, suggesting there some explanation; interrupting them at moments with a problem in mental arithmetic, scratching his head with a contented chuckle if that problem were solved.

"Pater," records his eldest daughter, "was very religious." He was, in fact, a presiding elder of the local Presbyterian church. The religious education of the Morrow children was thus no less intensive than their instruction in arithmetic. There were family prayers at half-past seven in the morning and again at bedtime. There were special Bible readings on Wednesdays, an ordeal rendered the more exacting owing to the inability of their father to understand how any Christian, however small, could fail to possess his own miraculous knowledge of the Concordance. Sunday was a day of strict domestic discipline, consisting of Sunday school in addition to both morning and evening services. All secular reading was on that day prohibited and no toys or visitors were allowed. This deprivation was not so serious as might be supposed. In the first place, the Morrow children possessed few toys, and Dwight and his brother would amuse themselves by cutting the semblances of soldiers out of magazine covers, at which they would fire through cannon constructed of spools of paper, pencils, and elastic bands. In the second place, Jay Morrow discovered that if one thoroughly pulled out the upper drawer which contained the Sunday books one could reach down to the drawer below, in which such unholy volumes as the biographies of Washington and Lincoln or the works of Dickens were locked on Saturday night.

Then there was the Catechism—the "Shorter Presbyterian Catechism"—which consisted of one hundred and seven questions which the Morrow children were expected to answer before the age of six.

"What," Mr. James Morrow would inquire sternly of Dwight, aged five, *"what* are the outward and ordinary means whereby Christ communicateth to us the benefits of redemption?" "The outward and ordinary means," Dwight would answer, "by which Christ communicateth to us the benefits of redemption are His ordinances, especially the word, sacrament and prayer, all of which are made effectual to the elect for salvation."

If he answered correctly all the hundred and seven questions he was given five cents with which to buy a stick of licorice.

He was not a strong child. He was frail and tiny, and even as an infant he suffered from those headaches which became the bane of his early and middle life. It may be doubted whether, had it not been for cod-liver oil, he would ever have survived. As it was, three of his brothers died in infancy. His physical development was moreover impaired by his falling out of an apple tree at the age of twelve. His arm was broken and was so ill set that it came to rest ever after at a slightly obtuse angle, thereby adding something incongruous to a frame which, even in later middle age, puzzled the superficial observer by its combination of force, delicacy, aggressiveness, and diffidence. Although between the ages of fourteen and fifteen he added several inches to his height, he always remained a very small man, whereas the later proportion between his short if stocky body and the magnificent calibre of his head imposed, at first meeting, a slightly disconcerting impression. The psychological anomaly of Dwight Morrow was from the outset indicated by a physical departure from all familiar type.

His father was aware of this physical debility and was careful, while stimulating his precocity, not to expose him to excessive strain. Dwight was thus able to graduate from High School at the premature age of fourteen. He was in fact chosen to deliver the valedictory oration for his graduating class. He selected for his theme the text of Deuteronomy XI, verse 29:

"And it shall come to pass when the Lord thy God hath brought thee in unto the land whither thou goest to possess it, that thou shalt put the blessing upon mount Gerizim, and the curse upon mount Ebal."

There are those who still recall the oration which Dwight Morrow delivered on that occasion. The pallor of his childish face reflected the white starch of his Eton collar. He rose tiny in the tribune, shaking a small fist wherewith he fulminated against mount Ebal or pointing a hopeful finger upwards when it came to Gerizim. His gestures on that occasion had been suggested to him by Miss Fanny Walker, the Allegheny instructress in elocution. Having disposed of Ebal with a final gesture of fulmination, Dwight Morrow devoted the rest of his life to the cult of Gerizim.

4

The most important influence of these early years was, it should be noted, the intensive study of mathematics. James Elmore Morrow, as has already been remarked, was a great mathematician. He impressed his children with the moral and esthetic beauty of that science, and the mental habits which Dwight Morrow then formed were essentially mathematical habits. In a letter written to a friend in July 1917 he has left on record the exact effect of his father's teaching upon the subsequent balance of his mind:

"The real difficulty of it was that we had been taught to multiply coefficients. We all forgot that the base 2 in the problem, as you have stated it, is not properly a coefficient because of the exponent that is annexed to it. That is to say, if you multiply $2^{2n} + 2$ by $2^{2n} - 2$ the answer is 2^{4n}. Most of us answered the question 4^{4n}, which, of course, was ridiculous.

"While I was at Amherst—and for two or three years after graduation—I tutored in mathematics. I always went out of my way to hammer in the very principle that was involved in that little problem. It is really rather a big principle of life. That is to say, to deal with realities and not appearances. It is the difference between having your feet on the ground and somewhere up in the air, and the principle is the same whether you are dealing with algebra, or law, or international loans.

"I sometimes think that one of the most valuable expressions that my father used in his mathematical teaching was one that he used to give me very often when I was ten or twelve years old. He was fond of saying that in mathematics you never asked a man to agree with you, but you defied him to disagree with you. This was his method of making you realize that spelling, in a sense, depended upon a convention; mathematics, on the contrary, depended upon something much more fundamental than that. There was no way of coaxing a man to agree that the three angles of a triangle make two right angles. Human beings could not make it anything other, granting our fundamental axioms with relation to space."

Meanwhile his brother Jay, having worked for a time in a coffin factory at Pittsburgh, was admitted to West Point, embarking thereby upon what proved a highly honorable career in the Engineer Corps of the United States Army Dwight, being three years his junior, was determined to follow this example. He obtained employment, first as board boy at the Pittsburgh Stock Exchange, and then with the Hostetter Coke Company. In the evenings his father would coach him in the technical subjects required for the West Point examination. He presented himself for that examination in the late autumn of 1890 and easily gained the first place. It happened, however, that a certain Francis Siviter, who stood second on the list, possessed political influence with the local congressman, Colonel Bayne. The appointment was thus accorded, not to Morrow, but to Francis Siviter.

Even if Colonel Bayne's ideas of justice had been as acute as his political sensibility, it may be questioned whether Dwight Morrow would ever have been admitted into the military academy. His small size, his delicate digestion, his constant headaches, and the disadvantage of his ill-set arm would in all probability have disqualified him on medical grounds alone. Yet the actual circumstances of his rejection inspired him with an acute sense of injustice which rankled for several years. He was never a man who accepted defeat with any readiness, having inherited from his father that tenacious quality which earned for the principal of the Fifth Ward School the nickname of "bulldog Morrow." Dwight, for his part, refused to submit to the injustice of Congressman Bayne without a further combat; he appealed direct to the President of the United States.

The text of this appeal, written in an angry boyish hand, runs as follows:

Allegheny, Pa.
January 3, 1891

President Harrison
Washington, D. C.

Dear Sir:

I do not want to trouble you or take the time for which you may have some more important duty; but I would like to state my case, if you would allow me a few moments. About three months ago in our district (the 23rd Pennsylvania) a West Point Competitive examination was announced and as I had always desired an education I studied hard for it and with several other boys was examined. When the result of the examination was announced I was notified by the Committee, appointed by Congressman Bayne, that I had come out first and would receive the appointment. It was published in the newspapers by the Committee and I thought the matter was settled, until I noticed in the paper that Mr. Siviter who came in second had been appointed by the Secretary of War. I wrote to Col. Bayne and he replied that as my brother (J. J. Morrow) now represents this district he had thought best to recommend the one who had come in second. He said that he was sorry but the matter had gone beyond his control. I have been working here in the city and it seemed very hard after being officially notified by the Committee that I would receive the appointment and after having laid aside a portion of the $100.00 deposit necessary to enter, to be debarred of my only chance of getting an education because my brother won the cadetship on a competitive four years ago. In the West Point register I can find no ban placed upon relatives of the present cadets. Indeed, I had always thought and had always been taught to think, that in America where everyone is supposed to fight for himself, no family ties either aid or retard one. We are told that the Military Academy is open to all.

When Col. Bayne wrote that Mr. Siviter had already been

appointed it seemed at first that I must give up all hopes of entering the Military Academy, but I see by the register that the President has the power to appoint ten every four years. I suppose that these are all promised or taken, but I have thought that in the event of the failure of any one of the present cadets appointed at large, you might see fit to appoint me in his place. I have no influential or political friends to press my suit.

I am only a poor boy with the one circumstance in my favor of having won the appointment once. Could you see your way to promise me that if any of the Cadets fail in the January examination you would appoint me to go in June? A dissapointment [*sic*] of the kind I received may not seem very much to a man in your position; but if you were ever a poor boy, with a poor boy's ambitions you can appreciate my position.

Anxiously awaiting a reply I remain

Very Respectfully Yours

Dwight W. Morrow

There is no record to show that this appeal received from the White House anything more than a perfunctory acknowledgment. Yet the situation, from Dwight Morrow's point of view, was serious enough. In the past four years he had devoted all his spare time to preparing for West Point; on January 11, 1891, he reached his eighteenth birthday; a military career had been denied him, and the only other profession which offered sufficient scope for his ardent ambition was the profession of the law; the law, in its turn, suggested the necessity of a college degree; yet how, with so short a time at his disposal, could he hope to master the many unknown subjects which were at that date required for matriculation?

His father, in 1889, had left the red brick, the asphalt, the huge flagstaff, and the iron railings of the Fifth Ward

DWIGHT MORROW, AGED ABOUT ELEVEN

School and had been appointed, after a spell at the Normal School of Slippery Rock, professor of mathematics at Allegheny High School, of which institution he became principal in 1891. The family meanwhile had migrated up the hill from Franklin Street, first to Pennsylvania, and then to Irwin, Avenue. These changes had effected but little improvement in the family budget. How could James Morrow possibly afford to send his younger son to college?

Dwight Morrow was able, by the infectious quality of his own self-confidence, to convince a father already prepared, for such high purpose to run financial risk and endure personal sacrifice. Dwight obtained a post at four dollars a week in the County Treasurer's office and gave such satisfaction that he was promised similar employment during his college vacations. While engaged in this function he evolved a technique which is of some phrenological interest. His duty was that of furnishing receipts for the taxes paid in over the counter of the Treasurer's office. By taking two pens and writing simultaneously with his left and his right hand he was able to fill in both the foil and the counterfoil at the same moment. This capacity for mental duplication remained with him throughout his life; he was one of those rare people who can speak intelligently and listen intelligently at the same time.

The County Treasurer's office, although it secured him a salary during those months when he was cramming Greek and Latin with a view to college matriculation, and while it offered him a prospect of pocket money during the vacation, provided no real solution of the financial problem. It was hoped vaguely that he would be able to support himself at college by tutoring the richer but less advanced of his fellow-students, and it was with this hope that he presented himself for matriculation at Washington and Jefferson. He was asked, on the first day, to work out a mathematical theorem. He produced the correct solution, but he arrived at it by an unconventional method. "We do not," said the examiner, "expect freshmen to do original work." Dwight Morrow was so incensed by such obscurantism that he lost all further interest in the examination. It was at this stage that his luck turned.

Professor Henry Gibbons, Amherst '73, had from 1874 to 1880 been teacher of Greek at Pittsburgh High School, and had come to know the Morrow family and to appreciate their ability and determination. In June of 1890 Mr. Gibbons received the appointment of professor of Greek at Amherst College. On hearing that Dwight Morrow had failed to matriculate at Washington and Jefferson he suggested that he should try for Amherst. There were only four days in which to prepare for his examination, and although Dwight did brilliantly in mathematics, he failed in Greek, Cicero, Virgil, Latin composition, and Ancient History. Professor Gibbons was able none the less to persuade the Amherst faculty to admit Dwight Morrow conditionally. There were eight separate "conditions" attached to his admission, and he was informed that unless he satisfied the faculty by passing tests in each of these eight subjects he would not be allowed to remain at Amherst after his first year.

It was under such disabilities that Dwight Morrow entered Amherst in September 1891 at the age of eighteen and a half.

This and his marriage were for him the most humanizing events in his life.

II. Amherst   1891–1895

THE Connecticut River, wide and powerful, flows from
New Hampshire to Long Island Sound. The meadows of
Massachusetts rise from that lovely valley, climbing in tiers
—half hill, half mountain—to Mount Holyoke in the south,
to Mount Lincoln in the northeast; forming a semi-circle
enclosed, at one end, by the firm outline of the Holyoke
Range and, at the other, by the more gentle contours of
the Pelham Hills.

Between the river and the uplands, some four miles distant from either, stands Amherst College, resting upon its
own dominant but unpretentious eminence. A few houses—
colonial, intimate, and sedate—flank the famous campus,
which spreads as a lawn within a group of splendid trees.
At the axis of this vista the college buildings are unsym-
metrically grouped. Even today the town of Amherst contains little more than five thousand inhabitants.

It was in 1759 that the settlers in East Hadley first peti-
tioned the Massachusetts Legislature for permission to constitute themselves a district, but it was not till 1775 that the
township was actually founded and christened in memory
of Jeffery Amherst, that once competent general, who, hav-

21

ing begun life as a page in the household of the Duke of Dorset at Knole, conquered Canada at the age of forty, thereafter refused to command the British forces against the American colonists, and degenerated finally into a Horse Guards pundit, subservient to the corrupt Toryism of his age.

In 1816, Elijah Dickinson, forbear of Emily Dickinson, persuaded his fellow-citizens to construct a school, largely with their own hands from their own material. In 1821, owing to the initiative of Noah Webster, the lexicographer, this academy was elevated to the dignity of a college, at first devoted to the training of ministers of the Congregational Church. It consisted, at that period, of Johnson Chapel (to this day the central feature of the college), flanked by two bleak dormitories to north and south. A period of decline in the eighteen-forties was followed by a revival under the administration of President Seelye, who realized that the reputation of a college depended upon the quality of its teachers. In 1891, when Dwight Morrow entered, the number of students had risen to 395, of whom 98 were freshmen. Today Amherst College contains some 770 undergraduates.

The love which Dwight Morrow conceived for Amherst remained undimmed until the day of his death. Even after graduation he kept in close contact with his college, becoming secretary, and later president, of the New York Alumni Association, and subsequently trustee, chairman of the finance committee, and chairman of the executive committee of the board of trustees. He took an active part in the campaign for a centennial gift to Amherst in 1921, a campaign which raised more than $3,000,000 in ten days. His own munificence to the college is evidenced by the Morrow dormitory, the Anson Morse professorship, the reconstruction of Johnson Chapel and the improvements in the campus. Yet it was not by monetary gifts alone that he sought to liquidate his debt of gratitude; he was lavish in devoting to Amherst the more precious resources of his energy and time. Today, in his final home at Englewood, the correspondence of his busiest years stands filed in cabinet after cabinet. And year by year, from 1905 to 1931, some twenty per cent of this correspondence is devoted to the interests of his old college.

How is this almost obsessive affection for Amherst to be explained?

It must be realized in the first place that Dwight Morrow was temperamentally grateful. The lavish generosity of his own nature enabled him to receive benefits with humility and without rancor. He possessed also a deep sense of dutifulness, an almost Roman quality of *pietas*. "Look," he would often repeat, "to the pit from which you were digged and the rock from which you were hewn." It is illustrative of his not infrequent intellectual inconsistency that the pit and the rock in his own case appeared always, not in the shape of West Virginia or of Allegheny, but in the lovelier New England shape of Amherst College. He would constantly render thanks to the destiny which had led his footsteps to that academic grove. Again and again, when visiting Amherst in later years, he would drive out to the neighboring township of Sunderland and gaze upon the dedicatory tablet affixed to the local library. "In gratitude"—thus runs the inscription—"to Him who permitted me to be born in this most beautiful valley . . ." Morrow felt that at Amherst he himself had certainly experienced a second birth.

The calm and loveliness of his surroundings—the open stretches of avenue and meadow, the glimpse of wide distances between the trunks of ancient trees—came as a refreshing contrast to the cobbles and congestion, to the smoke and clangor, of Franklin Street and Pittsburgh. Morrow was not a man of sensuous perceptions, nor was he always esthetically conscious of his own environment. Art, music, and nature had little meaning for him, and his interest in poetry was never an instinctive interest, but was directed generally to those poems which his wife and daughters either admired or composed. Yet subconsciously, the beauty of Amherst brought its deep refreshment, forming a sedative background to the more consciously realized excitements of study, companionship, and success.

At Amherst, again, Morrow first attained to a knowledge of his own powers. It was a hard battle and one for which, in all appearance, he was ill-equipped. He entered Amherst as an inconspicuous and rather uncouth freshman; when he left it he was already a man of reputation, influence, assurance, and achievement. Always he loved victory and hated defeat. For him Amherst was forever associated with this the first and most triumphant of many victories, and thus became for him an enduring reservoir of self-encouragement and self-esteem.

To these causes of affection must be added the intense enjoyment which he derived from corporate life. His capacity for friendliness, surpassing even his gift for friendship, amounted to genius. It was at Amherst that he first developed his unbridled taste for conversation. It was at Amherst that his humor, the actual twinkling merriment of his personality, first found their full recognition and their scope. And it was at Amherst that he became aware of his own genius for personal relationships, a talent by which he not merely won the devotion of all conditions of men, but was enabled to conciliate antipathies between other people and to create around himself circles of harmony where previous areas of discord had prevailed.

It was from Amherst, therefore, that he achieved a realization of, and confidence in, his own personality. His gratitude thereafter was colored by the relish of this discovery.

2

· Many of his Amherst contemporaries can still recall their first impression of Dwight Morrow as he arrived, a freshman, in that September of 1891. They can remember his little derby hat, the forelock which protruded below it, the mobile movements of his head, a coat buttoned almost to the chin, the way his little boots turned upwards at the toes, the way he used to slide and click his feet upon the brickwork of the passage, the way he whistled tunelessly as he ran upstairs. They can remember something diffident about him and at the same time something aggressive. They can remember how the fingers of his hands remained closed together, and how they would expand as unexpected digits when he once became either confident or amused. "Dwight," records one of his classmates, "was not popular and not known during his freshman year at Amherst. He did not begin to make his real friends or to count for anything until his sophomore year. He was unpolished and rather crude when he first came to Amherst."

There were other disabilities which precluded him from mingling immediately with the social life of Amherst. He was never an athlete, and his prowess in field sports was painstaking rather than distinguished. And during his first year he was obsessed by the necessity of working off those eight conditions under which he had been admitted.

He lodged, during those early months, with Professor and Mrs. Gibbons in a gay little house with white gables and green shutters set amid the apple trees which fringe Pratt Field. Upon the ceiling of his attic bedroom he inscribed with charcoal those eight conditions upon the elimination of which the continuance of his Amherst career depended. Profiting by the intensive coaching of Professor Gibbons, he was able, within three short weeks, to erase Greek from this depressing catalogue. The names of Cicero and Virgil were scratched off before his first term was finished. The other five conditions were easily eliminated before the end of the first year.

That these three first terms of elementary study were not wholly wasted is proved by a letter which he wrote to Professor Gibbons some thirty-two years later:

". . . The older I get the more I feel that the first year I spent at Amherst when I studied Greek in your home and saw Professor Morse occasionally in his home next door was one of the most valuable years of my life. The three succeeding years were much easier than the first because the deficiencies in my preparation were gradually made up. But it was the first year that meant so much to me because I was compelled to keep devotedly at work in order to keep my head above water. I know how much was my indebtedness to you during those first few months. . . ."

Yet even when the conditions were disposed of, his financial problems remained insistent. The fees for tuition amounted at that date to $110 a year. The sums which he had hoped to gain by tutoring pecunious classmates were not, in those initial years, forthcoming. He was obliged to invoke the assistance of his brother Jay, who had graduated from West Point in June of 1891 and was then receiving army pay to the enormous extent of $125 a month. Jay Morrow, affectionate always, was delighted to curtail his own pleasures for the needs of his younger brother's education.[1] His sister Agnes, who had married Mr. Richard Scandrett, a Pittsburgh lawyer, was also anxious to help. She furnished Dwight Morrow with her husband's discarded garments. Mr. Richard Scandrett was a dressy man: Dwight Morrow remained forever gloriously unaware of his own apparel. This arrangement was satisfactory to both.

His financial embarrassments persisted throughout the whole Amherst period and beyond. Dwight Morrow accepted the situation with humorous optimism, knowing that it could only be transitory. Towards the end of his fourth year at Amherst the dark clouds of financial depression began, here and there, to show a rift. The following letter, addressed to his sister Agnes in March of 1895, proves that he had already realized that the fortress of capitalism is not inexpugnable:

". . . I have worked hard this term. Have had Henry Clews, Jr, of New York to tutor in math. five hours a week and I have gently touched his family exchequer for two dollars per hour which will make $100.00 for the term. I am turning a few of my brains into money at last. I will probably have him next term in trig. if he doesn't get fired, and he will not if my prayers have any weight. We are going to get a $50.00 dividend from the *Lit*

---

[1] The accounts of this transaction happen to have been preserved. They begin by Dwight Morrow lending Jay Morrow the sum of $100 at six per cent interest. From 1891 onwards the position of creditor and debtor is, as so often happens, reversed. By 1898 Dwight Morrow owed his brother nearly a thousand dollars. By February 1902 this debt was liquidated with six per cent interest. "But," comments General Morrow, "there is no one who can say that these were not the best investments that I ever made."

so I will be able to graduate with all the extra expenses without touching Papa for a cent. From an occasional letter I get from Mamma I understand they are still down in the dumps financially. . . .

"Next year when I get home as soon as I get started I am going to make some effort to fund that debt of the pater's and pay Uncle Corry and Indiana. . . . In my four years here, which have cost me about $2500.00 I have only borrowed about $500.00 off Papa. Tell Dick that owing to my unexpected windfall from the *Lit* I can wait a month or so on that Building Loan $100.00 if it will save any interest. I didn't know I was going to get any money from that or from Clews at least until next May or June. Jay is saving up for his marriage and I want to let him off of $25.00 or $50.00 he promised me if I can possibly do so. . . ."

From time to time, moreover, some richer classmate, on leaving college, would bequeath his wardrobe to the members of his own fraternity. It was in this manner that Dwight Morrow inherited the shirts of Mr. Mortimer L. Schiff.[2] The shirts were richly embroidered upon their forefront with the initials M. L. S. When Dwight returned for the vacation these initials struck Mrs. James Morrow as alien and odd. She demanded an explanation. "Well, you see," he answered, "those letters stand for Morrow's Little Shirts."

On leaving the home of Professor Gibbons, Dwight Morrow boarded, first at Collins' boarding house and then at Wilson's. He obtained from these houses sufficient food for $3.50 to $4.00 a week. In his sophomore year, and before he could obtain a room in the Beta Theta Pi fraternity house, he took his meals at the Morse boarding house, a neat little mansion perched high above the embankment of the roadway. He occupied a table to himself to the right of the door

[2] Mortimer L. Schiff, 1877-1931; Amherst; New York banker, partner in Kuhn, Loeb & Co.

28

as one entered the dining room. At another table under the end window sat an even more exclusive student—freckled, silent, and aloof. His name was Calvin Coolidge. It was only in their last two years that he and Morrow achieved terms of friendship.

3

Gradually, as term succeeded term, Dwight Morrow's sturdy effervescence impressed itself upon his professors and his fellow-students. As his influence expanded, the original nickname of "Kid Morrow" tended to be supplanted by the more respectful intimacy of "Dwight." In October of 1893 he transferred his lodging to the Beta Theta Pi fraternity house, and in April of 1894 he made his Phi Beta Kappa. The record of his work shows an ascending scale of performance. It can be scheduled as follows:

FRESHMAN YEAR 1891-1892	Declamation	B.
	Rhetoric	C.B.
	Latin	D.D.C.
	Greek	B.B.C.
	Mathematics	A.
SOPHOMORE YEAR 1892-1893	Declamation	A.
	Rhetoric	B.A.
	Logic	B.
	Latin	C.B.B.
	Greek	A.C.
	French	C.
	Mathematics	A.
JUNIOR YEAR 1893-1894	Public Speaking	A.
	English Literature	B.
	Mathematics	A.A.B.
	Physics	B.
	History	A.
	Philosophy	A.

SENIOR YEAR | Debates | A.
1894-1895 | Philosophy | A.
| History | B.A.
| Political Economy | A.

Average for four years 88%.

The above schedule is indicative, both of the scope of his studies and of his performance in each branch.

During these four years he accumulated also certain prizes which helped to balance his embarrassed budget. In his first year he gained the Armstrong Essay prize, and thereafter followed the Walker prize for mathematics, the Lester prize for declamation, the Hardy prize for extemporaneous speaking, and the Bond prize for his commencement oration. These forensic triumphs were of actual pecuniary importance.

Nor were these his only activities. He contributed lavishly to such student publications as the *Amherst Olio* and the *Amherst Literary Monthly*. Of the latter publication he eventually became chairman of the editorial board and supplied to it as many as seven articles from his own pen. They are not, by modern standards, very interesting articles. They are little more than competent imitations of the magazine style of the period, being mainly concerned with the thesis that material success, unaccompanied by ideals or character, is an empty, and in fact a hollow, thing.

On occasions, however, when pressed for copy, he would draw upon autobiographical memories of a more sentimental nature. There is a story, for instance, entitled "The First Milestone," in which he recounts his own feelings when his sister Agnes became engaged. An illuminating episode is narrated, in a subsequent number, describing how he by chance entered the Roman Catholic Cathedral in New York and found himself, in an orgy of tolerance, kneeling side by side with a young man who was obviously of the Catholic, and not in the least of the Presbyterian, persuasion. Even more significant as an essay in self-revelation is a diatribe which he composed against the evils of conventional prejudice. "Nothing," he wrote, "dwarfs a man so much as hatred." Here, at last, one can identify the seed of much of his future philosophy.

He lived, during those final years, in the Beta Theta Pi fraternity house, sharing a bedroom with George W. Stone. This house, as it then existed, boasted several independent styles of architecture, among which predominated, but without much conviction, what might be called the Franco-American style of 1880. A new house has since been constructed on the same site; it is Georgian, comfortable and trim.

Dwight Morrow, after his admission to this fraternity, would spend many hours upon the front porch, swaying his rocking chair emphatically, expounding to his fellow-students his own views upon philosophy or politics. It was during the course of these discussions that he evolved those explanatory gestures which became the accompaniment of his later discourse.

These gestures, which were delivered with the elbows pressed close against the body, can be divided into two categories, the synthetic and the analytical. When combining a synthesis, Morrow would flatten his hand with the fingers glued together and outstretched; at one moment he would chop the sections of his argument vertically, while at another moment he would make jerky gestures, horizontal and dismissive, as if brushing from his knee the dust of some irrelevant detail. His analytical gestures were of a different and less emphatic order. His hands would then be raised, still with the elbows tight against the body, to the level of his shoulders; the fingers would diverge from each other and crook slightly; it would be as if he were holding up some crystal object, revolving the fragile polygon of his imagination, now rapidly, now slowly, in order that each separate facet might successively catch the light. On such occasions his little hands would dance like marionettes in front of the illumined scenery of his mind.

One had the impression of a clear-cut synthesis following upon vivid and volatile exploration. It was this fascinating fusion of the imaginative with the practical, of the cautious with the impulsive, of brilliance with solidity, which gave to Morrow's conversation a quality which can best be described as incandescent. He caused ideas to glow. He forced them, with abrupt tight gestures, to solidify. And the rays of this illumination can first be discerned in the spectrum of his Amherst years.

The judicial quality of his intelligence, as well as the influence which he was able to exert on men of different type, can also be recognized in an incident which occurred during his senior year. The annual game against Williams was impending and it was recognized that the Amherst team, as then constituted, was certain of defeat. The suggestion was made that the team should be strengthened by including some members of the Massachusetts Agricultural College—a neighboring institution the existence of which, in normal times, was completely ignored. A meeting was held to discuss this proposal, and it was warmly supported by the majority of those present, including Mr. Peter Davis, the athletic coach. Dwight Morrow, although anything but an expert in such matters, was invited to state his opinion. "I am," he said, "wholly in favor of the suggestion. We have always treated these people as our social inferiors. Now we can show them that in fact they are better than ourselves." The proposal, at that, was hastily withdrawn.

Enclosed within the expanding circle of his acquaintance was a smaller nucleus of intimate friends. Of all these friends, Charles Burnett [3] was the most dearly loved. To him, more than to anyone, Dwight Morrow confided his personal sorrows and ambitions; from him, more than from any other man, he accepted spiritual exhortation and even spiritual rebuke. Their paths, in after life, diverged into different channels. Morrow excavated for himself a channel to power through the rocks of law, finance, and politics. Burnett became a professor of psychology at a smaller college. Yet their intimacy was seldom interrupted and never dimmed. Only a few weeks before Morrow's death, Burnett could write to him of "a friendship unbroken through all these years, and enriched when Betty and the children came." No friendship (and he had many intimacies in later life) ever meant so much to him as his friendship with Charles Burnett.

The legend of his Amherst support of Calvin Coolidge has been exaggerated. Dwight Morrow was always fascinated by complicated propositions and Calvin Coolidge, as a proposition, was very complicated indeed. It is true that, partly from kindness, partly from curiosity, and partly from an insatiable appetite for things that other people failed to understand, Dwight Morrow paid more attention to the astringent unsociability of Coolidge than was accorded to it by any other member of the class of '95. His own early impression of

[3] Charles T. Burnett, b. Springfield, Massachusetts, 1873; Amherst '95; Ph.D. Harvard 1903 where he studied under Professor Hugo Münsterberg; professor of psychology Bowdoin College, Maine.

33

Coolidge is indirectly conveyed by a letter which he wrote to his son many years later when Dwight Junior, in his turn, was about to enter Amherst College. "In your class," he wrote, "there may be a sandy-haired boy with freckles and trousers which do not come down to his shoes who will some day be President of the United States. There may not. . . . It doesn't make much difference. The Pelham Hills will be there anyway." [4] It may be surmised, even, that Morrow assisted Coolidge to overcome his solitary habits and to create for himself a certain reputation in the college for reserved prudence and desiccated humor. There is a story that on the occasion of the "class statistics" at the end of their senior year, Morrow received all but one of the votes as being the man most likely to succeed in after life, whereas the solitary vote cast for Coolidge was that given by Morrow himself. This is not wholly authentic. Morrow did, it is true, obtain a majority vote on that occasion, but it was not an overwhelming majority; Coolidge, on the other hand, obtained more votes than one. There is a fibre, none the less, of something more than conventional admiration in the tone of Calvin Coolidge's later references to the Dwight Morrow of the Amherst period. There is a fibre, almost, of gratitude. "Perhaps," wrote Coolidge in 1930, "the most remarkable thing about this remarkable man is that, although his circumstances have greatly changed since those days, he has remained the same." And in a passage unusual in one to whom understatement had become a second nature, Calvin Coolidge sums up as follows the impression left by Dwight Morrow upon his contemporaries at Amherst:

[4] This somewhat Matthew Arnold reference to the Pelham Hills is not authentic Dwight Morrow. He caught the phrase one hot afternoon during the Meiklejohn controversy (for which see later) from Robert Frost.

"He was gifted with an ability that entered the field of genius, untiring in his industry, studious, thoughtful, of high rank, but without any of the attributes that usually characterize a man as a precise, exact, bookworm in college life. While he was simple and unassuming, friendly and sympathetic, he was always dignified. He was using what he had for what was best. He had no element of selfishness. He never strove to excel anyone, or defeat anyone, he was simply doing his best to perform his duties to his family, his class, and his college. He had character. Even then he was a public servant. His thoughts were not on himself but on the things and people about him." [5]

This indeed is serious eulogy. Yet it is not only in terms of his own influence on others that Morrow's career at Amherst can be valued. It must be estimated also in terms of what he absorbed. The shape of his intelligence was molded, during those four years, in the hands of three remarkable men.

4

Reference has already been made to the veneration with which Morrow regarded the calling of a teacher. "The curriculum," he said later when addressing a university audience, "does not make the college. The teachers make the college. And whether you are one year or fifty years out of college, in your sober moments the college means to you a lecture room, with a real man leaning over a desk—a real man, by the side of whom many of those who are now called great are shriveled into nothing." [6]

Of the three teachers who influenced Dwight Morrow at

[5] From Calvin Coolidge's introduction to "Dwight Whitney Morrow" by Hewitt H. Howland (March 1930), pages v-vi.
[6] Address to Marshall College, June 1928.

Amherst, the first with whom he came into contact was George Olds, professor of mathematics.[7] Writing to his sister a few weeks after matriculation, he informed her that "the finest professor we have is the math. man—and he is a daisy." Professor Olds reciprocated this admiration; he would often assert that Dwight Morrow possessed the finest mathematical mind of any student whom it had been his privilege to teach. The mutual esteem thus engendered remained unbroken to the end.

It was only in his third year at Amherst that Morrow came under the spell of Charles E. Garman,[8] professor of philosophy. He referred in later years to "the inestimable privilege" of being "thrown with one like Professor Garman," and readers of Calvin Coolidge's "Autobiography" will recall the enthusiasm with which the ex-President speaks of Garman, terming him "one of the most remarkable men with whom I ever came into contact."

The methods adopted by Professor Garman were in fact both brilliant and brave. He was aware that the majority of his pupils were the sons of parents whose religious beliefs were too simple and too inelastic to provide protection against what he foresaw would be an age of increasing skepticism. He thus set himself deliberately to destroy the fabric of dogma and to construct thereon a firmer edifice founded upon an intellectual belief in spiritual purpose. He divided his course into three main stages, the first dealing

[7] George D. Olds, b. Middleport, New York, 1853; educated at University of Rochester, New York, and at Heidelberg and Berlin, Germany; professor of mathematics at Amherst, 1891-1927, acting president and president, 1923-27; d. 1931.
[8] Charles E. Garman, b. Limington, Maine, 1850; Amherst 1872, Yale (Divinity School) 1879; instructor 1880, professor of moral philosophy and metaphysics, Amherst, 1882-1907; d. 1907.

with psychology, which was almost wholly destructive, the second with metaphysics, which was coldly explanatory, and the third with ethics, which was designed to inculcate a conception of the good. He would not allow his pupils to attend the first, or destructive, phase of his lectures unless they pledged themselves to follow the course to its constructive conclusion; and he would exact from them an undertaking that the notes which he circulated in the form of pamphlets should be regarded as secret communications to be mentioned only in the presence of the elect. This delicate and ardent man (muffled in shawls and greatcoats even though the temperature of his lecture room was kept at 75 degrees) removed from Morrow's mind whatever barriers, either to correct thinking or to tolerant feeling, his earlier education might have left. For this emancipation Dwight Morrow owed, and acknowledged, a heavy debt of gratitude.

If it was Professor Garman who released Morrow's intelligence from the fetters of prejudice, it was Anson D. Morse,[9] professor of history, who gave a definite shape and direction to his subsequent mental development. Professor Morse had an almost fanatical belief in the value of historical study and would inculcate upon his pupils the questionable theory that most problems of human conduct can be solved if their origins can accurately be traced along what he called "the corridors of time." Professor Morse was in fact a historian of the Guizot school and, as such, a little prone to accept sentimental analogies which a less imaginative scholar might have dismissed as fallacious or merely picturesque. His intellectual integrity is not in question. "History," he warned

[9] Anson D. Morse, b. Cambridge, Vermont, 1846; Amherst 1871, professor of history and political economy 1876-1907, professor emeritus of history until his death in 1916.

37

Morrow in later years, "is a sacred subject; and those who undertake to write of the meaning of history have need of great wisdom, great humility, and perfect devotion." Yet this almost religious conception of the function of history left his pupils with a perhaps exaggerated confidence in the historical method. With Dwight Morrow this confidence became a settled habit of mind. His first action, when faced with any new problem, was to explore its origins "along the corridors of time." The advantage of this method was that it provided information which was occasionally applicable, precluded impatience, and induced a belief in the inevitability of gradualness. The disadvantage was that it was occasionally misleading and frequently a serious waste of time.

It is a curious fact that Dwight Morrow (who was invariably reserved regarding his mathematical, legal, diplomatic, or financial abilities) was apt to expatiate sometimes on the subject of his historical reading, which was diverse and continuous, rather than profound. His references to Thucydides, for instance, or to Herodotus, were frequent but uncritical. His historical vanity was perhaps the only vanity which he possessed. And it can be traced to the influence of Professor Morse.

The value of this historical approach must not, however, be underestimated. "It was," records Professor Gilbert Murray, "Morrow's breadth of vision and understanding, his comprehension of the slow movement of history and human development, that made him one of the outstanding men of our time."

But his four years at Amherst were not entirely occupied in receiving the compliments of Professor Olds or absorbing the doctrines of Professors Garman and Morse. There were fraternity sleigh-rides to Deerfield, and in the summer long walks among the surrounding hills. There were social occasions also. "I have," he wrote to his sister in March of 1894, "used my dress suit about four times since Christmas." Morrow was not concerned with social ambitions or with social graces, and the society of women either left him indifferent or inspired him with alarm. Yet it was the custom at Amherst to take the 5.14 train into Northampton and to return on the caboose of a freight train at 9.00. The purpose of these excursions was to visit the young ladies of Smith College or to drink beer at Dick Rahar's. During his first year Dwight Morrow but seldom joined these expeditions. One evening, however, in the spring of 1893, he was dragged unwillingly to a small dance given at a girls' school in Amherst. He was there introduced to Elizabeth Reeve Cutter of Cleveland, who was already prominent among the students of Smith. They were each in a bad temper. Morrow was angry because he disliked dances. Miss Cutter was angry because she considered it beneath the dignity of a Smith student to attend a backfish party. It was thus on a basis of joint indignation that they first formed acquaintance. Thereafter Morrow's visits to Northampton became more frequent. Miss Cutter was invited to his Junior Prom at Amherst. The next year she returned the compliment. "I have," Morrow wrote to his sister,

"been invited over to the Smith Junior Prom which comes off on May 1st by Miss Cutter and of course count on having a fine time. I am going to have her over here for the Senior Prom if her folks will let her come. She is going to ask them when she goes home Easter vacation. Now, as soon as I hear from her definitely, I am going to write you and you can write her and tell her that you will be glad to chaperon her and invite her to stay with you while in Amherst. See! We will do the thing up in all propriety. It seems like an awful crusty thing for me to do to ask her over here for a week, but after mature deliberation I concluded that I had the crust to do it. You will like her awfully well, I know. She kind of reminds me of you sometimes. That is rather a dangerous statement to make in view of that story I wrote about you and on the whole I guess you had better consider the whole letter a personal one—at any rate with the Morrow family. . . ."

Miss Cutter, in the end, was obliged to decline this invitation.

5

Dwight Morrow's college career ended in a blaze of glory. The class statistics already referred to filled him with elation. He wrote to Mrs. Scandrett in excited triumph:

". . . I have been feeling quite a hoodoo over me for the last week or two for in the class statistics which come out in the class book I am relied upon as the one to be the most famous. It is a well-known fact that he who is picked out by a college class to be most famous always ends his life in an obscure corner. In the class statistics I also was elected the brightest man and the most popular. Please don't tear the letter up here and call me conceited. None of it amounts to anything but I feel just a wee bit proud when I think of those eight conditions I had when I wandered into town. Don't let Dick think he is going to have a college man with a swelled head in his office. I am willing to start in sweeping out the office if there is any show of me paying off my monstrous debts in the next five years. If the people are all hard up at home tell them not to come on my account. They wouldn't see much of me except on the platform and it is kind of selfish of me who has spent so much already to want a poor family to squander any more on him. . . ."

He was elected class orator and was able to expend the prize money he had accumulated in obtaining railroad tickets for his father, mother, and youngest sister from Allegheny to Amherst. "You want to be sure to come," he wrote home. "I am elected class orator. You want to be *sure* to come. Begin then to make all arrangements for I am sure to be one of the big toads, if not *the* big toad, in the puddle. . . . Of course the matter of gowns does not make any difference. People know that I am not rich, but I think a few of them are a little interested in seeing what kind of stock I spring from."

The day of June 25th arrived. When his turn came to speak, he spoke on "Dreams." His peroration was much applauded. "God pity," he said, "that one who has persuaded himself that his dream was false! The ideal must be true and eternal. It can never be shattered. We may forget it; we may barter away for dross that which is priceless, but whatever our weakness, the Dream is true, the Vision is He. If we can but carry away this truth, the scoff of the cynic means nothing. Let them scornfully say, 'The Dreamer cometh.' With the sobered confidence of youth, with all the humility of manhood, we can answer in the very words of cynicism, 'We *shall* see what will come of his dreams.' "

When the guests had departed he stood with Charles Andrews alone on the porch, watching the rain pour down in torrents through the elms.

III. Law School   1896–1899

THE RETURN TO PITTSBURGH. RESULTANT DEPRESSION AND HIS
ATTEMPTS TO ADJUST HIMSELF TO A LESS EASTERN ENVIRON-
MENT. FAILURE OF THESE ENDEAVORS. HIS CORRESPONDENCE
WITH CHARLES BURNETT. DURING THE PITTSBURGH INTERLUDE
HIS EARLY RELIGIOUS AND SUBSEQUENT INTELLECTUAL TRAIN-
ING ARE DIGESTED INTO A THEORY OF CONDUCT. ANALYSIS OF
THIS THEORY. HE ACHIEVES THE RUDIMENTS OF HIS OWN
FORMULA. IMPORTANCE OF THIS FORMULA. HE LEAVES FOR
NEW YORK. CIRCUMSTANTIAL DETAIL REGARDING HIS LAW
SCHOOL LIFE, ECONOMIES, AND FRIENDSHIPS. ALMOST BY CHANCE
HE BECOMES A CORPORATION LAWYER.

A REACTION, after such an apotheosis, was inevitable. The
eight months which followed were the most miserable in
Morrow's life. It had been arranged that he should return
to Pittsburgh and serve as an apprentice in the law firm
of Scandrett & Barnett, of which his brother-in-law, Mr.
Richard Scandrett, was a partner. The latter's interests were
concerned rather with local politics and business than with
the exact profession of the law. The class orator felt humili-
ated at being little more than "Dick's office boy," and soon
became restless under this lack of opportunity or enlightenment. Yet how, with debts unpaid, could he throw up a
position which, however meagre, did in fact provide him
with an immediate living wage?

In the depression which thereafter descended upon him,
three stages can be traced. During the first stage his longing
for Amherst, his homesickness for New England, numbed
his faculties. During the second stage he endeavored to
adjust himself to Pittsburgh and to silence all questioning
by an intensive study of law and history. During the third
stage his adventurism and his self-confidence revived. Why,

after all, need he spend his life in the office of a provincial attorney? Why should he lose all faith in the high promise of his Amherst years? Poverty he could well endure; study was his permanent delight; financial difficulties always settled themselves. He would take the bigger risk and aim at higher chances. He would go to New York. His father, with the indulgence he always displayed to Dwight's ambitions, encouraged this unreasonable enterprise. In the autumn of 1896 Dwight Morrow left his Pittsburgh employment for a three years' course at the Columbia Law School. Here again was a hazardous decision triumphantly justified by the result.

Before this solution imposed itself, many months of doubt and discouragement had to be endured. The office of Messrs. Scandrett & Barnett was situated on the eleventh floor of a bleak red edifice called the Carnegie Building. Dwight Morrow lived with his sister across the river in Imbrie Avenue, Allegheny. "My sister and I," he wrote to Charles Burnett, "have been more to each other than most brothers and sisters." With his brother-in-law he was seldom able to establish relations of confidence. His little nephew, Dick Scandrett —whom in later years he loved, trusted, and admired—did not at the age of four impress Dwight Morrow very favorably. "He is," he wrote, "a holy terror, sure."

To the biographer this interlude between Amherst and Columbia is of interest, since, during that period, he wrote some of his most revealing and outspoken letters. Dwight Morrow was not a letter-writer and in subsequent years his correspondence, though voluminous, was mainly stenographic. On leaving Amherst he had agreed with Charles Burnett that they should write to each other on the first Sunday after the fifteenth of every month. This resolution was not maintained, on Morrow's side, for very long. Yet sufficient letters have survived to convey an interesting picture of his doubts and his ambitions during that unhappy but pregnant period. There is in the first place his homesickness for Amherst:

"I got here yesterday," he writes on July 28, 1895, "and have been looking over the Amherst pictures. My boxes had arrived and I got my pictures and books out and am going to try and fix up a den for myself so that part of the day anyway I can get back to Amherst."

By August of the same year his homesickness is increasing.

"All I have been doing would really not rise to such a degree of importance as to deserve the honorable name of work. . . . I am getting very much discontented. I am beginning to get just a little bit homesick for Amherst. Just think! Only a few weeks now till the boys wander down to Pratt Field . . . and then when the shadows begin to fall over Mount Warner, little groups of seniors and juniors will wander up to the gym to make Doc's life miserable."

In November of that year he confides to Burnett his first hopes of leaving Pittsburgh for New York, only to relapse into a mood of despair at the hopelessness of any such enterprise. "Life," he writes, "does not have any knight-errantry left to it now." He plunges into a serious study of the law, taking special instruction from Mr. Thaddeus C. Noble, of Pittsburgh. He is deep in Blackstone, who convinces him that the profession of a lawyer has in truth a noble side. "It is really a fact," he writes, "that almost without exception the really great lawyers have been men with wonderful reverence for the laws of God." Bishop Stubbs also indicates to him that the study of law can open out wide vistas of scholarship and research. He consults Burnett regarding his own imagined failings. "I don't know," he writes on August 22, 1895, "anything more terrible to contemplate than being a hypocrite, and yet, sometimes, I think that it is such an easy thing to drift into, to allow people to think you are better, and know more, than you really do. I know I'm awfully prone to do that. I think that any fellow who is ambitious and eager for reputation is peculiarly open to such temptation." To these confessions Charles Burnett would reply with gentle psychological encouragement.

Gradually, as the months passed, his mood becomes one of wistful resignation.

"We think," he writes in December, "that we are in a poor place and everybody else is in a good one. I do that right along. My! what a commonplace town this seems to me! And then I get to thinking that if one could only love the commonplace what a jolly sunny world this would be! . . . It makes me so angry with myself that I cannot always apply that doctrine, but I can't: at times I find myself grumbling because I am doing so little and wishing I were in the East somewhere surrounded by Amherst friends. Such wicked discontented thoughts are getting less frequent now. When I get in my room on Sunday afternoon and get some good book to read or write a letter to a friend, I feel as though after all it is a good world and that the dull deserts are put in just enough to make the splendid mountain scenery more enjoyable. When I long for the good old days among the Massachusetts hills and when I hear of this thing or that thing coming around again, and remember how it was last year, I feel blue—until I remember what Amherst stands for, and then it seems to me that we ought to be able to do some good with all that advantage. . . ."

"Do you know," he writes again, "I have grown fond of Sunday evenings this year? I am more alone here than I have been before in my life, because I have so little time to revive old friendships, and I look forward to Sunday evenings when I can gather myself together in my room with my absent friends and write letters to them. I have just read over your last one and I have been thinking about letters and letter writing. You know I once told you that I never wrote more than a page or two when I was in college. That was true. I used to sit down and write a little scrawl to my mother, plead haste, and say that there was nothing out of the way to write about; when as a matter of fact there were thousands of little things which would have interested them had I not been too selfish at the time to write carefully. I believe I have gotten over that now. . . ."

"I see my end," he writes in March 1896, "make up my mind to reach it, and then fret because I do not reach it soon enough, which is a childish thing to do, and yet I haven't released myself from the chains though I consider, as do you, this an invaluable year in teaching me the philosophy lessons. In a college life where we have so much to attract us away from the blues we have little opportunity to learn to dictate to our moods. We balance our despondence by artificial pleasures which the society of others helps us to attain. In other words we push our moods aside but do not overcome them. When we get out, away from the crowd whose laugh and smile was our laugh and smile, we have to suppress our moods; we allow them no longer to dictate to us. Your last good letter with its 'potential' idea was very inspiring and helpful, Charles. I can't tell you just *how* helpful it was! I am hearing every day about what this man and that man has done and without going to the trouble that I am planning for myself, so that it is considerable of a temptation to alter our dreams a bit and reach the potential of material Pittsburgh. When I stop and think just how much our actions depend upon our environment I am appalled by the lot of caprice which it introduces into this world! Because 'A' was reared in a mechanic's cradle in a noisy dirty city and 'B' learned his first lessons

46

in some good professor's family in a sweet little town like Amherst, doesn't it seem wrong that the existence of both should depend so much on their environment? I suppose you will answer that upon both alike will some day break the lesson that man controls his potential and to the one who has the most to overcome, to him will be the greater reward, on the principle that the divine spark shines the brighter in him who has had to smash away so much rubbish to get it lighted. . . ."

Towards the end of that dreadful year his discontent began to fade. Amherst itself receded into the mists of memory:

"I hear," he writes in August 1896, "very little Amherst news now. Every now and then I wonder why it is that we drop our college life so quickly. I suppose it is because we are all changing.

"A constant friendship is one in which the changing of both friends is in the same direction. Constancy certainly couldn't be standing still. I used to think that I should rebel against dropping any part of my college feelings, and hated the idea of making new friends. Even in one short year we see what wretched creatures we would be if we went through life clinging to the old inspirations when we might be drawing new every day. . . ."

He began to consider politics. He took an interest in the "cross of gold" conflict between William Jennings Bryan and McKinley. So incensed was he by the fatuity of Bryan's economics that he became, and steadfastly remained, a Republican. He announced his intention of speaking at local meetings:

"One thing," he wrote, "I am going to try to do even at the risk of failing to please my audience (if I have one), and that is not to say anything which I shall be ashamed of in ten or twenty years from now. There is a sort of rule in this country that you must throw in a lot about the 'eagle' and a great deal of billingsgate concerning Democracy, if you would have the sterling sons of toil howl. It seems to me that people ought to be thinking seriously enough about this campaign to do something stronger."

These diversions did not overcome either his dislike of Pittsburgh or his love of New England. "The East," he wrote to Charles Burnett, "stands for a great deal more than a *locality*. It means my college and my college ideal." And in May of 1896 we find an abrupt letter as follows: "I have decided to go to New York. I think somehow, Charles, that this decision of mine to go to Law School is going to have a considerable influence on my life. Who knows but that ultimately I may land in New York?"

2

The Pittsburgh interlude (the phases of loneliness and self-criticism which it provoked) is important in that it gave Dwight Morrow the time in which to arrange upon the shelves of his consciousness that set of values with which Amherst had enriched the standards of his boyhood. During those eight months his ethical theories solidified into the concrete of intellectual habits; and it was perhaps fortunate that Charles Burnett, loving and reflective, was there to assist in deciding which of these habits were essential and which were not.

The Morrow legend, as it later developed, gives us a little man of gentle gaiety, of sweet unworldliness, of brilliant intellect. True it was that Morrow's unflagging zest, even in small things, titivated and amused; that his intelligence was as various, as volatile, but as intent, as a pack of hounds;

48

and that his absent-mindedness often gave to a superficial observer an impression of naïve indifference to mundane things.

Yet it would be a mistake to assess the mind and character of Dwight Morrow by such almost trivial symptoms. Essentially Morrow was a man of action. He was ambitious, determined, precise, cautious, unremitting, and shrewd. His hatred of failure was so intense that he might well have come to worship success. His realism, the actual importance which he attached to the orderly achievement of practical ends, might well, given the circumstances, have degenerated into materialism. His love of power, combined with his amazing resourcefulness, functioning through his genius for persuasion, might well have rendered him a politician.

There was no such degeneration. Had he concentrated his gifts upon material purposes, his achievement would have been greater. His example, less.

How came it that Dwight Morrow was able throughout his life to subordinate the quantitative standards of a man of action to the qualitative standards of a man of thought? It must be realized that he was living in a competitive and impatient age and that the areas of his activity were practical rather than philosophic. Many of his contemporaries were wont to dissociate the fluids of their idealism from the fluids of their realism, preserving each in separate flagons. It was because Morrow, in small things as in great, strove always to fuse the practicable with the desirable, the real with the ideal, that he stands out as an example of *the civilized man*. And it was from Amherst, as interpreted and reenforced by Charles Burnett, that he learned the secret of that fusion.

Such generalizations are unconvincing.

The above theory can, without undue anticipation, be fortified by an analysis of the main constituents of Morrow's mind. These constituents were faith, magnanimity, patience, and a perfect balance between imagination and reason. The ethical foundations of these qualities were laid by his father and mother; it was their intellectual applicability to the modern world that he derived from Amherst. "The peculiar genius of Dwight Morrow," wrote Walter Lippmann, "lay in the fact that he kept mystical faith in men without losing his own intellectual standards." As a symptom of this faith he possessed what Montagu Norman [1] has well called "creative confidence." "The working hypothesis of his career," wrote Walter Lippmann, "was to assume that every man was interested in the truth. . . . He proceeded on the assumption that they intended to be honest and by the very force of the assumption made them justify him." [2] One of the most potent of Morrow's intellectual implements was his trustfulness. He shared with Lord Grey of Fallodon the conviction that far more harm has been done to the world by lack of confidence than by excess of gullibility. He advanced towards duplicity with his little hands dancing expectantly in front of him and deception in its turn was disarmed. He dared, with his enlightenment, to cast away the heavy shield of doubt.

His magnanimity, again, was something more than a subjectively generous attitude towards life; it was a positive and energetic tolerance. "Remember," he would often repeat, "that we are all inclined to judge *ourselves* by our ideals;

[1] Rt. Hon. Montagu C. Norman, b. Hertfordshire, England, 1871; educated at Eton and Cambridge; Governor of the Bank of England since 1920.
[2] Walter Lippmann, author, editor, commentator on public affairs, in the New York *Herald Tribune*, October 7, 1931.

others by their acts." "Tolerance," records George Rublee,[3]
"had a special meaning for him"; and his intimates were
familiar with that wince of physical pain, that sharp intake
of the breath, with which he would recoil from any sign of
intellectual cruelty or arrogance. He never criticized motives;
he always tried to understand them. He never argued on
assumptions; he always sought to ascertain the facts. He was
never cynical; he was always, and sometimes unfortunately,
optimistic. For him the most improbous goose was always a
potential swan.

Amherst, or more specifically Professor Morse, provided
him also with a perfect intellectual balance between determi-
nism and free will. On the one hand, he was well aware that
in the stream of human experience the individual is but a
straw whirling in little circles of its own conceit. On the
other hand, he was convinced that some straws conducted
themselves "better" than other straws; and he was determined to belong to the more active category. This attitude
of mind explains what many of his contemporaries regarded as the enigma of Morrow's nature. They were perplexed at finding a man who (although avowedly ambitious,
although not abnormally modest or unselfish) would none
the less lose interest in a problem once it had been solved
and leave it to others to reap the ensuing laurels and applause. They did not understand that Morrow, being a believer in the gradualness of progressive evolution, had a
patient mind. He was in fact that most rare of all phenomena
—the ambitious but uncompetitive man. "The world," he

---

[3] George Rublee, b. Madison, Wisconsin, 1868; Harvard 1890, LL.B. 1895;
Washington lawyer; associated with Morrow on the Allied Maritime Transport
Council 1918-19, as legal adviser to the American Embassy in Mexico 1928-30,
and as adviser to the London Naval Conference in 1930.

once wrote to his son, "is divided into people who do things and people who get the credit. Try, if you can, to belong to the first class. There's far less competition." His genius for coöperation was thus something more dynamic than a merely virtuous habit of selflessness: it was inspired by creative convictions, as much intellectual as religious.

This perfect adjustment between the real and the ideal was reflected in the actual functioning of his intelligence, in the balance which he achieved between reason and imagination. "His imagination," writes Montagu Norman, "was as vivid and varied as his mind. The two seemed trained to work together in harmony and I like to believe that this harmony between imagination and intellect, this union between soul and mind, lies at the very root of genius. It is from this union that may be traced the personal sympathy which surely was the outstanding characteristic of Dwight Morrow. To him indeed it was the *way* of self-expression." To this harmony was due also his capacity to recognize the larger meaning of details and thus to see the essentials of any situation in great simplicity. "He dared," records Owen D. Young, "have fantastic thoughts," yet when it came to interpret those thoughts in terms of action, he would be wary, meticulous, precise.

Such were the qualities of mind and soul which enabled Dwight Morrow to exercise so great an influence upon his fellow men. These weapons were forged for him at Amherst from the rich ores of his heredity and religious training. In 1896 he already held them in his grasp. It is instructive to observe how, in the circles of experience which now opened before him, he learned to handle these weapons with ever-increasing dexterity, discipline, confidence, and power.

3

The Columbia Law School, in that autumn of 1896, was situated at the corner of Madison Avenue and 49th Street, upon the spot where today the New Weston Hotel rears its pleased pink face. To the east of the school there extended a wide gravel courtyard, running down to the edge of a dark canyon through which a network of railroad lines converged upon the Grand Central Station. The splendors of Park Avenue were yet to come.

It was in this courtyard that Dwight Morrow, during his first term at law school, was accosted by John Kerr. It transpired that they had played baseball together beside the banks of the Ohio River. That encounter led, as will be seen, to the whole Englewood connection and to a friendship of more than thirty years. In the second of Morrow's three years at Columbia, the law school moved its premises from Madison Avenue to Morningside Heights, and Morrow transferred his own lodging correspondingly from the top floor of 55 West 45th Street to the top floor of 344 West 123rd Street. In his third year he lived with John Kerr and the two Tyler brothers at 44 West 92nd Street. It is of this latter residence that the most detailed record has been preserved.

The house was built of brownstone and made no attempt whatsoever either at gaiety or charm. The staircase rose steeply from the little hallway, and on reaching the second landing there were two doors upon the right and a door opposite. The first door led into the bedroom tenanted by Dwight Morrow and John Kerr.[4] The windows looked to

[4] John Campbell Kerr, b. Allegheny, Pennsylvania, 1873; Princeton 1896, classmate of Morrow at Columbia; New York patent lawyer.

the north on 92nd Street and the furniture consisted of a double bed (shared nightly by Kerr and Morrow), two wooden tables, an open fireplace, two armchairs, and a washing stand with a cold marble top. The second door opened into the Tyler bedroom, between which and the front room was a small closet containing two basins. The door at the end of the landing led into a bathroom.

The young men washed in the closet, a circumstance which left the Kerr-Morrow washing stand free for other purposes. Every night they would damp the creases of their trousers, lay them carefully across the marble top, and place above them Hayer's "Cases on Evidence" or Chitty on "Pleading." It may be surmised that this year in 92nd Street was the only year in which Morrow's trousers showed any shape at all. Even in his ambassadorial and senatorial days, even in the days when Septimus Banks (most perfect of all valets) would iron those trousers, they invariably assumed the shape of a concertina before 11.45 A.M. John Kerr was a tidy man: Dwight Morrow was not.

The problem of finance was, as always, serious. He had hoped to maintain himself at law school by coaching younger men in mathematics. During the first year, there was an adequate supply of pupils, but at the outset of his second year the supply fell short. The spectre of having to return to Pittsburgh without completing his course at Columbia came to haunt his nights. Then suddenly the trickle of pupils swelled into a bright little stream. "As a result," he wrote to his sister, "I am seriously thinking of chancing another year of financial outlay." He was able, by such precarious methods, to maintain himself for the full three years.

It was not easy. He kept a little expense book crumpled in his pocket and entered every item of extravagance as it occurred. If it had rained that morning there would come the entry "Trolley to Law School: 5¢." His share of the morning newspaper cost him one cent and his share of the evening paper cost him half a cent. On Sunday he would read the foreign newsletters in the *Times*. "They enable one," he wrote home, "to keep track pretty well of what is going on in Europe." Few law students, at that date, would have possessed such entangling interests.

In the evenings he and Kerr would return to 92nd Street and at 6 P.M. would have their supper in the basement. They drank water only; they seldom allowed themselves a seat at the theatre; the meerschaum pipe was common property and shared by each in turn. Yet there was one luxury which Dwight Morrow allowed himself, perhaps the only luxury of which in the whole course of his life he was ever consciously aware. He loved an open fire. Every evening after supper he would carry up with him a few hickory logs and make a fire in the grate. The kerosene lamp would be lighted upon the table beside him and he would read till nine. He would then take the poker, crouch over the dying embers—poke and prod, poke and prod—sometimes plunged with wrinkled forehead in some mood of abstraction, at other times gesticulating with hand and poker as he discussed with John Kerr a point of jurisprudence.

There were but few interruptions in this routine. Once a month there would be an alumni dinner at the Murray Hill Hotel at 75¢ a head. Occasionally he would spend Sunday with his brother Jay, who was already an instructor at West Point. From time to time he would be laid low by one of his headaches and relapse into headache powders and darkness. And sometimes Professor Anson Morse would climb the

staircase and bring him news of Amherst and the Massachusetts hills.

On one such visit the Professor asked Morrow whether he
could come to Amherst for a term to lecture on history. It
was not possible for him to accept this offer, since his bar
examination was then approaching. But the fact that the
offer had been made filled him with excited gratitude. "The
very prospect," he wrote, "of being in Amherst for a spring
term and having business there makes one go almost wild."
The prospect came to nothing. Yet it was owing to the mediation of Professor Morse that but a few months later he
obtained an opening which determined his whole future
career.

Among Dwight Morrow's classmates at Columbia Law
School was Johnston de Forest, son of Robert W. de Forest,[5]
one of New York's richest and most worthy citizens. Writing to Mrs. Scandrett in November 1897, Morrow refers to
this friendship with a certain defensiveness. "De Forest himself," he writes, "I have got to know very well indeed. He is
a splendid fellow, one of the type who would be called an
aristocrat and yet who is a fellow of very serious earnest
purposes." [6] The de Forests lived in Washington Square, and
it was there, as well as at their country place on Long Island,
that Dwight Morrow obtained his first experience of luxury.
He was invited to stay for a Saturday to Monday at Cold
Spring Harbor, and even sailed down to Seabright in the
de Forest yacht. He was relieved to discover that the de
Forests did not seem to mind, or even to observe, the re-

[5] Robert Weeks de Forest, b. New York 1848; Yale 1870, Columbia LL.B.
1872; New York lawyer; president Metropolitan Museum of Art and other
civic, charitable and educational institutions; d. 1931.

[6] Johnston de Forest, b. Plainfield, New Jersey, 1873; Yale 1896, classmate of
Morrow at Columbia Law School; lawyer.

stricted nature of his own wardrobe. These visits were repeated, and one happy day in June of 1899 Dwight Morrow
found himself a fellow guest at Cold Spring Harbor with
Mr. Rudyard Kipling who, at that date, was the idol of
American youth. He was also invited to Washington Square:

". . . Last Friday I went to a dance at the de Forests' and had
a very good time although it was out of my class entirely. I met
some interesting people and some who were not so interesting
except for their names. . . . I met a son of Cornelius Bliss (the
retiring Secretary of the Interior) at the dance and several other
people of prominence, but as I said before, it was out of my
class. I would much prefer to meet people one at a time and get
to know them a little than to be thrown into a big bunch of
them whom you have never met before and probably will never
meet again and with whom you have little if anything in common. I suppose people are much the same everywhere, no particular locality or class having a monopoly on the bright and
interesting people or a monopoly on the dunces. From the people
I met Friday night I guess New York has its proportion of both
classes. . . ."

Dwight Morrow was never a snob, and in the elegances
of social intercourse he took no interest whatsoever. On the
other hand he was not so unfastidious in his social relations
as has sometimes been supposed. Little more than a year
after the above letter we find him writing to his sister in a
mood almost of social discrimination:

". . . I don't think I am anything of an aristocrat in my tendencies, and some of my very best friends are of course from poor
families, but as I get older I believe I find it true that the *best*
people to know are those with whom it is most difficult to get
acquainted. It is because they value friendship so highly that
they are not willing to take up with every newcomer. Of course

57

these 'best people' are not found in any class of society, but in all classes, and perhaps proportionately in all classes. . . ."

Whatever may have been the effect on Dwight Morrow of the de Forest circle, it is evident that he himself impressed the elder de Forest with his energy and brilliance. Early in 1899 Mr. de Forest offered him a position in the legal department of the Central Railroad of New Jersey, adding that if he accepted this offer his salary would start immediately pending his graduation from Law School in the coming June. Such an opening was better than anything Dwight Morrow had ever dreamed of, but before accepting it he consulted Professor Anson Morse. The latter feared that the proposal of Mr. de Forest, helpful though it was, might not afford Morrow sufficient scope wherein to deploy his talents. He therefore traveled down to New York and interviewed his old friend and classmate, Mr. John W. Simpson, of the firm of Reed, Simpson, Thacher & Barnum, and an Amherst man.[7] He urged Mr. Simpson to give young Morrow a post in his own firm. Mr. Simpson at once adopted Professor Morse's recommendation.

It was in this manner that Dwight Morrow became a corporation lawyer.

[7] John W. Simpson, b. Craftsbury, Vermont, 1850; Amherst 1871, permanent trustee 1908; Columbia LL.B. 1873; founder and senior member of the law firm of Simpson, Thacher & Barnum; d. 1920.

IV. Engagement and Marriage   1901–1903

MORROW BECOMES A CLERK IN THE FIRM OF REED, SIMPSON,
THACHER & BARNUM. HIS AFFECTION FOR MR. SIMPSON. HIS
APPEARANCE AND MANNERS AT THIS PERIOD. HIS INDUSTRY AND
INTELLIGENCE AT ONCE RECOGNIZED. HIS FIRST JOB. HIS LIFE
AT WEST 46TH STREET. MRS. GORREN. NEW YORK IN 1900. HE
STUDIES ECONOMICS, BANKING, AND TAXATION. OVERWORK. OOM
PAUL. THE STATEN ISLAND GROUP. MISS ELIZABETH REEVE CUT-
TER. EARLY OBSTACLES TO AN ENGAGEMENT. FORTUNATE INTER-
VENTION OF CHARLES BURNETT. THEY BECOME ENGAGED ON
JULY 26, 1901. THEY ARE MARRIED AT CLEVELAND, JUNE 16,
1903. EARLY MARRIED LIFE AT ENGLEWOOD. THE LITTLE BROWN
HOUSE IN SPRING LANE.

THE firm of Reed, Simpson, Thacher & Barnum,[1] although
not long established, was one of the most promising in the
United States. So great were the opportunities they offered
that, with other eminent law firms, it became their custom
to attach no salary to the privilege of acting as one of their
junior clerks. They felt, with justice, that any young
graduate would be honored to serve as unsalaried apprentice in such a house.

Mr. John W. Simpson acted as leading partner, and it was
to him that Dwight Morrow had to explain that he himself
would not be able to serve in a purely honorary capacity.
For eight years now he had preferred education to income;
when he looked back upon those four years at Amherst,
upon those three years at Law School, it seemed incredible
that such slender resources should have survived the strain.
He was now twenty-six years old. No longer could he allow
himself the luxury of not earning money; he had gambled

---

[1] Thomas B. Reed died in 1902, and Mr. Barnum resigned in 1904. The firm
was thereafter known as "Simpson, Thacher & Bartlett."

daringly upon his own talents, but it was time that these talents showed a dividend; from now onwards his whole energies must be devoted to liquidating past debts and to securing financial independence for the future. Mr. Simpson fully appreciated the force of this contention. He agreed to pay Dwight Morrow a salary of $60.00 a month.

The bond between Mr. Simpson and Dwight Morrow, which originated in the Amherst connection and their common friendship for Professor Anson Morse, strengthened as the years passed into deep mutual affection and respect. Simpson was an observant man and a quick judge of ability. As he limped from room to room of those early offices at No. 10 Wall Street,[2] he soon became aware that this new clerk was in some way different from other new clerks. His personal appearance, it was true, was not impressive. He was small, untidy, and much rumpled about the head. His clothes were anything but fashionable. His waistcoats were too high, his trousers were too low, and his jackets hitched up curiously around the right shoulder. Even Savile Row in later days never managed to remove from these jackets the impression that the owner was about to take them off. When he entered the offices of Reed, Simpson, Thacher & Barnum, Dwight Morrow was, moreover, wearing a tie pin which was not very good. He himself was fond of it. He described it as a "little stick pin, very pretty, being a wishbone with a diamond in it." Yet in fact this pin looked ill against a large plum-colored tie.

His manners, moreover, were dynamic rather than elegant; he had a way, when introduced to eminent clients, of making a sharp dancing-class bow and thereafter treating the

---

[2] The firm moved subsequently to the fifteenth floor of No. 25 Broad Street, and finally to the Harvey Fisk & Co. building at No. 62 Cedar Street.

DWIGHT MORROW, 1901

said clients as ordinary men or women. Having made his brisk little tribute to their eminence he settled down to their business. Some clients liked this form of procedure; others did not.

Yet even in those early days of 1900 there was something about Dwight Morrow that compelled attention. He appeared younger than his years, and that boyishness which in later years added such charm to his ambassadorial manner, seemed, in a lawyer's clerk, merely immature. The mobility of his intelligence was, however, buttressed by the solid precision of his industry, by the studious accuracy with which he did his work. Zest, imagination, and daring would twinkle from those kindly blue eyes; his very ingenuity of resource would both fascinate and disconcert; and then would come the realization that this electric incandescence was set firmly upon the rock of principle, cemented by the concrete of the most scrupulous industry. He seemed to combine the impulse of youth with the prudence of experience.

It was not long before Mr. Simpson was able to demonstrate his confidence by allocating to his young clerk a specific responsibility. An officer of the British Army, of the name of Arthur Lee,[3] had just married Miss Ruth Moore of New York City, who was a ward of Mr. Simpson. On leaving the United States for England Major Lee was anxious to entrust his wife's and his own American interests to reliable hands. He applied to Mr. Simpson. "We have just," the latter answered, "taken into this office a young man of whom we think very highly. He is a prize and will go far. I shall intro-

[3] Arthur Lee (now Viscount Lee of Fareham), b. Bridport, England, 1868; educated at Cheltenham and Woolwich; statesman, soldier, writer.

duce you to this young man and to him you can confidently entrust your affairs."

Thirty years later—by which time Major Lee had become a peer, a Cabinet Minister, and the inspired donor of Chequers—Dwight Morrow went to visit him in Richmond Park. "That," said Morrow, referring to their first meeting, "was a great day in my life. It gave me my first independent job."

The rapidity with which Dwight Morrow was able to secure the confidence and affection of the senior partners is also evidenced by the increases in his salary during the first four years. Having graduated from Law School in June of 1899, he became a clerk in the firm in the following October. In May 1900 his salary was raised from $720 a year to $900; in January 1901 from $900 to $1,200, and in July of the same year from $1,200 to $1,500; on the first day of 1902 it was raised from $1,500 to $1,800, and on January 1, 1903, when he was promoted managing clerk, it leapt from $1,800 to $3,125. During the first year he was able to supplement his salary by tutoring for the bar examination and by reviewing law books for the *Columbia Law Review*. Thereafter, having liquidated his own more urgent debts, he concentrated entirely upon the work of his firm.

He continued to live a life of the strictest economy. He shared rooms with Charles J. Fay[4] on the top floor of No. 67 West 46th Street, where he remained from October 1899 till June 1903. He took his meals at the boarding house of Mrs. Selma Gorren, a place much frequented by young lawyers. Impervious though he was to luxury, something of the sparse chill of this atmosphere appears to have penetrated

[4] Charles Jarvis Fay, b. Columbus, Ohio, 1871; Yale 1893, Columbia Law 1899; partner in the law firm of White & Case, New York.

even his indifference. He complains, at one moment, of "the slovenly, heathenish way of living which the New York boarding house superinduces." Mrs. Gorren, it transpired, was at that time passing through a financial crisis and her boarders suffered accordingly. Dwight Morrow, one evening before supper, found her weeping on the stairs. She thrust into his hands a tear-stained letter which is to this day preserved, with other perhaps more important documents, among his files. The letter ran as follows:

A. S. Barnes & Co.
156 Fifth Avenue, New York
September 16, 1901

Mrs. Selma Gorren
18 West 45th Street

Madam:

Notice is hereby given that four months' rent of 18 West 45th Street are past due and payable and that unless at least one month's rent, viz. $183.34 is paid by return mail the premises must be vacated.

Meantime I remain

Yours respectfully
Henry B. Barnes

Morrow was apparently able to settle this, his first experience of diplomacy, with Mr. Barnes, since two days later we find him writing to Mrs. Gorren the following firm but consoling letter:

September 18, 1901

Mrs. Selma Gorren
18 West 45th Street
New York

Dear Mrs. Gorren:

I am handing you herewith a copy of a letter which I wrote today to Mr. Barnes, the son of your landlord. Mr. Fay telephoned him this morning. While I know Mr. Barnes slightly, he is a very intimate friend of several friends of mine, and I have strong hopes that his father will grant you the additional time which you desire.

I should advise you to pay him the $50.00 which you have immediately and then be very careful to give him the October payment promptly. You should also make arrangements to set aside as much as possible in order to wipe out the back indebtedness. I see no immediate prospect of finding anybody who will loan you anything upon your furniture, but I have strong hope that you will keep your courage and pull yourself out of your difficulties safely. You will, of course, realize that while neither Mr. Fay nor I have assumed any legal obligation for your fulfilling your promises to Mr. Barnes, we have in a certain measure staked our reputation upon your ability to straighten the matter out.

With very best wishes for a successful outcome, believe me,

Faithfully yours,

Enc.   Dwight W. Morrow

2

The summer of 1900 was torrid even for New York and the attic room at 46th Street became a furnace. Down in Philadelphia the Republican National Convention nominated William McKinley for a second term and Theodore Roosevelt as Vice President. Away in Kansas City the Democratic National Convention nominated William J. Bryan upon an anti-imperialistic platform. The memory of the Spanish war had ceased to be a pleasing memory. The Dewey Arch still reared its dazzling white plaster on Fifth Avenue, but the Dewey legend was already in decline.

America, having for one hysterical moment tasted the wine of jingoism, having shouldered for a space the White Man's burden, was already tiring of the "Little Brown Brother," was morally much embarrassed by the rebellion of Emilio Aguinaldo in the Philippines. Senator Beveridge and William Allen White might still inform them that it was their manifest destiny to go forth as a world conqueror; the American public had no desire to fulfill any such destiny. The expansionist typhoon had lasted but a few excited hours; the great waters of American pacifism had resumed their habitual calm.

Internally, also, the social unrest, which had reached a climax in 1896 around the person of William J. Bryan, was tending to subside. The psychological shock occasioned by the End of the Frontier in 1890, by the closing of the glamorous period of free land, by the realization that America's opportunity, and her resources, were not in fact limitless, had been mitigated by the ensuing romance and self-satisfaction of the Cuban episode. Wall Street, it is true, was still regarded with deep suspicion and the movement against the "boss" system in politics was increasing. But the great inflation controversy of the middle 'nineties had been all but silenced by a welcome increase in the supply of the world's gold. The year 1900 stands out, flanked by the anxieties of 1896 and the anxieties of 1902, as a year of relaxation. And thus, at the turn of the century, New York relaxed.

It was the period of Mr. Dooley and Charles Dana Gibson, of the shirtwaist and Richard Harding Davis, of "Richard Carvel" and "Monsieur Beaucaire." People in 1900 were reading "The Master Christian" by Miss Marie Corelli, but they were also reading "When the Sleeper Wakes," by Herbert G. Wells. The theatres were crowded. Sarah Bernhardt acted in

"Camille" and Coquelin in "Tosca." Henry Irving and Ellen Terry journeyed to New York with "The Merchant of Venice" and "The Bells." Mr. William Gillette was repeating his impersonation of Sherlock Holmes, and Miss Maxine Elliott was winning great applause in "When We Were Twenty-one." The street organs still played the "Swanee River," with more modern additions from "Florodora." There was as yet no jazz; there was only the cakewalk.

Dwight Morrow took but little share in all these gaieties. He would return late to 46th Street, pursuing "along the corridors of time" the problems which had arisen during the day. It was a period of great activity in the City of New York; companies were being fused almost daily and combines were being formed; the office of Reed, Simpson, Thacher & Barnum hummed like a hive.

Morrow, with characteristic thoroughness, would work far into the night studying the past history and basic principles of the subjects with which he had to deal. He acquired in this manner a varied knowledge of economics and an expert acquaintance with the origins of banking and the history of financial legislation. He studied Bagehot assiduously and could quote long passages from "Lombard Street" by heart. The influence exerted upon him by the writings of William Graham Sumner [5] was even more important, and, although he never became a dogmatic free-trader, yet he acquired from Sumner a definite belief in Herbert Spencer's organic theory of society. Nor were these studies wholly academic. The Supreme Court in 1896 had, amid general indignation, declared invalid the graduated income tax bill of 1894. Morrow

[5] William Graham Sumner, economist, b. Paterson, New Jersey, 1840; Yale 1863; professor of political and social sciences, Yale, 1872-1909, emeritus 1909-10; d. 1910.

foresaw that the income tax controversy was one which would become of central importance in the next decades. He plunged into an intensive study of taxation, analyzing Seligman with the greatest care. "There is one subject," he said in after life, "which I really *do* know about. And that is taxation." This knowledge was of the very greatest use to him in the years that followed.[6]

Mr. Simpson became uneasy when he noticed this voracious industry. "Never," he said to Morrow, "never work on Sunday, not for any man." Morrow disregarded this advice. True it is that he joined the Harbor Hill Golf Club, played tennis occasionally, and never failed on Sundays to attend Dr. Purvis' Presbyterian Church. Yet he continued to work more than was either necessary or wise. No subject could be too indigestible or too arid for his insatiable appetite. He actually enjoyed things more when they were dull. "The older I get," he wrote to Charles Burnett, "the more I feel that our real satisfaction in life is to be gotten from the way we do our work, rather than from the work we do."

There was evidence, none the less, that his health was suffering. "I notice with alarm," he wrote, "that my mind during the evenings keeps running upon office questions." "I am afraid," he wrote again, "that I have come to be something of a fatalist in regard to headaches. You see I have had them for a long time. I sometimes think they belong to me as fairly as does the taste for mathematics."

Charles Burnett was equally preoccupied with the spiritual health of his friend. "Win a little time," he wrote to him,

[6] The depth of his study of income tax problems can be gauged from a scholarly article which he contributed to the *Columbia Law Review* in May 1910. In 1917 he took a leading part in securing the passage through Congress of the Hollis Amendment whereby gifts to charity up to 15 per cent of income were exempted from income tax.

"from this stirring vigor for the contemplative life and you will be the richer. The latter is in you and wants only the chance for its appearance." Morrow accepted this advice with affectionate modesty. "My work," he wrote to Burnett in November 1900, "has been most interesting and inspiring. My health has been fine and the hard work seems to make me flourish both in body and mind. About *soul,* I am not so sure. If I did not have a good man like you to keep track of me I am afraid I should be forgetting some of the better things."

There would be moments, however, when the pressure of study and the airlessness of his top-floor bedroom would become unendurable. He would descend in his shirt sleeves to the street and spend an hour or two talking to an aged Dutch tobacconist who kept a cigar store on the east side of Sixth Avenue, between 45th and 46th Streets. Morrow was fond of this old Boer, whom he called "Oom Paul." There would be much talk about the Tugela River and Spion Kop, about Magersfontein and Paardeberg, about Cronje and De Wet. Oom Paul was anything but an Anglophile; Dwight Morrow was anything but an imperialist; their agreement was complete.

During these conversations Morrow would smoke a cigar of the brand known as "Bouquet de Paris." He continued to smoke these cigars even at a date when they could no longer be excused on the grounds of poverty. His friends loathed the "Bouquet de Paris" and protested strongly. "Well, you see," Morrow would answer, "they serve a very useful purpose. They prevent me, and you, from acquiring the tobacco habit."

In the spring of 1901 he and Charles Fay decided that they could not possibly face another summer under the grilling roof of 46th Street. It was agreed that they should migrate for the hot weather to Staten Island. A boarding house, entitled the Hotel Belleview, was discovered on Grymes Hill, where once had been the home of Bache Cunard. Other young lawyers combined in the enterprise, and some twenty-five young men would thus cross New York bay every evening in the ferry. After supper they would sit out on the porch, looking down upon the lights of the harbor and listening to the Italian singers who rowed close to the shore yelling Neapolitan songs. The young men would answer with songs from their own college repertories. Dwight Morrow much enjoyed these ditties, although he was not always able to tell one from the other. He was contented in this irresponsible circle. It was amid the gaiety of the Staten Island group that he first met Joseph P. Cotton, later Undersecretary of the State Department and his firm supporter during his Mexican mission. It was here also that he met Charles W. McCandless, who became thereafter one of the dearest of his family friends.

Yet there were other reasons why Dwight Morrow was so uproariously happy in the late summer of 1901.

3

There had been occasions, during the last two years, when he would be assailed by some brooding obsession. Suddenly he would thrust his books aside, crouch close to the embers of the fire, and let the poker thud softly among the dying embers. Charles Fay knew that on such occasions he was thinking about Elizabeth Reeve Cutter and the non-arrival of an expected letter from Cleveland. Already in 1899, during the first weeks of their joint sojourn at 46th Street, Charles Fay had been admitted into the secret of what he then regarded as a hopeless romance.

Morrow, one evening, had risen abruptly from his chair and hurried to the little black trunk in the corner where he kept his personal treasures. He had returned with a photograph. "Charlie," he had said, "here is the girl whom I am going to marry." It was a photograph of Elizabeth Reeve Cutter. "I am *going* to marry," repeated Dwight Morrow, his young face taut with lines of determination. Charles Fay, who until then had never known Morrow to express any interest in romance, was much impressed. He relapsed into appropriate murmurings of approval. "Here again," he thought, "is an instance of Dwight's powers of concentration." He had little conception of how intense, how compelling, those powers could be.

From the day when he first met Elizabeth Cutter at Amherst in 1893, Dwight Morrow never for one instant diverged from his admiration of her provocative independence or his respect for the strength of her intellect and character. For ten long years he concentrated upon this resolve. His tenacity was overwhelming; his constancy superb; his eventual triumph a victory by which everyone was conquered and none defeated. It was not an easy struggle; there were many obstacles; and it took him eight years before he was assured of success. But his achievement, when finally realized, was enduring. It assured the unclouded happiness of two exceptional people over a period of twenty-eight years.

The stream of this romance, as has been said, did not run smoothly. Elizabeth Cutter had been nurtured in circumstances similar to, but not identical with, those of Morrow himself. There was the same background of principle. Yet there was a difference of practice. "Betsey," he would tease her in after years, "you cannot claim that you were strictly brought up. Your parents played cards and you were taught to dance. No, Betsey, you cannot claim that you were strictly brought up." There was, in fact, a difference between the Cleveland and the Pittsburgh backgrounds which it is necessary to define. It was a difference in culture and in horizon. Elizabeth Cutter was herself deeply interested in literature and art. In the Cleveland circle there were many friends who shared these interests. Dwight Morrow, especially during his Amherst period, was impervious to the esthetic, even as he was indifferent to the more elaborate graces of human intercourse. In the early stages of their acquaintance she regarded him as a brilliant rather than as a romantic figure. The very certainty, the actual concentration, of his devotion, while it irritated her strong instinct for independence, failed to stimulate her imaginative impulses. He was unaware of these insufficiencies. In the rush of his affection he brought brother Jay up to see her at Smith College. It was fortunate perhaps that he did not, at the time, realize the effect of this stratagem. "Mr. M.," recorded Miss Cutter in her diary, "brings his brother to see me. I like his brother more than I like Mr. M."

The efforts by which he endeavored to secure the presence of Miss Cutter at the Amherst commencement exercises of 1895 have already been recorded. Shortly afterwards she herself graduated from Smith College with distinction. She returned to Cleveland where, for a space of time, she taught in a private school. Dwight Morrow visited her there in December 1895 (they even went to the theatre), and again

in June of 1896. Such visits were not repeated. Their corre-
spondence seems, on one side at least, also to have languished.
"Do I ever hear from Cleveland?" he writes to his sister in
March of 1899. "About once a year or thereabouts."

In the summer of that same year 1899 Miss Cutter and her
sister Annie left for Europe with an English uncle. A few
months later they were joined by their parents and youngest
sister Edith and remained absent for almost two years. This
expedition was undertaken, partly in the interests of Mr.
Cutter's health and partly in order that Elizabeth Cutter
might complete her distinguished record at Smith College
by a finishing course at the Sorbonne and in Florence.

During this long absence it was considered fitting that
Dwight Morrow should curtail both the number and the
tone of his letters. He agreed that he would write imperson-
ally and only on the occasion of some "holiday." This obligation did not prove very restrictive to a man of his resource:
the number of the "holiday" letters which reached Paris or
Florence gave the impression that, instead of studying for a
bar examination, this young man was celebrating every feast
of the Established Church, every event in American history,
and the birthday and other anniversaries of his remote relations and most distant friends. These letters produced an
effect. They reminded Miss Cutter of the incisive brilliance
of his conversation and of the actual zest which he was
able to impart to ideas. She found herself comparing the
quality of his mind and character with those of her super-
ficially more cultured friends. Such comparison was all to
Morrow's advantage.

Early in 1901 the Cutter family returned to Cleveland.
Dwight Morrow had abandoned not one jot of his persist-

ence, but there were moments when even he became discouraged. During one of his moods of depression he confided in Charles Burnett who, as usual, was affectionate and philosophic. It was almost by chance that this devoted friend was able, much to his own surprise, to be of practical assistance.

In the month of June 1901 Charles Burnett decided to take a holiday at Annisquam, near Gloucester, Massachusetts. He asked Morrow to accompany him. The latter was busy at the moment but promised to join him at Annisquam in the course of a few days. Burnett arrived alone at the little inn kept by Mr. Publicover. He found that Elizabeth Cutter, in charge of an invalid relative, was staying under the same roof. He warned her that Dwight Morrow was expected shortly and asked whether it would be more tactful to tell him not to come. She replied that it would *not* be more tactful to tell him not to come. He arrived on July 24th. On July 26th they became engaged.

Two months later he broke the news to his mother:

> Law Offices of Reed, Simpson,
> Thacher & Barnum
> 25 Broad Street, New York
> September 23, 1901

Dear Mater:

Your letter came today. I am sorry you are not coming down this fall, but perhaps it will be wiser for you to come when Agnes is able to come with you.

One reason why I wanted you to come down was to tell you a little secret. I have gone and got engaged to be married. Please don't shout out loud until you read my solemn exhortation not to tell anyone. The girl is Elizabeth Reeve Cutter of Cleveland, Ohio. She is a fine, dear, straightforward little girl who has been my best girl friend for some seven or eight years, although it is but a few weeks since she told me that she loved me. Dear old Mater, I hope this makes you happy. I know you will like her very, very much and she will surely like you and love you dearly. She is a girl who has been brought up not essentially different from the way our little brood was reared—in a good Presbyterian family. She is pretty nearly my own age—between Hilda and me.

There! That's all there is to say except that I know what a serious step I have taken and am very happy over it. It isn't necessary for me to tell you that I don't expect to be married until I am firmly enough on my feet here in New York to be sure that I'm not bringing a girl to share hardships with me. It will probably be two years before I can support two comfortably.

You must remember that you are still to come to New York and let me tell you about it.

Now, inasmuch as it is to be some time before I am married, I don't want anybody told. You may tell the good Grandmother and the Pater and Alice *but no more*. In order to give you the news first I have not written Agnes yet but will write her tomorrow, if I don't get the chance today.

Good night, dear Mater. I'll be satisfied if my wife makes as good a wife as you have made to the Pater and I pray that you may have many years left you in which to see her do it and that as many of them as you wish may be spent with us.

Your boy,

Dwight

A long engagement followed, but for him it was a period of inspired work and happy anticipation. The immediate condition of his finances did not allow of marriage or even of a public announcement of his engagement. Yet, in the centre of his soul, there was no further cause for alarm. The echo of his confidence rings thereafter sharp as the sound of horseshoes galloping through the night:

Association of the Bar
42 West 44th Street, New York
February 8, 1902

My dear Mater:

With Jay in the Philippines and Agnes on the way there and with Hilda married and away from home and me in the city of New York planning to get married, you must feel that your little brood of chickens have pretty well fled from the hen coop. I meant to write you so that you would get the letter on your birthday but I kept putting it off because of work and here I am sitting down and writing you when your birthday is nearly over.

Maybe when your next birthday comes around I will be able to invite you down here to a home of my own. I haven't any definite plans yet as to getting married, but if things go well in the office this year, I shall expect or hope to be married in about a year. I sent Jay a check for $75.00 the first of this month, being the final payment on the $775.00 I owed him when I left Columbia a little over two years ago.

I'm getting $1,800 a year now and an occasional extra. The extra which promises to come this month may be as high as $500.00, that being the amount I am to get for a little extra work if a particular matter goes through. That however is something you must say nothing about, yet. I don't expect to get married until they give me $3,000.00, but I rather expect they will do that next year if I tell them I need that much in order to get married. Unless you and the Pater are intending to build a house I think I shall let myself remain in your debt for awhile. My present insurance will more than pay you if anything should happen and when I get married I'll carry enough of it for you to make you safe.

Meanwhile I am going to subtract from my savings a small bill and enclose it for you to buy a new hat or pair of shoes.

Some time when you have a moment of leisure I wish you would sit down and write a letter to my Elizabeth. Her address is 1174 E. Madison Avenue, Cleveland, and her full name is Elizabeth Reeve. I think she would appreciate it very much if you would write her and tell her that you want her to come down and see you as soon as she feels that she is ready to announce our engagement—or before—if she chooses. Mayhap she will feel reassured if you tell her that I'm not a half bad sort of a fellow and have never beaten my mother.

Well, good night, Mammy! I wish you would write the little girl and hope you may have many, many happy returns and I wish the enclosed five dollars were five hundred.

Dwight

They were married at Cleveland on June 16, 1903. Among the wedding presents were thirteen cut-glass bowls. Dwight Morrow wore a frock-coat and a white waistcoat. Charles Burnett, as was fitting, acted as best man.

4

The honeymoon lasted from June 17th to July 20th and was spent among the New England hills which they both loved so dearly. From Greenfield they drove to Brattleboro, and from there to Spofford Lake. A long visit was paid to Annisquam, where they were greeted by Mr. Publicover, and a shorter visit to Amherst, where they saw Professors Garman and Morse. A note to his mother is typical of those breathless letters which sons and daughters write to their parents during the first days of a honeymoon:

The Brooks House
Brattleboro, Vermont
June 21, 1903

Dear Mother:

We left in such a hurry last Tuesday evening that neither of us got a chance to say goodby to you as we wanted. We came directly from Cleveland to Greenfield, Massachusetts, and from Greenfield to Brattleboro. We have been climbing and tramping over the hills here and having a fine time. You've got a fine new daughter, Mater—finer than you know, however much you may like her now. Some day when you come to visit us in New York you will have a little better idea of how good a girl she is—but you'll never know how completely happy she makes me.

We go from here to Spofford Lake tomorrow—driving; and then the next day drive from there to Keene, New Hampshire. From Keene we plan to go to Deerfield and from Deerfield to Northampton and Amherst and then to Annisquam for a long quiet rest.

I hope that you got home safely from the wedding, were not too tired, and that you had a good time. With love from my wife to my mother,

Yours in haste
Dwight

From Boston they took the boat to New York and spent a few days with Mr. and Mrs. Robert de Forest on Long Island. For Dwight Morrow this visit was merely the continuation of his honeymoon and the gaiety which sparkled in his blue eyes was triumphant. For Elizabeth Morrow, who since June 16th had been living in some other-world of delight, the arrival at Cold Spring Harbor marked a return to reality. The rooted dignity of the de Forest home reminded her that she had lost her Cleveland background,

77

and that it would take her many, many years to re-create in the unfamiliar East an environment worthy of her husband's future. It was during those days that she realized how protracted and how solitary, how wise and tentative, must be her endeavor to build up around their mutual devotion a social atmosphere which should both soothe and stimulate her husband's intellectual restlessness; an atmosphere which, while satisfying her own fastidiousness, would entail no lowering of the proud standards of her independence. The contemplation of this responsibility filled her with a sudden seriousness. In the years that followed she was to prove that a perfect marriage can, while remaining an idyll, become an epic. At Cold Spring Harbor so creative an achievement seemed difficult and distant; her courage, for the moment, quailed. "Have felt very quiet here," she records in her diary, "and unlike myself."

She soon recovered her identity. On July 20th, Dwight Morrow returned to his office desk, and after spending a short time at Como, New Jersey, they joined the group at Staten Island. The bachelor survivors of that fraternity greeted them with acclaim: the table allotted to them in the dining room was decorated with huge white ribbons. In the gaiety of these surroundings Elizabeth Morrow settled down to the problem of a permanent home.

It was at this stage that her husband developed a sudden, and wholly unexpected, taste for social status. He explained that it was impossible for anyone in their position to live on the west side of Fifth Avenue. Such a thing simply "wasn't done." They must find an apartment on the East Side. To this day it is unknown from what sources Dwight Morrow, who in general was contemptuous of social distinctions, had derived this obstinate piece of information. It was pointed out to him that any apartment in the more fashionable areas would cost them three times their total income. He insisted none the less that his Elizabeth could not live west of Central Park. The only alternative was to abandon New York completely and to concentrate on the suburbs. It happened that John Kerr lived at Englewood, New Jersey. He invited the Morrows to stay with him for August 10th and 11th, to examine the locality with a view to permanent residence. They decided at once that this was the place in which they wished to live. They therefore lived there for twenty-eight years.

Englewood is a small city situated in Bergen County, among the woods which clothe the western escarpment of the Hudson River. It extends for some three or four miles along the Northern Valley. There is a nucleus around the main railroad depot of shops and gasoline stations, of banks and churches, of drug-stores and real estate agencies. The town then wanders westward towards the Teaneck ridge, and in the east climbs the hill, dispersing itself into detached houses of wood and brick dotted brightly among the surrounding trees. The hill rises in terraces from the Northern Valley until it culminates in the long line of the Palisades, dominating the deep canyon of the Hudson River. The trees continue to the edge of this cliff barrier, and tumble down the clefts to the edge of the river itself. From the summit of these cliffs a wide view can be obtained, westwards toward the hills above Paterson, eastwards to the dim distant outline of Long Island, and southwards across that splendid river to where, twelve miles away, New York City rears its minarets. The scenery is, in fact, suggestive both of Reigate and the Rhine.

On their very first visit they started to look for a home. The budget which, during their evenings at Como and Staten Island, they had drafted so carefully allowed them $45.00 a month for rent. There was "a dear little old-fashioned house" which came within these requirements. On the other hand there was another, larger, and far dearer house which Dr. Van Horne had just constructed on Spring Lane. The monthly rent for this mansion was $62.50. It was brown and warm and cheerful: there was a bilberry hedge beside it: the station was only a few hundred yards away: and Dr. Van Horne consented to put an open fireplace into the back sitting room, or "library." They knew that this house was beyond their income; they also knew that it was exactly what they desired. They started negotiations with Dr. Van Horne. Would he put in more bookcases? Dr. Van Horne replied that there were already two bookcases and that "no sensible man required four bookcases." Would he remove the stained glass windows in the doorway? He refused to do anything of the sort. They signed the lease with jubilation. They decided to economize by omitting to install a telephone.

It was some time before the painters and plumbers left the house. Mrs. Morrow's diary bears the following entry under the date of October 28th: "Our moving day! Bought groceries in the morning. Tonight dear supper in our dining room, Dwight and I, and then a fire in the library! This is home!" And four days later: "Our first Sunday in the new home. A happy day! Read the Psalms together before the fire."

The furniture began to arrive. They were much alarmed by a bill from Messrs. Schwegler of Cleveland for furniture transport and packing. In spite of this, the mahogany library table arrived broken. The packing cases made an excellent dressing-table for the spare bedroom and were draped with cheap muslin. The green sofa was installed in the library.

Morrow wrote triumphantly to Charles Burnett:

". . . The house is fine. It has a parlor, library, dining room and kitchen on the first floor, four bedrooms and a bathroom on the second floor, and two bedrooms on the third floor, a good concrete cellar with a laundry and a furnace, and something of a front porch. I am about two minutes' walk from the station on a quiet little street called Spring Lane. The house has no number, there being only three houses on said Spring Lane. If we choose to claim it I suppose we could call ourselves Number 1. The fine room in the house is the library which has a big open fireplace in which we pile logs every evening. Every room has Georgia pine floors which gives us a chance to use rugs instead of carpets.

"Elizabeth by much ingenuity and carefulness has eked out our store of cash so providently that I find myself the possessor of two mahogany sofas—one in the parlor and one in the library —a fine mahogany library table, and a mahogany dining table and chairs. In the morning—I state it with *awe*—we take our chops or eggs off *doilies!* And we make our coffee in a little copper French coffee pot, which operates on the table and makes fine coffee while you wait. That same coffee pot reposes on your beautiful tray every evening in the library and makes after dinner coffee while we sit around the library fire after dinner. Truly it is grand! . . .

"Elizabeth has been fortunate in getting a good girl from Richmond, Virginia—a colored girl who makes fine rolls and good buckwheat cakes. We like her much and are glad that Lydia, our Annisquam girl, went back on us. Then I have a fine man named Pat who comes three times a day and shovels coal into my furnace. All in all, I feel like a 'grown-up' for sure. You must come and see it. . . ."

Gradually the routine of that happy active life established itself. Dwight Morrow would leave the house at 8 and hurry to the station—"three minutes if I walk," he wrote, "two minutes if I run." He would return at 6.45. His wife would light the lamp on the table by the library window so that he could see it as he hurried up the hill. After supper they would read together by the fire. There would be the "Life and Letters of T. H. Huxley," and subsequently Morley's "Life of Gladstone." Morrow was wont to affirm that the former of these two books influenced him more than any biography he ever read. Of Gladstone he remarked, "What impresses me most is that you always have the feeling that he is primarily learning from history, not from introspection."

The atmosphere of these early years is best conveyed by some extracts from Mrs. Morrow's diary:

1904. *January* 21. The stained glass windows are to be taken out in the spring.

February 9. Dwight came home tonight with the news of an "extra." I sat and guessed from $15.00 all the way up to $250.00!! We can pay Schwegler entire and the coal bill and have money besides to put into the bank. It has been such a happy evening.

February 11. Dwight came home tonight saying Schwegler is paid!! We don't owe a cent.

June 15. Tonight Dwight and I have been sitting on the little green sofa talking about a year ago tonight. It has been such a short happy year!

September 25. Dwight and I have had a perfectly happy time together. Elisabeth lay on the floor after dinner and kicked and crowed and almost crawled. She is irresistible. Wrote Agnes and Mother. Later Dwight and I read "Shall We Understand the Bible?"

December 26. Another happy evening together alone, Dwight and I. We are just as happy together as two people could be I believe.

1905. *February* 12. Finished "Life of Gladstone." Reading Judges aloud tonight—also George Adam Smith's "Geography of Palestine."

March 2. Dwight has been taken into the firm! His name goes on the paper. We have had such a lovely talk about it. I said, "Well anyway I was your first partner." "Yes, dearie, and you will be my last."

March 10. Tonight Dwight has really talked religion—his own beliefs. I wish I had his brains, but I have his heart, which is better.

It was in this house that their first three children were born.[7]

By the end of 1909 their financial troubles were a thing of the past. The diary for 1910 opens with the following extract: "January 1. Tonight we have been talking over our prospects. We have passed the period of struggle. Dwight says it will not be so much fun now—but wherever we are together there will be fun."

---

[7] They had four children, namely: *Elisabeth Reeve,* b. March 17, 1904, married December 28, 1932, Aubrey Niel Morgan, d. December 3, 1934; *Anne Spencer,* b. June 22, 1906, married May 27, 1929, Charles Augustus Lindbergh, and had issue (a) Charles A., Jr., b. June 22, 1930, d. March 1, 1932; and (b) Jon Morrow, b. August 16, 1932; *Dwight Whitney, Jr.,* b. November 28, 1908; and *Constance Cutter,* b. June 27, 1913.

V. Corporation Lawyer   1899–1914

DWIGHT MORROW'S ACHIEVEMENT LESS SIGNIFICANT THAN HIS
PERSONALITY. THE COMBINATIONS OF THAT PERSONALITY AS
AMOUNTING TO A NEW TYPE OF CIVILIZED MIND. HOW FAR HIS
PROFESSION HAMPERED THE EXPRESSION OF THIS PERSONALITY.
THE CONTEMPORARY PREJUDICE AGAINST CORPORATION LAW-
YERS. MORROW'S DISCOMFORT IN FACE OF THIS PREJUDICE. HE
THEREFORE CONCENTRATES ON THE WORK IN HAND. HIS EFFI-
CIENCY AS AN OFFICE LAWYER AND HIS REFORM OF LEGAL
DRAFTSMANSHIP. MR. THACHER'S TRIBUTE. HE BECOMES A PART-
NER AND ELABORATES HIS LEGAL METHOD. DESCRIPTION OF THAT
METHOD. BRILLIANCE CONTROLLED BY CAUTION. FANTASTIC
GOOD SENSE. TOLERANT REASONABLENESS. HIS ACTUAL OCCU-
PATIONS. TWO EXAMPLES OF HIS METHOD. THE AFFAIRS OF THE
EQUITABLE OFFICE BUILDING CORPORATION. THE AFFAIRS OF
THE UTAH POWER & LIGHT COMPANY. HIS BRIEF ON BEHALF OF
THE LATTER.

THE career of Dwight Morrow is less interesting than his
personality. The former was hampered by circumstances and
truncated by premature death. The latter remains as a standard. His achievement, although remarkable, was not unique.
What renders Dwight Morrow so fascinating a subject for
biography is that, in the varied and rapid expansion of his
career, he developed a new type of civilized mind.

An endeavor has been made in preceding chapters to
indicate the central focus from which his intelligence
throbbed out in ever-widening arcs. It is a sad circumstance
that Morrow, who longed to be a teacher, never lived to
recognize that he had become a master to them that know.
There would be moments when he would be conscious of
the full potentialities of his own powers, when he would
feel upon his cheek the wind of the wings of genius; such
moments filled him with awe. There were other moments

when he would doubt his own capacity and regard as accidental the influence he exercised upon his fellow men. In his moods of diffidence—and they were frequent—he would cling to admiration as some frightened child clings to an adult sleeve; in his moments of self-awareness he would be calm, concentrated, and indifferent to external approval. Across this cleft between his self-trust and his self-distrust was suspended a liana bridge of charm, humor, boyishness, and self-assertion. Many observers were so fascinated by these connecting ligaments that they ignored the confronting rocks of practicability and desire which were thus garishly, tenuously, and bravely joined. Even as F. S. Oliver wrote of Alexander Hamilton, "The power of his intellect was hardly suspected under the ambush of his extraordinary charm."

The essence of his genius, the type of civilized mind which he evolved, was, as has already been indicated, a creative combination between the taut and the elastic, between the rigid and the mobile, between the reasonable and the fantastic, between romance and science, between the tolerant and the firm. He showed how organization and individualism could, in fact, be rendered compatible. The fact that this demonstration was effected by the combination of opposites was apt to bewilder even his admirers. "Dwight," they would say, "is a wonderful little fellow." They seldom endeavored to translate this irrelevant gesture of surprise into any coherent opinion. The admiration which he aroused was undiscriminating. Only the more intelligent among his contemporaries realized the profound seriousness of his mind.

It was unfortunate that so interpretative a man should have been accorded, for the arena of his performance, the over-illumined amphitheatre of Wall Street. His resentment of those arc-lamps, which threw the delicate gradations of his aims into crude contrasts of black or white, may partially account for the moods of restlessness which form so curious a counterpart to his concentration upon the work in hand. Again and again we find him struggling to escape from the precisions of the law, from the excitements of high finance, either to the seclusion of some academic grove or to the more distant forests of national or international politics. It is no sufficient explanation to say that Dwight Morrow was indifferent to money or that he actually resented the large sums which almost automatically accrued. The mathematical side of his temperament welcomed such monetary accretions as demonstrably correct. Yet he was more than a mathematician: far more than a lawyer. His imaginative impulses were cumbered by the machinery of corporate law and high finance. It was not unworldliness, since Morrow was too human to dissociate himself from human activities. It was not lack of ambition, since Morrow was a most ambitious man. It was not a prejudice against capitalism, since Morrow, being temperamentally a nineteenth century liberal, was a firm believer in rewards for personal energy. It was a conviction, rather, that his own peculiar genius did not find its amplest expression in terms of material success.

Dwight Morrow was a man of action predominantly interested in ideas. Although a mathematician, and as such intent upon certainties, he was also a romantic, and as such fascinated by the unexpected. He was a fervent sculptor, ever seeking for some less malleable material; it was the obdurate always that he sought to mold.

His career as a lawyer will be examined, therefore, not so much in terms of the actual cases with which he dealt, as in terms of the expansion given to his mind and destiny by those first fifteen years spent in the very centre of capitalism. It matters little whether Dwight Morrow did or did not succeed in reorganizing the Guanajuato Power & Electric Corporation or American Gas & Electric, Inc. It matters a great deal whether, in developing the ingenuity and resourcefulness required of a corporation lawyer, he succeeded at the same time in expanding his own vision and integrity. It is of minor import to what extent he came to be regarded as an expert upon company taxation, public utilities, and water rights; what is of major significance is the confidence, the respect, and the affection which, in the course of this unceasing activity, he managed to inspire.

In the old Amherst days, Calvin Coolidge, on one of those rare occasions when he abandoned his habitual reserve, had told Dwight Morrow that his principle in life would be so to fulfill the functions of the moment as to be able, when called upon, at once to take on some more exacting function. "One should never," he said, "trouble about getting a better job. But one should do one's present job in such a manner as to qualify for a better job when it comes along." Dwight Morrow never forgot that lesson. He avoided the habit of regarding any single occupation as an end in itself; he always regarded his functions as steps to something more important. It was from this angle, with this reservation, that he flung himself, as a pack of beagles, upon the practice of the law.

2

It will be recalled that during the Pittsburgh interlude Dwight Morrow had been relieved to find in the pages of Stubbs and Blackstone confirmation of his theory that a lawyer can become eminent without compromising any of his moral, intellectual, or religious standards. In the first decade of the present century this theory was put to a severe test.

In the period between the end of the Civil War and the end of the Frontier, American opinion had on the whole been grateful to the captains of industry for their energy in opening up the country. So soon, however, as opportunity ceased to be limitless, so soon as there was no more country to open up, this attitude of admiring thankfulness was succeeded by a mood of envious criticism. The "common man" began to feel that while he had himself been occupied in cutting down trees, his more sly compatriots had been occupied in organizing a strangle-hold of trusts and other trade monopolies and in subjugating the political machine to the interests of big business. He was correct in this assumption. His resentment, however justified, was indiscriminate and ill-informed. He did not realize in the first place that a development as impatient and as wide as that which took place between 1870 and 1900 could not, under a capitalist system, be carried out without extreme egoism, ruthlessness, and avarice on the part of individuals. He failed, in the second place, to distinguish between results which were caused by personal greed or selfishness, and results which were the inevitable concomitant of rapidly improving machinery and transport. And in the third place he came to confuse the innocent with the guilty, and to group under such opprobrious terms as "Wall Street," "Big Business," and "Politics," activities which were often valuable and sometimes disinterested.

This growing tide of popular criticism had, towards the end of the century, led to a conflict between the capitalists and the people, culminating in the Sherman Anti-Trust Act of 1890 and the New York and Ohio court decisions of 1890 and 1892. Although these legislative and judicial enactments did in fact put an end to the trust-organizations as they then existed, yet the monopolists were able, with the assistance of their lawyers, to dodge these restrictions and to continue their activities under another name. During the administration of President McKinley the Sherman Act was, in fact, allowed to slumber; and the close alliance which existed, on the one hand, between McKinley and Mark Hanna (the boss of the Republican Party), and on the other hand between Mark Hanna and Wall Street, offered every hope that these slumbers would not be interrupted.

This hope was shattered by a Polish maniac of the name of Czolgosz who, on September 6, 1901, fatally wounded President McKinley at Buffalo. "Now look!" exclaimed Mark Hanna on returning from the funeral, "that damned cowboy is President of the United States!" And in truth Theodore Roosevelt was not sensitive to the feelings either of Wall Street or of the Republican machine.

It was not long before the new President declared war upon the monopolists. The Sherman Act was disinterred and prosecutions were launched against those by whom it had been violated. The campaign culminated in a victory for Roosevelt when, in March 1904, the Supreme Court of the United States reversed its own previous decision and declared illegal the vast merger known as the Northern Securities Corporation. The triumph of the President was, at the time, complete.

In the course of this embittered controversy it was divulged that many captains of industry had relied upon their lawyers to advise them how the provisions of the Sherman

Act could legally be evaded, and that the several *aliases*—such as mergers, holding corporations, syndicates, and alliances—which the Trusts had thereafter assumed had been contrived by the ingenuity of the legal advisers to the parties concerned. It thus resulted that the corporation lawyers of New York City became tarred with the Wall Street brush and that even a firm of rising and unsullied reputation such as Reed, Simpson, Thacher & Barnum could not at the time escape the popular prejudice which arose from this generalization.

Dwight Morrow resented the unfairness of this prejudice. It irked him to feel himself, or those with whom he was identified, exposed to criticism. His confidence in his own firm was absolute, his conviction of their integrity unequivocal. He always regarded himself as a liberal democrat and was distressed to find that the profession which he had acquired after such hard sacrifices was regarded by Demos as illiberal. To him the Law was an honorable, and indeed a sacred, thing. He felt acutely uncomfortable at finding that this view was not shared by the majority of his compatriots. Something of this disquiet lives in a letter, written three years after the crisis, to Charles Burnett:

". . . If a man is a wise lawyer he says to his friend the philosopher, 'I realize that most of the rules of conduct with which I deal are those which concern only the externals of life.' To this I take it the philosopher should reply, 'You are right in dealing only with such rules of conduct in your courts, but you must take care lest you come to believe your statutes are absolute rules like the rules of right and wrong which I discover.'

"To which the lawyer will reply, 'Oh, Philosopher, nobody who readeth the statutes which are now made is in danger of thinking that they have aught to do with right and wrong.' This last retort would show that the lawyer is something of a humorist without the power of continued philosophic thought. . . ."

The last words of this letter are significant. Morrow was well aware that as a managing clerk in a single firm he could not reform the whole legal system of the United States. All he could hope to accomplish was improvement within the immediate orbit of his own activity. He thus concentrated upon doing his own work ideally without seeking to impose the ideal system upon others. That, throughout his life, was the method he adopted. He always preferred tiny idealisms in practice, to vast idealisms in theory. He influenced by the force of small but numerous examples. His function at the moment was that of a lawyers' clerk. He would perform that function more honorably and more efficiently than it had ever been performed before. He therefore concentrated, during those years of controversy and abuse, upon his actual daily task.

3

The force of that concentration was tremendous. With voracious energy he seized upon the briefs which were entrusted to him. He examined, explored, verified, substantiated, analyzed, and advised. Four years after he first joined Reed, Simpson, Thacher & Barnum, he was promoted managing clerk. It was not long before he became the nerve-centre of the whole firm.

Morrow, essentially, was an "office" lawyer. He was never an exceptional advocate. Only four times in his career did he actually appear in court, and on such occasions his performance was satisfactory rather than brilliant. "This," he wrote after his initial appearance as an advocate, "is the first time that I have been paid to talk and others have been paid to listen to me. I could not make them listen." Yet when, in later years, he appeared at Denver, Colorado, on behalf of the Utah Power & Light Company, he was able to overwhelm his audience by the cataract of his specific knowledge and general erudition. It was not, however, as a forensic lawyer that he made his mark.

There was in the first place the office itself. His methods of organization and procedure were both authoritative and gay. "He was," records one of the junior clerks, "the boss in our office. When he went home the day was over for the rest of us." He was almost pedantic in his insistence upon the value of economical drafting. He would assert that each statement should be composed on the assumption "that every unnecessary word costs ten dollars." When he first arrived at Reed, Simpson, Thacher & Barnum the conventional style of drafting was archaic in the extreme. Corporate papers were not considered effective unless the old formulas were repeated and engrossed with heavy reiteration. Dwight Morrow, as one of his colleagues records, "took the old forms and made them new." He insisted that the essence of legal statement was that the correct ideas should be formulated in the correct order. He condemned all parenthetical sentences and all qualifications. "Think," he would say to the junior clerks, "what it is that you want to say. And then say it in the fewest possible number of words. Good English can be recognized by a single test. Is this sentence simple and precise? That is the only test which need worry you about good English."

It came to be noticed, after a few years, that the documents which emanated from the firm of Simpson & Thacher were more intelligible and more crisp than those which were drafted by less newly established firms. They were both scholarly and vernacular. There was no attempt to resort to the indolent pedantry of established jargon. They gave to opinions a dash of outspokenness, even of realism. The modernity of Morrow's drafting affected the legal correspondence of the time.

There was also the problem of personal relations. With the partners and the staff he was almost at once on terms of intimacy and affection. Mr. Simpson and Mr. Thacher came, within a few months, to regard him with unlimited confidence and esteem. The clients of the firm were at first disconcerted by his youthful appearance, and by his indifference to the accustomed formulas of impressiveness. In the end, they came also to rely on Dwight Morrow as the most substantial and sympathetic member of the firm.

"He had," records Thomas D. Thacher, "an uncanny knack of quickly finding the common ground upon which the conflicting claims of divergent interests could be resolved. . . . In many of his negotiations he became the acknowledged leader in working out a complex situation, even though he represented but one of the parties interested. In such cases he quickly gained his opponents' complete confidence—inspired by his integrity of mind and sincerity of purpose, not merely to protect the selfish interests of his client but to preserve the substantial interests of his opponent in a common understanding of mutual advantage to both. Men mutually desirous of accomplishing a common object turned naturally to him to iron out the difficulties of agreement arising between them. . . . Thus he earned an enviable reputation at the bar, and very quickly gained the respect and confidence of many men who were preëminent as leaders in the world of business and finance." [1]

There could be no more accurate or comprehensive description of Dwight Morrow's subsequent technique as diplomatist and statesman.

Such capacity, such industry, such erudition, earned him, within less than ten years, a high reputation in his own profession. People began to quote Dwight Morrow's opinion as something which created effect even in the highest circles of big business. On one occasion Mr. Simpson, the senior partner, meeting James Elmore Morrow, Dwight's father, addressed him as follows: "Mr. Choate, Mr. Root, and I have the reputation of being the best corporation lawyers in the City of New York. Your boy is better than any of us." James Morrow scratched his head and chuckled.

That Mr. Simpson's eulogy was inspired by something more than Amherst sentiment, or personal affection, can be deduced from his action when, in the spring of 1905, Dwight Morrow was invited to join the faculty of Columbia Law School. He was much tempted by this offer and hesitated for a few days whether he should accept it or no. At that date he was no more than a clerk in the office of Simpson, Thacher & Bartlett, and such an offer was flattering in the extreme. He informed Mr. Thacher both of the offer and of his own temptation to accept it. Mr. Thacher was deeply perturbed. He cabled to Mr. Simpson, who at that moment was spending a holiday in Europe. "Under no circum-

---

[1] Thomas D. Thacher, b. Tenafly, New Jersey, 1881; Yale 1904, member of Yale Corporation; Solicitor General of the United States 1930-33; now associated with Simpson, Thacher & Bartlett as counsel. The passage quoted is from Mr. Thacher's contribution to the New York Bar Association memorial of 1931 to Mr. Morrow.

stances," came the reply, "let him go. Make him a member of the firm at once."

It was in this manner that Dwight Morrow became a partner in Simpson, Thacher & Bartlett's and that his name appeared, as such, upon the firm's notepaper.

The immediate impression that he created was thus one of rapid resourcefulness, even of ingenuity. This impression was shortly succeeded by surprise at his extreme caution. He would dart at an idea, and having caught the idea would sit down and examine it with the most scientific concentration. Impulse and imagination would at once be succeeded by prudence and reflection. It was at this point that his clients would become impressed by the width of his knowledge and the depth of his industry. Having by these methods analyzed his own original idea and submitted it to a series of almost chemical tests, he would then hold it up to the light, turning it this way and that in order that each successive facet should be illumined. Occasionally he would set the idea down upon his table and walk around it, scrutinizing it from every point of view. Having satisfied himself that the idea was advantageous to his client and sound in law, he would then pass on to the final stage of his examination and consider the proposition in terms, not of immediate or one-sided expediency, but in terms of its own intrinsic value. For this particular test he would place himself in the frame of mind of the opposite side. Was the proposition one which would appeal to them as fair, reasonable, and just? Was it one which they would accept without mental reservations and be able to execute without undue strain or difficulty? Every contract, in his view, entailed for its fulfillment the coöperation of both parties: that coöperation implied the *will* to coöperate, and such a desire must in its turn be based

95

upon reasonable satisfaction. Dwight Morrow, in all the affairs of life, worked on the principle that a hard bargain was always a bad bargain. Such were his powers of persuasion that he was able to induce even the most obdurate captains of industry to share his view. It was upon his unflagging reasonableness, as much as upon his astounding brilliance or knowledge, that his ultimate reputation was based.

It was in such a spirit that he contributed to the organization or reorganization of such companies as the Electric Bond & Share Company, of the American Gas & Electric Company, of the Electrical Securities Company, of the Central Colorado Power Company, of the Animas Water & Power Company, and of the Equitable Office Building Corporation. He was also continuously concerned with the affairs of the American Locomotive Company, the Railway Steel Spring Company, and the Pacific Coast Company.

These activities brought him into intimate contact with such commercial magnates as Mr. C. A. Coffin [2] of the General Electric, Mr. Henry Cannon [3] of the Pacific Coast Company, Mr. S. Z. Mitchell [4] of the Electric Bond & Share Company, and General T. Coleman du Pont [5] of the Equitable Office Building Corporation.

[2] Charles A. Coffin, b. Somerset County, Maine, 1844; president General Electric Co. to 1913, then chairman of the board; active in American Red Cross work during World War; d. July 1926.

[3] Henry White Cannon, banker, b. Delhi, New York, 1850; U. S. Comptroller of the Currency 1884-86; president Chase National Bank, New York, 1886-1904, chairman of the board 1904-11; d. 1934.

[4] Sidney Z. Mitchell, b. Alabama; U. S. Naval Academy graduate 1883; head of Electric Bond & Share Company to 1933.

[5] T. Coleman du Pont, b. Louisville, Kentucky, 1863; graduate Massachusetts Institute of Technology; president E. I. du Pont de Nemours Powder Co. 1902-15; chairman of the board Equitable Office Building Corporation; active in local and national politics, U. S. Senator from Delaware (resigned 1928); d. 1930.

His work also included a great many bond issues with mortgages, a subject on which he became one of the leading New York experts, being particularly skilled in the development of a new feature which provided security for the bondholder while giving adequate freedom of action to the mortgagor companies. His grasp of commercial and financial problems was no less original and firm than his handling of the problems of corporation law.

An illustration of his capacity for rapid constructive labor is furnished by the constitution of the Equitable Office Building Corporation. The old Equitable Life Building had been completely gutted by fire, and all that remained of its once magnificent offices was the statue of Henry Baldwin Hyde gazing with distressed paternity upon the ruins of its Grand Central Hall. It occurred to General T. Coleman du Pont that it was unfortunate to leave the ruins of this unhappy enterprise as an encumbrance and an eyesore. He decided to purchase the site and to form a corporation for the construction of a new building containing suites of the most modern offices. Negotiations were opened and a board of directors was formed under the chairmanship of Judge Day. It remained to draw up the articles of association. It was at this stage that Judge Day announced that he was obliged to leave for Europe within a week and that the formation of the company must be postponed until his return. Mr. Louis Horowitz,[6] acting for General du Pont, hurried to the offices of Simpson, Thacher & Bartlett, with whom he had conducted many previous negotiations. His idea was that a firm of such experience might possibly be able to draw up articles

[6] Louis J. Horowitz, born 1875 and educated in Poland; former president of Thompson-Starrett Co., Inc. (builders); chairman of the board since 1928; director and trustee of various commercial and charitable organizations.

of association, even in so complicated a matter, before the departure of Judge Day. He found to his disappointment that all the senior partners were absent. He was told that the junior partner, Mr. Dwight Morrow, would shortly be available. He left a message asking Mr. Morrow to come round immediately to Judge Day's office for a conference with General du Pont.

"In about ten minutes," records Mr. Horowitz, "a little fellow came in with his hair mussed up and his vest buttoned wrongly. I explained to him our difficulty, warning him at the outset to interrupt me if there was anything he did not understand. He listened with a far-away look in his eyes. I said to myself, 'This youngster not only does not understand what I am talking about, but he hasn't got sufficient sense to stop me and ask questions.'"

At the conclusion of the interview Dwight Morrow rose, assured them that the papers would be ready within three days, made his little dancing-master bow, and hurried from the room. He worked the whole of that night and the whole of the day following. On the third day the articles of association were accurately completed and the corporation was formed. Judge Day left for Europe. General du Pont and Mr. Horowitz remained to spread the fame of this achievement through the city clubs.

4

Of the many cases on which he was engaged during those years, the one in which he himself took especial pride was that arising out of the appeal lodged by the Department of the Interior against a decision given in favor of the Utah

Power & Light Company by the Utah District Court. It may be taken as a specimen of his legal work.

In the early years of the century the large electrical combines of the eastern states had begun to extend their operations toward the Middle West. Such companies as the General Electric and the Electric Bond & Share Company had come to be interested in the exploitation of water-power in Colorado, Utah, and Nevada. It was soon apparent that the legislation governing water-rights in the arid middle western districts was different both in form and intention from that prevailing upon the well-watered Atlantic seaboard. Dwight Morrow had in the early years of his legal career become interested in these differences, and had specialized in both the federal and state statutes governing the subject, in the ensuing court decisions, and in the interpretations given to these by the Interior and other Departments at Washington. He came to the conclusion that the prevailing practice and opinion was ill-formed and as such anomalous.

The general issue can be simplified as follows. Under the common law which the original thirteen colonies had drawn from England the owner of property possessed, subject to certain very minor restrictions, unburdened rights over the water originating in, or flowing through, that property. In the arid areas of the Middle West, in which water became a matter of essential public utility, it was found that such rights of property must be curtailed in the interests of the community. It was thus enacted that the owner of land could not monopolize any water situated upon that land, or deny right of access to that water, if it could be shown by third parties that the said water could be put "to beneficial use."

The administration at Washington, in a desire to meet the immediate objections of local farmers rather than the ultimate interests of the community as a whole, endeavored to obstruct the operations of the Power Companies. It was not so much a question of whether they were wrong or right in this attitude of opposition; they were probably right; the point is that they based their obstructions upon a faulty legal basis, namely, upon the law as it existed in the watered, and not as it existed in the arid, States.

A test case was provided by the Utah Power & Light Company. Since 1900 this company had been engaged in the exploitation of hydro-electric power works upon the Logan River in the State of Utah. In 1903 the land upon which the company's reservoir was situated was made part of the Federal Forest Reserve, and their activities were therefore brought to a close. They instituted an action against the Department of the Interior in the District Court and were successful. The Department appealed against this decision, and the Power Company entrusted Dwight Morrow with their brief for the defense. It was in this brief that he was able, by superior knowledge, to demonstrate that the Administration was wrong in law.

The Company based its claim upon the Act of 1866. The Department argued, firstly that the Act of 1866 did not apply to hydro-electrical exploitation, since electricity was at that time unknown, and secondly that the Act of 1866 had in fact been repealed by the Act of 1896, which gave power to the Department of the Interior to grant licenses for reservoirs and conduits in federal properties or reservations. Dwight Morrow answered the first contention by showing that the Act of 1866 obliged the owner of land to grant hydraulic privileges when it could be shown that such privileges would be employed "for beneficial use," and by challenging the Department to prove that the operations of the

Utah Power & Light Company were anything but useful and beneficial to the public at large. Their second contention he demolished by showing, with a wealth of detail, that if it were upheld, two-thirds of the companies working on irrigation, mining, lumber, and electric power west of the Alleghenies would have been operating upon an illegal basis.

It may be well, as an illustration of his legal style, to quote a passage from the brief he then composed:

". . . The country acquired from Mexico was an arid or semiarid country. The use of water in the development of mining was a necessity, and the water was at once turned to a beneficial use in complete or substantial disregard of the English common-law doctrine of riparian rights. Entirely apart from the use of water directly in mining, it was inevitable that the mining industry should call into existence communities to minister to the miners' needs. Crops must be raised to feed these new communities; mills must grind grain and furnish clothing. Thus it came to pass that in the main industry of the new country, and in those secondary industries that contributed to the main industry, water was a prime necessity. The rapidly growing population in this new land, with climatic conditions differing from those that prevailed in any other portion of the United States, soon evolved a new system of property law, the very keystone of which was the appropriation of water for beneficial uses.

"Parallel with the mining development in California and Nevada, but entirely independent of any mining law or customs, the doctrine of appropriation of water found a foothold in the Salt Lake Valley in 1847 prior to the acquisition of the territory from Mexico. From the outset the doctrine of appropriation prevailed, entirely regardless of any problem of mining. Small woolen mills were established as early as 1851, and cotton mills as early as 1862. Here, as in the mining region, the local necessities created the law that the man who could put the water to service must be permitted to do so. Here, as in the mining region, the water was an element of absolute necessity. No man could hold it idle if another man was ready to use it. From the beginning, beneficial use was the basis, the measure and limit of the right to the use of water. . . .

"The doctrine of appropriation absolutely required the subordination of land in certain cases to an easement for water. As Judge Hallett said in Yunker *vs.* Nichols, *supra,* necessity required that the law should withhold 'from the land-owner the absolute dominion of his estate, which would enable him to deny the right of others to enter upon it for the purpose of obtaining needed supplies of water.' To permit a farmer in a New England state to condemn a right of way over an adjoining farm in order to secure water, might well be in contravention of the fundamental principles of that common-law which we had drawn from England. Notwithstanding this, however, the climatic conditions in the arid region created a new law. California and Nevada, if they desired, could provide by their constitutions and laws that an owner of land must submit his land to the burden of a ditch in order that the land away from the stream might receive the water without which that land would be worthless."

Morrow was, as has been said, pleased with this particular brief, mainly, we may suppose, because it combined historical with purely legal research. It is in fact an example of lucid and temperate reasoning, fortified by scholarly evidence. His study of this subject entailed upon him several successive trips to Colorado and to Salt Lake City. These brought him into touch with many ruggedly creative people, such as Mr. Stephen Birch,[7] an experience in which he always delighted. And the solidity of his conclusions did much to enhance his already growing reputation in the City of New York.

[7] Stephen Birch, b. New York, 1872; Columbia University School of Mines; president, later chairman, of the Kennecott Copper and other mining companies.

VI. Digressions 1909–1914

"THIS—" Morrow would remark to his wife during these strenuous years—"this, Betsey, is not the life for you or me. Once we have made $100,000 we shall retire from the practice of the law. I shall teach history: you will write poetry: the children will earn their own living."

The fact that, even when his fortune had reached a total of seven figures, he never effected this renunciation does not detract either from its sincerity or from the constancy with which it returned, if only in the form of a daydream, to his mind. Being a practical man and one who had experienced the cramping anxieties of poverty, he was determined to harvest the crop which, at such risks and with such endurance, he had sown. He was determined to justify those seven years which he had with apparent unwisdom lavished upon his own education. He was determined to secure for himself, for his own family, as for his brother and sisters, a tolerable financial independence. Only when this primary objective had been achieved would he indulge in the luxuries of an academic career.

As an undertone of his whole business life, as a constant

motif in the rhythm of his philosophy, recurs again and again the old prayer from the Phaedrus:

Socrates. Should we not offer up a prayer first of all to the Gods of this place?

Phaedrus. By all means.

Socrates. Beloved Pan, and all ye other Gods who haunt this place, give me beauty in the inward soul; and may the outward and the inward man be at one. May I reckon the wise to be the wealthy, and may I have such a quantity of gold as a temperate man and he only can bear and carry. Anything more? The prayer I think is enough for me.

Phaedrus. Ask the same for me, for friends should have all things in common.

This prayer, amid the rush and rattle of Wall Street, was continuously on his lips. It was read above his coffin when he lay dead.

He never realized his ambition of retiring, once independence had been achieved, into a life of contemplation. The scheme, as so often happens, created—by the very process of its execution—other responsibilities. The industry and acumen necessitated by his primary objective imposed upon him, once that objective had been secured, ever wider obligations and opportunities. He became responsibly involved in important affairs and found it difficult, at any given moment, to divest himself of that responsibility. Moreover, during his later years as a corporation lawyer he came to taste the stimulant of influence and the wine of power. The scholarly, the didactic, the almost pedagogic, approach remained with him, as will be seen, until the end. But as circumstances and his own energy enlarged the circles of his influence from the initial circumference of Cedar Street to the wide arcs of international affairs, his function in life became the education of the adult rather than of the adolescent; not of Amherst only, but of the world. He was himself too modest to realize the nature of this enlargement. "Other things," he would say, "became more important."

His personal fortune, his actual savings, did not, until he became a partner in J. P. Morgan & Co., show any startling increment. His share in the profits of Simpson, Thacher & Bartlett was calculated on a percentage basis and did not, owing to the number of less active partners who claimed a higher percentage, represent any vast sums. Until he went to Morgan's he never bought an automobile, and even then the car which he owned was no more glorious than an open Packard. True it is that by August 1911 he had prospered sufficiently to allow himself the luxury of a personal secretary and to engage Mr. George Foley of Englewood at a salary of $20.00 a week. In April 1915 Mr. Foley's place was taken by Mr. Arthur Springer who to this day occupies for the Morrow family the position of guide, philosopher, and friend. Yet the most Dwight Morrow ever made in one year at Simpson, Thacher & Bartlett was $35,000, and that figure was only reached in 1913, the last year of his partnership. The total capital which he was able to accumulate during his fourteen years of arduous labor as a corporation lawyer did not exceed the figure of $100,000.

Dwight Morrow was never an acquisitive, or even a thrifty, man. When once his immediate debts had been liquidated he displayed no desire either for ostentation or for economy. He bought expensive books which he read carefully and marked with heavy pencil lines upon the margin. He was generous to his relations. And he indulged, without stint, in the delights of foreign travel.

Being a dynamic person, Dwight Morrow remained intellectually malleable until the day of his death. His mind was always in process of formation; he was always a student hungry to learn new things. His early journeys to Europe, although undertaken at an age when a less intelligent man would already have become unreceptive, were for him immensely formative. Some account of these early expeditions must thus be given.

2

The first time that Dwight Morrow crossed the frontier of the United States was in the summer of 1901, when he made a simple camping excursion into Canadian territory. His visits to the Dominion were repeated in 1904 and 1905. It was not, however, till the early summer of 1907, the year of the great Wall Street panic, that he crossed the Atlantic. This, the first of innumerable visits to Europe, lasted from May 25th to July 11th, and the whole five weeks were spent in England. Morrow had equipped himself for this journey with "a brownish suit" from the shop of Charles Leifert in Stone Street, and a letter of credit for five hundred pounds sterling.

Among those letters to his mother which have been preserved is a hurried note, written from the R.M.S. *Etruria* on June 1, 1907, which shows that even at this age of thirty-four Dwight Morrow was capable of boyish excitement:

Dear Mater:

Here I am almost in sight of Queenstown which we should reach this afternoon. When I finish this note I will go out on deck and watch for the first look of Ireland whence my ancestors sailed about one hundred years ago. I suppose they came over in the steerage, if we had such things in those days. . . .

I never was so far away from you before but I never felt better. . . .

Dwight

Since writing I have looked out of the porthole and seen the Ireland of my forefathers. My heart is swelling with the "Wearing o' the Green."

From Ireland they crossed to England, and after a tour in Devonshire and Cornwall they visited the town of Rugby. This eccentric destination had been suggested to Mrs. Morrow by her admiration for Matthew Arnold, and to Dwight Morrow by the pleasure and profit he had derived from reading "Tom Brown's Schooldays." They left the station, wandered for a while about that ugly town, visited Rugby Chapel and Upper School, and then realized that they had lost their way. It was at this moment that an incident occurred which became very familiar to those who, in after years, had the privilege of negotiating with Dwight Morrow on financial or diplomatic affairs.

They accosted a little Rugby boy of twelve or thirteen years of age. "Could you," they asked him, "tell us the way to the station?"

"Well," he answered, "you turn to the right there by the grocer's shop and then take the second to the left. That will bring you to a place where four streets meet. And then, sir, you had better inquire again."

This answer came to symbolize for Dwight Morrow his own method of approaching complicated problems. It implied in the first place a realistic skepticism regarding the capacity of human intelligence. The human mind is a small vessel and cannot, at any one moment, hold too much. It was, in the second place, an object lesson in the inevitability of gradualness. And in the third place it was a parable of how, when the ultimate end is uncertain, one should endeavor to advance, if only a little way, in the correct, rather than the incorrect, direction.

Whenever, in later years, Dwight Morrow reached that stage of negotiation when all hope of a final conclusion seemed obstructed by obstinacy and blurred by fatigue, he would lean back in his chair and allow the twinkle of reminiscence to smooth from his face the frown of concentration. "Well, gentlemen," he would say, "I shall now tell you a story. On my first visit to England in 1907 I visited the town of Rugby. I realized that I had lost my way and might indeed be wandering away from my destination. I stopped a little schoolboy wearing a colored cap. . . ." And then would follow the story culminating with "And then, sir, you had better inquire again." "I propose," Morrow would continue, "I propose, gentlemen, that we now take the first turning to the right there by the grocer's shop."

Many a negotiation was, by this story and the method it symbolized, rescued from collapse.

A second and more elaborate visit was paid to England in the summer of 1908 and lasted for seven weeks. It was not till the spring of 1911 that the great continental tour was undertaken. Accompanied by Fräulein Matter and the three children, they sailed on April 13th on the *Prinz Friedrich Wilhelm* for Bremen. The children and the governess were deposited in the picturesque Harz Mountains while Dwight Morrow and his wife, accompanied by Grosvenor Backus,[1] undertook a walking tour in the Austrian Tyrol. They

[1] Grosvenor Backus, b. Poughkeepsie, New York, 1874; Amherst 1894, Columbia 1897; New York and Washington lawyer.

walked from Jenbach over the Rainer Alp along the Te-
gern See and thus to Munich. And here they parted. Morrow returned to America and Mrs. Morrow joined the children for an educative summer in the Villa Montana at Bad
Harzburg. The entry in her diary for June 4, 1911, runs as
follows: "Simmen's Hotel, Munich. Dwight has just said
goodbye. It is for four months and we have never been separated for longer than four weeks." The family were not,
in fact, reunited until October 2nd.

The effect of these pre-war journeys was important. Mrs.
Morrow had, as has been seen, completed her education in
Europe and was able by her knowledge of foreign cities and
languages to render these holiday periods of leisure and con-
tentment rather than the harassed ordeals endured by less
experienced travelers. Morrow himself was predominantly
interested in sites of historical association and in the lives
and characters of the ordinary people. They conducted themselves, not as tourists tied to time's winged chariot, but as
leisurely observers. From these happy and sensible expeditions he acquired an enlargement of sympathy. Many Anglo-
Saxons, when visiting Europe, are apt to be impressed by
differences rather than by similarities. To the wide humanity
of Dwight Morrow nothing could seem alien. He returned
to the United States with the useful conviction that the average European and the average American, in all essentials of
thought and feeling, are much the same.

3

In May of 1909 the Morrow family moved from the little
brown house in Spring Lane to a site known as the Miller

property, on Palisade Avenue, higher up the hill. This new home, which has since been demolished, is described by the eldest Morrow daughter as "a mild example of late gingerbread architecture with fancy trimming around the windows and a little tower over the front door." The tower and the trimmings were removed and bathrooms were added. The house contained an acre of garden including two especially fine trees, a tulip tree and a sweet gum tree, under which the children would play. From the upper windows a wide prospect opened to the west, over the trees and roofs of Englewood and down to the Northern Valley, to where, above the glinting curves of the Hackensack River, the skyline was edged by the hills above Paterson. At night time the sound of trains hooting in the valley below would rise insistently. All around were trees and lawns. "If," wrote Dwight Morrow, "we keep to our present resolutions and ill fortune does not overtake us, we shall live here for the rest of our lives."

The Morrows, by that time, had become leading members of the Englewood community. Prominent in that community was Henry P. Davison,[2] a partner in the firm of J. P. Morgan & Co. and fully enjoying the prestige—the "superbia Morganorum"—attached to that office. Another neighbor was Thomas W. Lamont,[3] who in his turn was shortly to be admitted as partner to 23 Wall Street. A third Olympian in

[2] Henry Pomeroy Davison, b. Troy, New York, 1867; president Liberty National Bank 1901; vice president and director First National Bank a year later; one of the organizers of the Bankers Trust Company 1903, and of the Astor Trust Company 1907; adviser to the National Monetary Commission 1908; partner in J. P. Morgan & Co. 1915; chairman of the war council, American Red Cross; d. 1922.

[3] Thomas W. Lamont, b. Claverack, New York, 1870; Harvard 1892; Bankers Trust Co. 1903-09; vice president First National Bank 1909-11; partner in J. P. Morgan & Co. since 1911.

the banking world was Seward Prosser,[4] who occupied the house behind the Morrow home on Palisade Avenue.

A legend has since arisen that if one lived at Englewood, if one took daily the 8.22 train up to New York City, and if one acquired thereby the friendship of Henry P. Davison, the road to fame and fortune was thereafter open. This legend, in so far as Dwight Morrow was concerned, is apocryphal. He had but a slight acquaintance with Davison in Englewood days, since Davison left Englewood for Peacock Point, Long Island, in 1909. Far more intimate was Morrow's friendship with Seward Prosser. The latter would call for him on his way down to the station. "Little Judge," he would shout from the garden, and then would begin that breathless scurry, those last minute omissions and reminders, that flurry of things forgotten and things found, which were the accompaniment of all Morrow departures.

His friendship with Thomas Lamont, although close, was not so close as it became in later years. Mrs. Lamont had been a college mate of Elizabeth Cutter at Smith, and the relations between the two families became intimate as the years advanced. The children of the neighborhood would play endless games under the trees, and the parents would meet at the Shakespeare Club, reading "Othello" together or "The Merry Wives of Windsor." The Morrows remained well contented with the friendships which they had formed in their early married life. True it is that the eminence which Morrow subsequently acquired in the wider world of finance and politics brought him a host of glitter-

---

[4] Seward Prosser, b. Buffalo, New York, 1871; started career with Equitable Life Assurance Company of U. S.; vice president Astor Trust Company 1907-12; president Liberty National Bank 1912-14; president Bankers Trust Company 1914-23, now chairman of the managing committee and member of the executive committee.

ing acquaintances and a very few valued friends such as
Mr. and Mrs. Cornelius N. Bliss, George Rublee, and Jean
Monnet. But the friendships which, in those early days of
the little brown house, he had formed with such staunch
neighbors as Mr. and Mrs. Charles Hulst, the Vernon Munroes, or the John Kerrs, were forever cherished undimmed.

"Many of the neighbors," writes Morrow's eldest daughter,
"were young married couples like our father and mother who had
also just moved to Spring Lane, and in a short time they all became good friends. The Kerrs were across the street, the Backuses
next door, the Vernon Munroes on Hillside Avenue, the Prossers
around one corner and the H. V. D. Moores around the other,
while on Engle Street were the Hulsts and the Harlan Stones.
They formed a bridge club called the Simple Club, and on Saturday evenings there were dancing classes over the Woman's Exchange. . . . Life in Englewood during those days was simple
and leisurely. There were few automobiles, even Dr. Holmes
made his rounds in a two-seated buggy. One could not call a taxi
of course, but instead telephoned Englewood 18 and asked Mr.
Leacy to send one of his carriages, a square black box on wheels
which became hermetically sealed as soon as the door was closed.
One leaned back in musty grandeur against the faded green
cushions. . . .

"It was all very neighborly and casual. In those days people
leaned over their fences to ask how things were going at the house
next door, and there was never a more solicitous neighbor than
Mrs. Fitschen, the sweet German lady who lived beside us. When
she came out to garden she always beamed across at us and inquired in her soft foreign voice if little 'Lisbeth and Annchen'
were quite well today."

Even when they moved up to Palisade Avenue, even when
in 1919 they acquired a sumptuous apartment on East 66th
Street in New York, even when they built their present

DWIGHT MORROW AND HIS SON, 1911

home upon the hill, these early associations remained unbroken. Dwight Morrow and his wife considered it the height of vulgarity to lose contact with early friends. Throughout his life he was always available for the affairs of his own community, helping in their charities, assisting them to construct an Armory, contributing his energy to hospital and other drives. During the year 1911 much of his time was occupied with the reorganization of several Englewood charities in the functioning of which serious wastage and overlapping had been observed. There were the Civic League, the Babies' Dispensary, the Tuberculosis Relief Association, the Bureau of Associated Relief, the Visiting Nurses Association, the Englewood Hospital, the Daisy Fields Home for Crippled Children, the Young Men's Club, and the Woman's Exchange. All these separate and sometimes competitive associations maintained their own staffs at a cost to a community of only 10,000 inhabitants of $5,041 a year. Dwight Morrow consented to serve on a committee to investigate this duplication of energy. Expert guidance was asked for from the Charity Organization Society of New York, and a Miss Margaret Byington was lent to the Englewood community in the capacity of consultant. She recommended that five of these nine separate organizations should be fused together under the title of "Civic Association." It was largely owing to Morrow's tact and persuasiveness that this fusion was achieved without undue ill feeling.

4

The affairs of Amherst College also provided a diversion from the practice of the law. Morrow was to learn from bitter experience that the "Amherst spirit"—a spirit of energetic but tolerant idealism—was not as operative among the elder alumni as in the class of '95. A foretaste of later controversies was furnished him in 1908 in connection with the candidature of Grosvenor Backus for the position of trustee.

A vacancy having occurred upon the board of the Amherst Trustees, it became necessary for the nominating committee to suggest to the alumni the name of a new candidate. This committee was presided over by Mr. Luther Ely Smith,[5] and its two most active members were Mr. Lawrence Abbott and Judge Whitman. The latter advocated the candidature of Governor Fletcher Proctor of Vermont, whereas Mr. Smith himself favored Grosvenor Backus. The discussions were at first carried out by correspondence, and Mr. Smith was delighted to receive one morning a telegram from Mr. Abbott from which he derived the mistaken impression that the other members of the committee agreed with his own proposal. He telegraphed jubilantly to Mr. Backus informing him that he had been nominated. It then transpired that the name mentioned in Mr. Abbott's telegram had not been that of Grosvenor Backus but of Governor Proctor. Mr. Smith, in his enthusiasm, had misread the one for the other. On hearing of this Mr. Backus offered to withdraw his candidature. Mr. Smith begged him not to do so. Mr. Abbott and Judge Whitman were incensed. They circulated to the 3,500 alumni of Amherst a pamphlet recounting these events in a disobliging spirit under the title of "A Protest and Explanation." Dwight Morrow then intervened in the controversy. He joined with Harlan Stone[6] in circulating a coun-

[5] Luther Ely Smith, b. Downers Grove, Illinois, 1873; Amherst '94; St. Louis lawyer.

[6] Harlan Fiske Stone, b. Chesterfield, New Hampshire, 1872; Amherst '94; college mate of Morrow at Columbia 1898, dean of the Law School 1910-23;

ter-pamphlet contending that the insinuations made against the good faith of Mr. Smith and Mr. Backus were unmerited and unfair. The Amherst spirit degenerated for a few weeks into fratricidal strife.

His friends begged Morrow to desist from taking sides in this unhappy controversy. "I have a burning sense," he replied, "of the injustice that has been done to Backus and Smith, particularly Backus." A classmate wrote to suggest that this quixotic espousal of a cause which was not popular with the main body of the alumni might diminish Morrow's own influence with that body and affect his chances of eventually becoming, in his turn, trustee. "I think," Morrow replied, "that you will agree with me that it is hardly a sound reason for keeping silent that one's influence hereafter may be lessened by one's speaking."

The incident in the end was settled by Grosvenor Backus insisting on withdrawing his name from the list of candidates. "The sooner," wrote Dwight Morrow, "we forget about it, the better." Yet he did not himself forget the incident or the hornet nests into which the alumni councils had suddenly developed. When next a controversy arose at Amherst (and it was of a far more public and embittered nature), Dwight Morrow, as will be seen, acted with greater patience and circumspection.

That he had not in fact lost any influence by this intervention was shown four years later when it became known that Professor Harris was about to resign the presidency of the college. There was a strong feeling among the younger alumni that Dwight Morrow should be asked to accept the

Attorney General of the United States, now Associate Justice of the Supreme Court of the United States by appointment of President Coolidge in 1925.

post. This feeling was voiced in a letter addressed to him by Mr. George B. Mallon in January 1912:[7]

"My own idea," wrote Mr. Mallon, "if I had the choice, would be to get away from the ministerial-teacher type and select an Exhibit A like yourself as an illustration of what a college course and a proper application of it can be made to accomplish in a profession. I have talked to a dozen or more Amherst men on this subject and I have not found one who has not been enthusiastic in hoping that the board of trustees would at least give you the opportunity to consider the thing seriously. There is no question of your having the enthusiastic support of the alumni and, I am sure, of the undergraduates."

Morrow was not at the time able to consider this proposal. The then state of his finances did not permit him to dream of such retirement. Yet he took a deep interest in the appointment of President Harris' successor and wrote many letters to Amherst men in which his own views on the matter were expounded at length. Typical of such letters is one which he addressed to Henry P. Field in March of 1912:[8]

"I understand that the suggestion of Professor Walker has been made with considerable force by those who feel that the President of Amherst should be a leader in the religious life of New England. Personally, this seems to me the wrong end to begin with. I do not know Professor Walker personally. He may be the best man for the place. I do not think, however, a man should be elected because he is a great religious leader, nor should a man be barred out because he happens to be a minister. I feel strongly

[7] George B. Mallon, b. Malone, New York, 1865; Amherst 1887; reporter and editor New York *Sun* 1882-1912; associate editor of publishing company to 1917; Director of Publicity Bankers Trust Company 1918-1928; active in New Jersey War Savings campaign 1917-18; d. 1928.

[8] Henry P. Field, b. New London, Connecticut, 1858; Amherst 1880; first employer of Calvin Coolidge; Special Judge of Probate, Hampshire County, Massachusetts, since 1909.

that Professor Garman shortly before his death put it about right
when he said that during the first period of Amherst's history
it had been its main function to train ministers; that during the
second period which is about ending it had been its main function
to train professional men other than ministers; that during its
next period it would probably be its principal function to give an
all-round training to men who would take a large part in the
business affairs of the nation. I am quoting Professor Garman
from memory but you will find some such statement in his public
speeches. If anyone other than Garman were the author of such
a heterodox statement he would probably be accused of trying
to turn the college into a business college. Of course, what Garman really meant was that with the big problems that are being
worked out in social reform through our business organizations
it should be one of the high aims of the college to train men not
only of cultured minds but with minds of strong enough fibre
to distinguish the essential from the non-essential, in the continual
struggle which any enlightened state is making for the social bet-
terment of its members. Amherst College needs for its head a
man who is a scholar and who knows other scholars when he sees
them; a man who is an idealist but whose idealism is based not
upon what Garman would have called a 'leaky' mind, but upon
a buoyant faith braced and sobered by a calm survey of history;
and above all a man with wide enough sympathies to reach the
hearts of good, bad and indifferent men."

Here again we have evidence of the durable effect exercised by Professor Garman on the shape and color of Dwight
Morrow's mind.

5

It was in the course of these years that Morrow first
emerged as a politician. His interest in politics dated from

the day when, at the age of seven, he accompanied his brother in the Fifth Ward procession from Allegheny to Pittsburgh during the Garfield-Hancock campaign. This was the occasion of his first expedition across the bridge. He shouted loudly and he marched republicanly; his elder brother became alarmed at the sudden exhaustion which subsequently assailed him. This first political demonstration, which ended in bed and tears, was not in the very least a successful experiment.

His second excursion into politics was even less encouraging. In 1896 he spoke and canvassed for his brother-in-law who was seeking election to the Central School Committee at Pittsburgh. "I have," he wrote on that occasion to Charles Burnett, "had my first contact with the great unwashed American sovereign, and to say that I am discouraged and disgusted with City political methods is putting it mild."

The fact that Mr. Scandrett was on that occasion successful did not diminish Morrow's disillusion. "This," he wrote, "makes one realize more than before that a rich man's duty is to the State, while a poor man's is to his family; when I have earned enough money practicing law I am going to do what little in politics I can and until then I am going to formulate methods and wait."

He waited until 1912. When in 1909 he was invited to stand for election as Mayor of Englewood, he refused, "although," as Mrs. Morrow's diary records, "he would really like to do so if he could afford it." The year 1912 offered him his first opportunity to play a part in national politics. President Taft was seeking reëlection as the official Republican candidate, and was opposed both by Theodore Roosevelt, representing the Republican insurgents, and by Woodrow Wilson, the Democratic candidate. Morrow took the side of Taft.

In April of that year he allowed his name to be advanced as district delegate from Bergen County to the National Republican Convention. "Dwight," records Mrs. Morrow in May, "absolutely absorbed in politics. He has spoken seven times today." He induced President Taft to visit New Jersey and accompanied him on his tour of the principal towns. "The people," he recorded, "are apathetic and generally disgusted with the whole situation. Most of them have a feeling of pity for Taft, but then one does not vote from a feeling of pity." Dwight Morrow, at that time, was not an admirer of Theodore Roosevelt; he resented the fact that that dynamic genius had split the Republican elephant into two parts; he was too sober a party man to approve of such disintegrating individualism. "I believe," he wrote to Charles Burnett, "that if Roosevelt should be nominated he will be elected, especially if the Democrats nominate Bryan against him. Roosevelt, after a month's rest, will make one of his astounding turns and will outdo Burke as a conservative. It is all in the day's work, but I can't help wishing I were an assistant teacher of philosophy in your department."

Dwight Morrow, on this occasion, was not elected, although he was pleased at obtaining 90 per cent of the Republican vote in Englewood itself. "Now," he remarked after the election, "we know exactly how *not* to run a campaign." Yet his activity on that occasion must have been remarkable. It lived in the memory of President Taft. "I remember," the ex-President wrote to Morrow in 1921, "with great gratitude the service you did me in 1912 when was 'the winter of my discontent.' That ride through northern New Jersey and those speeches will never, I think, disappear from my memory. One values friends who show themselves to be such under conditions like that."

It would be premature at this stage to examine at any length the political convictions of Dwight Morrow. Such examination must be reserved until we come to consider the nature of, and the reasons for, his ardent support of Calvin Coolidge in the campaign of 1920. It should suffice for the moment to indicate that his political theory was illustrative of his general habit of mind. In that theory many apparent inconsistencies, and even contradictions, might be discerned. He was a loyal Republican, yet he often spoke and acted against the official policy of his party; he was an advanced Liberal, yet he supported the standpatters against the progressives; he was a constant upholder of the rights of property, yet he disbelieved in unearned increment even as he disbelieved in hereditary wealth; he was a free-trader by instinct even though he stood for a system which had been created by, and was still based upon, protective tariffs; he was an ardent democrat and yet, as early as 1900, he could write, "Had I lived one hundred years ago, I certainly should have followed Hamilton rather than Jefferson"; he worked for twenty-seven years in Wall Street and yet, in December 1912, we find him writing, "My own feeling is that I would rather the stockholders got a little less dividends and have the employees paid a little bit more"; he read *The Manchester Guardian* with as great a pleasure as the New York *Times*.

Such inconsistencies were only apparent. Morrow's political theory was in fact in complete harmony with his general tone of thought. He was loyal to the Republicans, not so much because he felt that they were necessarily more enlightened than the Democrats, but because he had been convinced by historical study that the two-party system was essential to the stability of the State. His adherence to his party was thus neither an emotion nor a feeling, but a deliberate form of belief. He supported Taft against Roosevelt, not because he had confidence in the static forms of conservatism, but because he objected to seeing the principle of the two-party system endangered by strenuous, even if brilliant, egoism. He indulged, as will be seen later, in socialistic sympathies, while serving as a Levite in the temple of capitalism. Yet in all this, the central girder of sincerity can be identified as a constant endeavor to adjust the balance between the practicable and the desirable; as a habit of thought which led him, in all the affairs of life, to prefer the tentative footsteps of correct tendencies to the impatient strides of what might prove incorrect experiments; as a conviction that any given set of circumstances, however defective it might be, represented some organic growth within the womb of history; as an intellectual distrust of all extreme opinions or impatient remedies; and as a belief that the practical idealist must proceed from within, and not from without, the circle of conditions in which chance or his own abilities may happen to have placed him.

That, even in his younger days, there was a certain relativism about his political theory is shown by a letter which he wrote to Professor Morse in November 1912 towards the close of that undignified and embittered year of party warfare:

"If we drift into a conservative and a radical party, my surroundings and historical study will lead me toward the conservative party, especially if we should be fortunate enough to get a conservative party which would put the emphasis upon the performance of duties rather than upon the protection of rights. I am not sure, however, that a conservative who really wanted progress would not be of more service in a radical party helping to hold the party back, than in a conservative party trying to push that party on. Probably a man that was either a radical or a conservative during the whole of his lifetime would be on the wrong side about half of the time. At all events, we will hope that we may be fortunate enough to have leaders of both parties who will still think it worth while to read history."

6

The year 1912 had been for Dwight Morrow one of intensive activity both political and legal. He had been obliged to abandon his annual summer holiday and to spend many exhausting weeks in the Middle West, endeavoring from Salt Lake City to further the interests of the Electric Bond & Share Company and Mr. S. Z. Mitchell. The autumn found him exhausted and depressed. Just before Christmas he developed symptoms of illness. "Dr. Holmes," notes Mrs. Morrow in her diary for December 20th, "thinks Dwight has typhoid fever. Dwight insists that he has nothing but malarial fever which he had once twenty years ago." On the following day a consultation was held. "Dr. Foster," writes Mrs. Morrow on December 21st, "came out and said that Dwight has bronchial pneumonia." The attack was short but sharp. Within a week he was pronounced convalescent, but in need of a long holiday in a milder climate. "Just at present," he wrote on January 2, 1913, "I have not got much life in me. I have been flat on my back for three weeks with a bad attack of bronchitis and a dab of pneumonia. The doctors are going to ship me off to Nassau just as soon as I am strong enough to go. I don't suppose I have been very sick, but inasmuch as I have not been in bed longer than two days ever before in my life I feel like a worn-out old man with one foot in the grave."

Two months were spent in the Bahamas, and when he returned in March he was able to grapple with the affairs of the Utah Power & Light Company and to prepare the brief which has already been quoted and which he always considered as the highest achievement of his legal career. Yet his illness, and that first of many holidays at Nassau, had enabled him to step back for a few moments from the unremitting machinery of business, and to consider his career and utility in terms of the good life. He was not encouraged by this confrontation. He was now forty years of age and could expect another quarter of a century of active service. Must these twenty-five years be the same thing all over again? He had now experienced all that the legal profession had to offer him in so far as work, responsibility, and reputation were concerned. Was he forever to go round and round in the same cage? Already in 1910 Mrs. Morrow had observed signs of restlessness and discontent. "I think," she noted in October of that year, "that Dwight is a little dissatisfied with his work. Would like politics or law school teaching."

It was at this moment, when his gaze was already fixed upon ampler or more gentle horizons, that an offer was made to him which determined his whole future life.

ONE night, in the little brown house on Spring Lane, Mrs.
Morrow had been startled from her sleep by yells of pain and
fear. She hurried to her husband's assistance. "Betsey," he
panted, "I have had the most horrible nightmare. It was
truly horrible. It was all so vivid, it was all so ghastly. It
seemed real, Betsey, it seemed so *real* . . ." and at the recollection of his nightmare he groaned repeatedly aloud. "What
was it?" she asked him. "What was it that you dreamt?" "It
was terrible," he groaned. "It was all so vivid, somehow. I
dreamt, Betsey, that we had become rich. But *enormously*
rich." "But, Dwight," she answered, "that's nothing to be
scared about! You can trust me to set *that* right." He was
comforted by this assurance and silence again descended
upon that happy little house. But the nightmare came true.

It has already been shown how, towards the end of 1912,
Dwight Morrow began to tire of being a corporation lawyer
and to turn restless eyes in search of other approaches to
what he called "the greater adventure." He toyed for a
moment with the idea of accepting the post of counsel to the

General Electric. At one period he considered applying for the appointment of solicitor, or legal adviser, to the Department of State in Washington. The salary attached to this post was no more than $7,000 a year, but the quality of the work appealed to him (and rightly) as exactly suited to his temperament and gifts. Neither of these nebulous ideas materialized.

It happened that the firm of J. P. Morgan & Co. of 23 Wall Street were at this time considering an addition to their senior staff. They began, with their usual circumspection, to look round for a man possessed of character, reputation, energy, ability, charm, and legal knowledge.

It was in 1912 that Thomas W. Lamont prematurely suggested to Henry P. Davison the name of Dwight Morrow. At the moment the proposal did not commend itself to Davison, whose estimate of Morrow's importance was derived from a quite casual acquaintance in the early Englewood days. In June of 1913 Davison happened to revisit Englewood and to hear Dwight Morrow make a speech in the Armory on behalf of the rebuilding of the hospital. He was impressed both by the energy of his intelligence and by the influence which, since those early days, he had been able to acquire in his own community. A few weeks later Davison was hurrying down Cedar Street in the pouring rain: he collided with a very short pedestrian, and their umbrellas became interlocked: in the process of extrication which thereafter ensued, Davison looked downwards and recognized his assailant as Dwight Morrow. Lamont's original recommendation, fortified by his recollection of the Armory speech, recurred to his mind. He made inquiries in the City of New York and heard nothing but praise of Morrow's character and ability. He again spoke to Lamont on this subject and, thus united, they approached Mr. Morgan. It was in this manner that the suggestion was first raised.

One would have assumed that a man so dynamic as Dwight Morrow, and one who was admittedly restless under the routine of corporate law, would have jumped at an offer which would not only bring him into touch with the main problems of his age, but which would also open vast vistas of personal opportunity and power. Dwight Morrow did not jump: he crept towards the proposal, perplexedly and inch by inch.

The first tentative suggestion was made to him by Thomas Lamont on December 30, 1913. Morrow replied that he would be prepared to consider the proposal in principle. Three days later a dinner was arranged at which he was introduced to Mr. J. P. Morgan. The introduction was successful, and Mr. Morgan thereafter authorized his partners to suggest to Morrow that he should become associated with the firm for a period of mutual trial, with the prospect, should this experiment prove satisfactory to both parties, of eventually being admitted as a partner. Dwight Morrow asked for time to consider this proposal. The period which followed was more than a period of cautious deliberation; it was a period of nervous strain. His hesitation was due to something more fundamental than any normal desire not to embark without due reflection upon a new career; it arose from an endeavor to assure himself that this new career, however promising, would not conflict with those values which he had elaborated as essential to the good life. The weeks that followed were not in any sense weeks of practical reasoning; they were weeks of acute spiritual crisis. By the end of January he had worked himself into a highly nervous condition.

The tension which he endured is reflected in Mrs. Morrow's diary:

1913. *December* 30. Dwight has had a most remarkable offer! Tom Lamont speaking for J. P. Morgan asked Dwight today if he would consider joining himself to J. P. Morgan & Co. with a view to becoming a partner later. It is a tentative offer, and Dwight is not sure whether he wants to go that way.

1914. *January* 2. Dwight in town tonight, dining with J. P. Morgan. He is being looked over!

January 8. Dwight still uncertain and much torn over Morgan offer. He asks me what we should do but I cannot tell.

January 10. Dwight hesitating about the Morgan offer, I don't know what I hope he will decide. I cannot help him.

January 14. I think Dwight will accept.

January 15. Tonight Dwight planning a unique "dignified refusal" of Mr. Morgan's offer.

January 30. Dwight much used up over this Morgan question. He has asked for more time. We leave tomorrow for Bermuda.

The first three weeks at Bermuda were devoted to the recovery of his intellectual balance. With the renewal of health came a renewal of clarity and self-confidence. Gradually his hesitation veered towards the point of acceptance. By February 21st a decision had almost been formulated, and it was then fortified by a chance incident. In the reading room of the Princess Hotel, Bermuda, he came across a cartoon in a New York paper in which Mr. J. P. Morgan was represented as a vulture preying upon the entrails of the shareholders in the New Haven Railroad. He well knew that, but for the support given by the firm of Morgan, the said shareholders would have had no entrails at all. He was incensed by the injustice of this cartoon, and the flame of knight-errantry which always gleamed as a little lamp among the arches of his intelligence blazed up in a fuse of indignation. "Well, if I am going in," he said to his wife, "I am glad to go in at a moment when brickbats are flying." Dwight Morrow always had a protective passion for the misunderstood. He spent the next day drafting a letter of acceptance. It was addressed to George Case,[1] who as a close friend of both parties and as a lawyer, had acted during the last weeks almost as an intermediary. After dinner, in their sitting room, Dwight Morrow and his wife discussed this letter until 2 A.M. They decided to send it. Before sleeping that night the letter was signed and sealed. Morrow crept down the dark stairway and posted it in the hotel letter box. When he returned he paused for a moment in the doorway. "Now," he said, "we are no longer lawyers: we are henceforward bankers." The letter ran as follows:

> Princess Hotel
> Bermuda
> February 25, 1914

Dear George:

The day before I left New York I had a short talk with Mr. Morgan. I told him that I had hoped and expected to reach a final decision before I went away but that I had not been able to do so. He very kindly told me that I had been thinking about the matter too much, that I should drop it out of my mind entirely until I have had some vacation and that I might let him know when I returned unless I came to a decision while away. I have been down here now about three weeks and have had a fine rest. I have succeeded in forgetting New York much better than I expected. With a rested body my mind seems to be work-

---

[1] George Case, b. Kansas City, Missouri, 1872; Yale '94, Columbia Law '97; Mr. Morrow's friend and adviser.

ing more clearly and directly, as well as more positively. This week for the first time a real conviction has come to me of what I should like to do. I am putting it down frankly on paper—partly to clarify my ideas and partly to get the benefit of your judgment.

Mr. Morgan's proposition is in substance that I go with Messrs. J. P. Morgan & Co. as an understudy for Mr. Steele, with the expectation on both sides that this will lead to a partnership when the estate of Mr. Morgan senior is settled. It is contemplated that this will be in about two years. Mr. Morgan very properly wants all of my time.

This apparently puts two questions before me: first, whether I want to leave the law to become a banker; second, whether I ought to abandon permanently the law before Mr. Morgan has had an opportunity to satisfy himself personally that I am the man that he wants to associate permanently with his firm.

In the perplexities of my last four weeks in New York, trying to do my ordinary work and at the same time reach a decision on so vital a matter, I think I confused the two questions, and of course they do run together. At this distance, however, I think I have separated them.

On the first question I am entirely satisfied that I am willing to give up the law for this banking association. The work seems to me larger, the responsibilities greater, and I am not afraid. As to the second question, I have not been able to free my mind from some reluctance to abandon permanently the law before Mr. Morgan knows that I measure up to his requirements.

In this situation, would the following course be proper, and if so, practicable? Could I go to Messrs. J. P. Morgan & Co. without making any formal announcement that I was abandoning the law? I could simply give up my present office and desk and move over to Messrs. J. P. Morgan & Co. to whom all of my time would belong. This would involve of course a complete surrender of any participation in the business or profits of Simpson, Thacher &

Bartlett, and no participation by them in my compensation from Messrs. J. P. Morgan & Co. I would be in a sense on an indefinite leave of absence from the law. Such a course would seem to me to have these advantages:

From my personal point of view it would avoid a public renunciation of the law prior to the time that I had proved my fitness for the new life.

From the point of view of S. T. & B. I think it would considerably ease my going.

From the point of view of Messrs. Morgan & Co. I am not fully qualified to judge. And this of course is the most important point of view, because I want as much as they do the manner of my going to be such that I shall be of the most use to them. I think the proposed course might have one advantage for them. If for any reason I did not fit—and this might happen without discredit to either side—neither the firm nor Mr. Davison nor Tom personally would need have the slightest embarrassment in looking for a better or more adaptable man. Of course the circumstances might well be that I could not or would not desire to go back to my old firm, from which severance in fact would be complete. The general practice of the law would still be open to me however, without the record of a formal and public abandonment of it.

Having said so much, I want to say something more. When written down all the above sounds *too* logical and prudent, and after all, the big decisions of life are not made by logic but by intuition—by faith if you please. What is making me go in is not only the high standing of the firm and the character of its members, but the direct straightforward way that Mr. Morgan and Mr. Davison and Tom have talked with me. When I left Mr. Davison in New York, he told me that he had no doubt that I would come and I had a note from him from the steamer, forwarded here, in which he says it will all look clear in the retrospect. Such confidence is contagious. I want to avoid the appearance and the reality of bargaining with such men. I therefore tell you that I am going anyway. The conditions and the manner of my going Messrs. J. P. Morgan & Co. may determine. I want to start right with them however by putting down what is in my own mind.

I had thought first of writing directly to Tom. I am writing to you because you have a detached position that the others of us do not have and because you have perhaps a fuller understanding of the point of view of one who has put his heart into, and rested his weight upon, the legal profession for fifteen years. I need not tell you how highly I have valued your own advice in the whole matter. I shall prove that by following your advice rather than your example. I expect you of course to show all or any part of this letter to Tom. Do not bother to write me unless the impulse come.

We leave here March 10th, reaching New York on the 12th. I wish you and Mary could have been here with us. We have had a fine rest and I am eager to get back. When a little salt water blown into one's face can serve as so fine a tonic for the mind, it is a pity that we ever let our bodies run down.

2

The above letter sets out, in precise and logical terms, the practical considerations which caused Dwight Morrow to hesitate. There were other and more interesting elements in his perplexity. "They wanted him," wrote Calvin Coolidge in later years, "not merely because of his talent, for talent was plentiful and easy to buy, but they wanted him for his character, which was priceless." Dwight Morrow was fully aware that he was staking his reputation. He already knew too much about the firm of J. P. Morgan & Co., about the men who composed it and the principles on which they acted, to fear for one moment that by entering No. 23 Wall

Street he would be compromising any particle of his soul. Such an apprehension never assailed him. Yet he was undoubtedly rendered uneasy by the fear lest some of his friends, and particularly those who knew little of the more civilized aspects of corporate business, might be tempted to regard it as unfortunate that Dwight Morrow, whom they had always cited as indifferent to material advancement, should, at the age of forty, seem suddenly to bow down in the Temple of Mammon. A slightly defensive note, a note almost of self-justification, can be detected in the letters which he dispatched at this period.

"I do not think," he wrote to Robert de Forest, "I need to tell you how hard it was for me to leave my old associations. After a great deal of thought, however, it did seem to me that the larger task was here. And, after all, when we speak of 'advancement' do we not mean the accepting of the larger task?"

The slight tone of self-defensiveness which underlies this letter suggests that Morrow, who in his authentic moments never for one instant rendered unto God the things that were Caesar's, was at this juncture not wholly convinced. An unwonted note of self-explanation can also be detected in his letters to his two academic mentors, Charles Burnett and Professor Morse:

"I can only believe," he wrote, "that at the end of ten years' experience in such an organization I shall be better prepared for the performance of any task which I may be asked to perform than if I continued in the work I have been doing for the last fifteen years."

"Although," he assured Burnett, "the matter means a change in a financial way and, if it works out as both sides expect, will mean a very great change, Betty and I are not conscious of having let the money consideration affect us. In fact, I think that feature has been a deterring element in reaching our decision. I have been very much impressed with Mr. Morgan's candor and frankness and his plans for the future of his house. Of course I have known Davison and Lamont for a long time and greatly admire them. I have a feeling that in the changes that are to come in the next five or ten years there is a very great opportunity for real service in such work."

"Mrs. Morrow and I," he confided to Professor Morse, "are not conscious of having let the money side of the question affect us, although it makes considerable difference in that respect. We have not any idea, of course, of changing our method of living and it has been a deterring factor rather than an inducing factor that if the thing works out it may throw on us some duties and obligations to which we have not been accustomed. The thing that makes me go is the size of the work and the character of the men with whom I will be associated. I think there is a very great opportunity for real service there in the next five or ten years.

"I am not sure that the character of my work will be changed very much. At first, at least, it will consist in dealing with the same kind of legal problems that I have had, but perhaps a little larger. There will, of course, be the tendency to get more and more into the business side.

"I, too, have always felt that I should like the academic life if an opportunity which I could meet offered itself. Perhaps even that dream need not be permanently given up. So far in life I have always felt that it was not the particular work that a man was doing, but his attitude toward it, which determined his usefulness and his happiness. If the new work changes me for the worse I am going to blame it on myself rather than upon the work."

Apart from this uneasiness regarding the effect of his decision upon his academic friends, he was fully conscious that,

in the then state of public feeling, a prominent and prolonged association with the house of Morgan would be of
disadvantage if and when he decided to embark upon a
political career.

The campaign conducted by Theodore Roosevelt against
the trusts had led to an hysterical mania for exposure which
had in the end degenerated into what Roosevelt himself
described as "muckraking." A mood of disappointment
afflicted the average American so soon as, with the closing
of the Frontier, opportunity ceased to be limitless. Theodore
Roosevelt had ministered with exuberance to this discontent.
With reckless though magnificent energy he had struck out-
wards to right and left. Such phrases as "down-trodden millions," "corporate greed," and "representatives of predatory
wealth," had become part of public memory. It is no dis-
paragement to a great, if impatient, man to say that he
failed absolutely to teach his country the art of discrimination. The prejudices that he created, fostered, and instilled
were to a large extent valuable and dynamic; yet in the resultant suspicion of Wall Street were included both those
who were guilty and those who assuredly were not. The
house of Morgan for this reason was not, for all its intelligent rectitude, an advantageous avenue towards either representative or administrative office. Morrow well knew that as
a Morgan partner he would be seriously hampered in his
political ambitions.

He approached this side of the problem with his customary
tolerance. On the one hand he did not deny the influence
which organized wealth could and would still exercise upon
democratic politics. "Capital," he wrote, "has a tremendous
influence directly and indirectly upon government. I suppose
this will continue to be true until the capitalistic system is

abolished, which it may be some day. Meanwhile, some owners of capital will use their power wisely and some will use it
unwisely. In all ages there will be small men like Mulhall
who will throw out their chests and feel that they are running the government." On the other hand he did not believe
that the popular prejudice against Wall Street need, for a
sincere democrat, prove invincible. "I shall," he was accustomed to say, "need one good licking in the political field
before the American public will forgive me for being a
Morgan partner." He did not possess the cynicism to fore-
see that neither Coolidge nor Hoover would have the intellectual courage themselves to ignore such a disability on
his behalf.

More immediate and more personal was his actual distress
at severing his fifteen years' connection with Simpson,
Thacher & Bartlett. Morrow always felt the need of a
friendly, even of an intimate, perhaps even of a protective,
covering to that intensive cell in which he worked. He hated
any new environment, and was peculiarly, and perhaps
morbidly, sensitive to the "freshman" feeling. His personal
affection for Mr. Simpson and Mr. Thacher rendered the
wrench all the more painful. It was no good pretending that
they did not resent his departure; they minded terribly.
"For me," Mr. Thacher recorded many years later, "all the
romance of the law business went with him." And it is true
that the incandescent quality in Dwight Morrow cast a
romantic glow over the most material and prosaic objects.

One person, at least, was unreservedly delighted. When, in
July of 1914, it was publicly announced that Dwight Morrow
had become a partner in the firm of J. P. Morgan & Co., the
sensation created in Allegheny was vivacious and extreme.
His mother, much to her self-satisfaction and amusement,

became a public figure over night. She wrote in disordered jubilation to her daughter-in-law:

Dear Betty:

July 4, 1914

My hand is clear out of joint and with all the gloves I had one week ago I think I have only one that has a whole right hand to it. I went out on the street yesterday and it seemed that I met everyone who had ever seen Dwight and they all fairly fell all over me. I never felt so puffed up in all my life and really I do not know how I can live much longer. Just think of Dwight, my boy Dwight, having such a future before him. Isn't it grand? How soon it came—the first I knew of it was in the morning paper, and before I got fully dressed the reporters came buzzing in—oh! my poor old head was all upset. I was afraid to open my mouth; when I got to myself I had to sit down for a good cry. . . . I am simply awed when I think of so much grandeur and I feel that I will not be able much longer to fit in with the *plutocrats.* . . .

Clara Morrow need have had no such apprehension. Dwight remained unplutocratic to the end. And to the end she continued to upbraid him for his reckless extravagance, for his unfitting, and indeed unrighteous, generosity.

3

Dwight Morrow entered the office of J. P. Morgan & Co. on April 15, 1914. On July 1st of the same year he was admitted a partner. According to the custom of the house, he simultaneously became a partner in the associated houses of Drexel & Co. of Philadelphia; Morgan, Grenfell & Co. of London; and Morgan, Harjes & Co. of Paris. Yet he was in no sense elated.

In its early stages, his depression can be explained by actual homesickness for Cedar Street and the familiar desks and bookshelves of Simpson, Thacher & Bartlett. He returned, on that first evening of April 15th, to confess to Mrs. Morrow that he had been "pretty lonely and blue all day." This feeling of loneliness was a strangely reiterant fibre in his nervous composition. To the end of his life he was subject to moods of nervous diffidence, when the sunshine of his self-assertive gaiety would suddenly be blotted out. At such moments he required around him a consoling phalanx of subordinates and friends. In Cedar Street there had always been available the affectionate admiration of his partners and the respectful admiration of his clerks. The atmosphere of J. P. Morgan & Co. was, in comparison, less familiar, less domestic, less subservient, and, as such, less consoling. Before long, it is true, he came to regard his partners, not in New York alone but also in London and Paris, as a charming Christmas family, whom he loved dearly and by whom he was dearly loved. But during those first days he was actually awed by J. P. Morgan & Co., feeling himself to be a very small new boy in a school in which the older boys appeared unnecessarily large, strong, superior, and initiated. The impression of not being wanted very much by anybody was increased by the fact that No. 23 Wall Street was at the time being rebuilt and that the office had been temporarily transferred to an annex in the Mills Building on Broad Street. He confessed to Louis Horowitz that he felt "like a cat in a strange garret." "I seem," he said, "to have no particular place."

How are we to account for this diffidence?

A large proportion of it can, as has been said, be explained by his temperamental dislike of all unfamiliar environments.

Yet he was intimate with Thomas Lamont, he liked Henry Davison, and his feeling for Mr. Morgan was one of grateful respect. Some further explanation must be sought if we are to understand why his diffidence lasted.

Dwight Morrow possessed almost no acquisitive instincts, but he had a very strong possessive, or, more accurately, "protective" instinct. It will be seen later how his passion for such problems as French currency, Cuban loans, Mexican finances, or naval ratios, was essentially a "protective" passion; he knew as much about these subjects as any living expert; they thus became *his* subjects, and the fact that the French, the Cubans, the Mexicans, and the whole Naval Conference became dependent upon him actually stimulated his imagination, his clarity, and his zest. It was not a question of egotism, it was certainly not a question of personal vanity; it was merely that he worked more gaily and more brilliantly when his protective passion had been aroused.

There is a story which he would frequently recount that illustrates this curious aspect of his character. He had read somewhere of how Sir Charles Napier, the conqueror of Scinde, when congratulated upon the battle of Hyderabad, had answered: "Yes, but I would rather have finished the roads of Cephalonia." Morrow would expound at length his personal sympathy with that remark. "You see," he would say, "Napier had ruled that little island as an autocrat; he had built hospitals and schools; he had almost completed a network of roadways. The islanders depended on him; he was their protector and their friend; and then, when his work for them was but half completed, he was recalled. He achieved, in later life, more obvious successes; but the roads in Cephalonia were *his* roads; they represented the little job that he loved as his own. I understand that man."

In those early months at Morgan's there were no Ionian roads to assuage his protective instincts, no creative work with which he could be personally identified. Important matters were dealt with coöperatively between the partners and responsibility was seldom individually involved. The authority and experience of others were far greater than his own. He felt out of gear in the main machinery of the organization and for the first time in his life a sense of ineffectiveness came to damp his energies. He had expected "the wider adventure." He found only that he was occupied with business, similar to, but less intimate than, his cases in Cedar Street. And what was more discouraging was that he foresaw no moment at which these problems would become predominantly his own, no moment when his possessive instincts would find their full satisfaction.

From time to time, during those early weeks, some dusty file would be brought to him, some forgotten relic of old Mr. Morgan's days. In this way he was given the Père Marquette dossier to study. "That's a lemon," remarked Charles Fay when told of it, "they took that off the shelf and gave it to you." A fortnight later the file of the New Haven Railway was also placed on his desk. "That," remarked Charles Fay, "is another lemon."

Gradually, however, he became interested even in these desiccated and abandoned problems. A few months later Mrs. Morrow met J. P. Morgan at a dinner party. "I don't know," he said to her, "about this husband of yours. We had a lot of moldy securities—then Dwight comes along, spits on his hands, and we start making money on them."

This was all very satisfactory. But it was not the "larger task."

4

What was the larger task? Five weeks after Dwight Morrow became a partner in J. P. Morgan & Co. the European War burst upon an unexpectant world. From then onwards No. 23 Wall Street became the centre of vast international affairs. No private firm in the history of mankind has ever dealt with affairs of such magnitude as thereafter devolved upon the house of Morgan. Dwight Morrow's whole future development was determined by the circumstance that he joined J. P. Morgan & Co. a month before August 1914. Yet before we trace the curious circles into which that opportunity expanded, we must consider what, but for that dramatic circumstance, would have been his scope. We must consider, that is, whether the routine of banking was that to which Morrow was best adapted.

It must be realized that in April of 1914 the whole banking system of America was undergoing a vital transformation. To an authentic banker these transformations would have proved of fascinating interest; the attention which Morrow paid to them was, for him, a languid attention; it may be concluded, therefore, that he was accidentally rather than essentially a banker.

This point requires emphasis. The importance of the banking problem must first be explained. At that period the Federal Reserve System was not in operation, and until November 1914 the old illogical and ill-coördinated methods persisted. In July of 1914 there existed some 7,500 national banks with combined capital, surpluses, and deposits of some $9,000,000,000. There were in addition some 20,000 State banks, private banks, and trust companies whose capital, surpluses, and deposits totaled some $14,000,000,000. The national banks, in spite of their name, were isolated and independent; there were forty-nine different sets of banking laws; and the whole system led to decentralization, inelasticity of credit, cumbersome transfer methods, and a lack of coördination between the fiscal operations of the Washington Treasury and the movements of commercial credit. It was to meet this chaotic regionalism that the Federal Reserve System was, in November 1914, inaugurated. Yet until the Federal Reserve Board came into being the responsibility for financial guidance fell, as was clearly shown in 1907, upon the shoulders of the leading New York bankers, who acted together under the leadership of J. P. Morgan & Co. as an entity which they all trusted. The system might have worked well enough had there existed between the Treasury at Washington and the bankers that degree of coöperation which exists between the British Treasury and the Bank of England, or had the leadership of the house of Morgan and other bankers been as unquestioned throughout the country as is the influence, in Great Britain, of the five central banks. No such discipline existed, and the country was for this and other reasons exposed to recurrent panics which, under a more centralized system, might have been avoided or at least controlled.

It is significant that Dwight Morrow did not accord to this fascinating problem that degree of concentrated interest which he devoted to other, and less professional, controversies. He was interested in law; he was interested in diplomacy and international finance. But banking, as banking, left him cold. It is a curious fact that in all his vast correspondence, in all his many articles and speeches, there are but scant references to such problems, for instance, as the centralization of the American banking systems or the proper relations between the large banks and the Federal Administration. He described himself in later years as "a lawyer in a banking firm." "Although," he would say after his retirement from Wall Street, "I never helped J. P. Morgan & Co. to make much money, I certainly prevented them from losing it." He was invaluable to them, as will be seen later, as a conciliator of opposing opinions: he did much skilled and thorough work in the reorganization of companies in which his firm or his partners held an interest; he frequently made brilliant suggestions and even more frequently counseled patience and discretion; he was able, by the radiation of his intelligence, to render the most opaque problems translucent; he was industrious, imaginative, and sound. When, thirteen years later, he resigned from the firm, his partners were in despair. "He left," writes Mr. Russell Leffingwell,[2] "a hole and a void in the office that have never been filled. I thought when he left us that I would never recapture the savor and joy of work." All this is uncontested. Yet it may be questioned whether Morrow would have found so full a scope for his talents had not the war and the reconstruction period that followed created opportunities for the exercise of his unequaled diplomatic powers. He was not a natural banker: by nature he was a statesman. It was indeed a fortunate circumstance which made him a member of a firm to which statesmanship has always seemed more important than routine banking.

His observations upon the theory and practice of banking are not, therefore, either important or profound. They reflect the *laissez faire* philosophy which he had derived from a too

2 Russell C. Leffingwell, b. New York 1878; Yale '99, Columbia Law 1902; Asst. Secretary of the Treasury 1917-20; partner in J. P. Morgan & Co. since 1923.

uncritical study of William Graham Sumner. They reflect also his more personal skepticism regarding the ability of the legislator to advance the happiness of mankind. He was suspicious, for instance, of legislation tending to restrict the freedom, or to "protect the interests" of the individual investor. "The question," he wrote to Sir Walter Layton,[3] "I would like some time to talk over more fully with you is how much government control there should be of this subject. All my inclinations are for complete freedom. Governments can easily get into a dreadful mess when they begin to interfere with the freedom of investment."

The same theory was expressed at greater length in a letter which he wrote to Ellery Sedgwick[4] at the end of 1925:

"As I get older, I have more and more respect for the wisdom of the English as an investing nation. In the case of banks, for instance, there are very few restrictions upon the character of assets in which the banks can invest. Roughly speaking, they can take the savings of the English public and put them all in the River Platte, if they want. This results in investors being obliged to put their reliance upon the people who are managing the business rather than upon the statute. In the last analysis, can we get away from this fundamental principle, and is it not well that people who have savings to invest should be taught that no statute can really take care of them? It is the person who is managing the property in which they take an interest that they ultimately must rely upon. This confidence may often be abused. In some cases there is actual wrong-doing. In many more cases, in my opinion, there are just bad mistakes of judgment. If the thing

[3] Sir Walter Layton, eminent economist. b. London, England, 1884; University College, London and Trinity College, Cambridge; member of the Balfour Mission to U. S. 1917; active in reconstruction financial matters; editor of the London *Economist*.

[4] Ellery Sedgwick, b. New York 1872; Harvard 1894; editor *Atlantic Monthly*.

goes wrong all cases of bad judgment are looked upon as wrong-doing."

It may be concluded, therefore, that, had the war not intervened to give him the large excitement of world politics, Dwight Morrow might never have felt that he had found the sort of opportunity which he desired. Even so late as February 1915, when already the Morgan firm had assumed world responsibilities which were vast even for them, his moods of hesitation would recur. Yet in the months that followed he also was whirled into the central hurricane of those tremendous years.

MORROW'S LIFE TOO HOMOGENEOUS TO BE SEPARATED INTO DE-
TACHED PERIODS. IT IS CONVENIENT NONE THE LESS TO DEAL
SEPARATELY WITH HIS NON-POLITICAL WORK AT MORGAN'S IN
ORDER TO LEAVE THE FIELD CLEAR FOR EXAMINATION OF MORE
IMPORTANT ACTIVITIES. DIFFICULTY OF DEFINING WHAT WAS
PERSONAL WORK OF AN INDIVIDUAL AND WHAT CORPORATE
WORK OF FIRM AS A WHOLE. EARLY CASES, PERE MARQUETTE
AND NEW HAVEN COMMON STOCK. THE ERIE RAILROAD MORT-
GAGES. THE KENNECOTT COPPER CORPORATION. OTHER ACTIVI-
TIES. THE MUTUALIZATION OF THE EQUITABLE. THE AFFAIRS OF
INTERBOROUGH RAPID TRANSIT COMPANY. THE RESCUE OF MR.
W. C. DURANT. HIS HOME ATMOSPHERE. REMINISCENCES AND
SKETCHES BY HIS TWO ELDER DAUGHTERS.

THE point has now been reached where Morrow's activities,
which have hitherto been confined within the orbit of the
United States, expand in ever-widening circles. From this
moment onwards he becomes a factor, not in New York
only, but in world affairs.

It may be felt that too much detail has already been accumulated as circumstantial to what might be called his pre-
paratory stages. Such criticism would underestimate the
continuity of Morrow's life, or the strange circumstance that,
whether he was dealing with the problems of Mrs. Selma
Gorren or with the problems of Great Britain and France,
he was continuously the same. The evolution of his character
did not proceed by a sequence of jumps, impulses, starts, or
revelations; it was a gradual deduction from certain ethical
and intellectual premises, arrived at by an energetic process
of experiment and research. This process was unremitting;
it continued to the day of his death. It would be an error to
divide so homogeneous a life into arbitrary sections labeled

"Period of Preparation" or "Period of Action." Morrow lived for ever in a period of preparation; he never for one instant regarded himself as a completed man. The distinction which exists between his pre-war and his post-war occupations is not a sharp distinction. Until 1927 he was continuously engaged in problems which were not essentially different from those of his legal career. Conversely, his participation in international affairs, although expansive and intense, was not, until 1927, continuous.

It will be convenient, none the less, to dispose in this chapter of those of his functions as a Morgan partner which, important as they are as illustrating his methods and explaining the growth of his great reputation, were unconnected with the war or with the development of his political aptitudes and ambitions. The field will then be left clear for the story of his political and diplomatic labors from the date of that first breathless crisis in August 1914, to the moment when, on October 5, 1931, President Hoover, telephoning to summon him urgently to Washington, was informed that Dwight Morrow had died.

As has already been stated, the system followed by J. P. Morgan & Co. was a coöperative system. No specific branch of business was, except in special circumstances, assigned to any individual partner; the responsibility was pooled. The partners would meet Mr. Morgan either in his private office, or less formally at luncheon, and would discuss together the problems of current business. It would thus be a mistake to attribute to the wisdom or initiative of any single partner policies which were in fact the corporate contribution of them all. "You ask me," records Mr. Russell Leffingwell, "what was Dwight's function in our office. He had none.

He was not charged with any particular duties. He partici-
pated in nearly everything we did. His job was to think."

Subject to this general reservation, it may be asserted that,
in the early months at least, Dwight Morrow specialized, not
so much in the operations of high finance, as in straightening
out many minor tangles into which the various corporations,
in which J. P. Morgan & Co. held an interest, had become involved. His work in this connection was of great value, and
not merely to his own firm. He was able, by applying his
dynamo of creative confidence, to vivify moribund concerns.
He became the physician of sick businesses, and the breadth
and depth of his reputation were largely based on the skill,
and above all on the magnanimity, with which he healed.

2

Reference has already been made to the indignation
aroused in Morrow by what he considered to be the unjustified attacks made upon J. P. Morgan & Co. in connection
with the affairs of the New York, New Haven & Hartford
Railroad. It is unnecessary to disinter the details of that forgotten agitation. A succession of unfortunate events, including the fall in price of the New Haven shares during the
panic of 1907 and the antagonism aroused by the attempts
of Mr. Charles S. Mellen (the very aggressive president of
the railroad) to acquire control of the Boston & Maine
system, had led to an investigation by the Interstate Commerce Commission early in 1912, supplemented in 1914 by a
more intensive inquiry conducted under a resolution of the
United States Senate. This inquiry developed into an
attack, not merely on the administrative methods of Mr.

Charles Mellen, but also upon the responsibility of Mr. J. P. Morgan senior, who had died in the previous year. One of Morrow's first and most welcome tasks, on entering the office, was to defend the memory of Mr. Morgan against these unfair attacks. He was able by the lucidity and frankness of his evidence to demonstrate that such errors as had been committed had been made without Mr. Morgan's knowledge and in some cases in direct opposition to his instructions. He was not able entirely to remove from the public mind the adverse sentiments which had been aroused; but he was certainly successful in creating a juster estimate in all reasonable minds.

In 1915 he was able to devote his powers of conciliation to more constructive purposes. In January of that year he was of the greatest assistance to the Erie Railroad in the matter of their mortgages. Two such mortgages existed under which the company had issued 4 per cent bonds, saleable only at heavy discounts under the then money conditions. Morrow evolved the plan of creating supplemental mortgages, providing for an increase in the interest rate, under terms consistent with the conditions then prevailing, and carried his negotiations to a successful conclusion.

An even more intricate, and for him more fascinating, task was that of the capitalization of the Kennecott Copper Corporation. For several years prior to 1914 J. P. Morgan & Co. had shared with the Guggenheim brothers an interest in the Alaska Syndicate. This syndicate owned copper mines, fisheries, landed properties, and even a railroad. It was desired to dissolve the syndicate and to reorganize the properties upon a broader basis, thereby releasing what had become a frozen investment. This task was entrusted to Dwight Morrow who, with characteristic thoroughness, proceeded to study the copper industry in all its ramifications. "Six months," recorded Mr. Daniel Guggenheim,[1] "after Morrow had started upon this investigation he knew more about copper than I or any of my six brothers." The original syndicate was transformed into a public corporation with an issue of convertible bonds, subsequently retired through conversion into stock, and a substantial interest in the stock of the company was bought privately by friends of the two original owners. The scope of the Kennecott Copper Corporation was thereafter extended by the purchase of a large interest in the Utah and Braden Copper Companies. The Kennecott company thus became one of the three greatest copper-producing properties in the world.

Dwight Morrow worked for months upon this reorganization, which gave full scope to his ingenuity and resource. The problem appealed both to his practical zest in simplifying the complex and to his romantic passion for history in the making. On the one hand, there was an immensely intricate tangle to unravel, a mass of facts and figures to be mastered and absorbed. On the other hand glimmered that vast, once Russian, province, the memories of the Klondike fever of 1896, the glamor of something remote, mysterious, imperial, and huge.

It was during this period that he renewed acquaintance with Mr. Stephen Birch, subsequently president of the Kennecott Copper Corporation, who became one of his dearest, heartiest, and most convivial friends. When the negotiations had been completed, Morrow composed a detailed report which he submitted to Henry P. Davison. "You have," Davi-

[1] Daniel Guggenheim, mining capitalist and philanthropist, b. Philadelphia, Pennsylvania, 1856; identified for many years with the most valuable and important copper properties in the United States and elsewhere; founder of the Guggenheim Fund for the Promotion of Aeronautics; d. 1930.

149

son remarked, "provided for every eventuality and for even the most minute contingency. But you have forgotten one thing. You have forgotten to provide for our commission. You have left out the part which says how much J. P. Morgan & Co. are to be paid for their hard work on this job." And in fact that was the only item in the whole business which had escaped Morrow's attention.

Before he left the office for the night he would dictate to his secretary the agenda for the next day's business. This agenda would be typed upon a pink paper slip and would be waiting on his desk the following morning. A number of these agenda slips have survived among his papers (generally as bookmarks), and the following, chosen wholly at random, indicates the multiplicity of his tasks:

D. W. M.   Saturday, December 5, 1914

Père Marquette
City Loan bonus
Alaska
Southern Railway unpaid coupons
Imperial Copper Company
Erie
Exchange
Equitable
Republican Congressional Committee
Port of New York Reorganization
Write Daniel Willard
Miss Simmons, Englewood High School
Civic Association Special Committee

Nor were these all. In the course of those years he assisted in such diverse problems as the reorganization of the H. B. Claflin Company, the disposal of the properties owned by

J. P. Morgan & Co. in California, and the closing out of the old liens on the Madison Square Garden sites. The correspondence of those years deals with interests as varied as those of the Niagara Falls Power Company, the United Dry Goods Company, and the Baldwin Locomotive Works; and touches on such subjects as company legislation, income tax on non-resident aliens, Amherst, Englewood, begging letters, New York clubs, the Bar Association, the latest books on economics or history, and the welfare of his friends and family. All this is distinct from the labor arising from the operations of J. P. Morgan & Co. in financing the payments for orders placed by France and Great Britain in the United States. These operations form the subject of the chapter which follows.

It has been necessary to catalogue these activities in order to convey something of the formidable nature of his employment. It would be impossible to deal in detail with these wearisome operations. Some mention must, however, be made of three problems, the solution of which was a source of lasting satisfaction to himself, and the cause of astonishment and admiration on the part of his fellows. These three problems were the mutualization of the Equitable Life Assurance Society, the financial readjustment of the Interborough Rapid Transit Company, and the rescue of Mr. William C. Durant.[2] They are not, even as business problems, wholly uninteresting. As illustrations of Morrow's magnetic methods they are significant and useful.

[2] William C. Durant, b. Boston, Massachusetts, 1861; educated in Michigan; organizer of Buick Motor Car Co., General Motors Co., Durant Motors, Inc., and others.

3

When Henry Baldwin Hyde, the founder of the Equitable Life Assurance Society, died in 1899, the control of his vast interests, the burden of his immense responsibilities, passed into the hands of his son, James Hazen Hyde, at that date a Francophile youth of the age of twenty-three. The more elderly directors of the Equitable did not fully appreciate the charm of this young man, who seemed to them to devote to the French Symbolists an interest greater than that which he accorded to the policyholders of the Society. They so harassed young Mr. Hyde that in 1905 he transferred his majority holdings to Mr. Thomas F. Ryan and retired permanently to his spiritual home in Paris.

The disagreement between Mr. Hyde and his fellow directors had attracted public attention, and Mr. Joseph Pulitzer profited by the occasion to launch a press campaign against the whole system of American insurance companies. This campaign led, in the autumn of 1905, to an official investigation, in the course of which Charles Evans Hughes gained that public reputation which, but for the more mobile tactics of Theodore Roosevelt, would have earned him the Presidency. As a result of this inquiry, legislation was passed, which, by restricting the powers of insurance directors, gave greater security to the policyholders.

This legislation, however, did not go as far as the public demanded. It was widely felt that it was unwise for an insurance company such as the Equitable, with millions of policyholders and assets running into upwards of a billion dollars, to continue as a private corporation. This uneasiness was not diminished by the fact that Mr. Thomas Fortune

Ryan, who had acquired the controlling interest in the Equitable, was not considered a man of sufficient calibre to execute so large a responsibility. It was because of this feeling that Mr. J. P. Morgan senior, who was subsequently joined by George F. Baker[3] and James Stillman,[4] acquired the majority holdings from Mr. Ryan, believing, and rightly, that public confidence would, in this manner, be restored. Mr. Morgan placed his own block of shares in the hands of three trustees.

On the death of Mr. Morgan senior the situation was reviewed. Mr. Morgan junior and the other partners felt that whatever guarantees might be given and accepted, the principle of private ownership was still an unwise one to follow, and that efforts must be made to transform the Equitable from a private corporation into a mutual corporation. In June 1915 Mr. Morgan disposed of his own block of shares to General T. Coleman du Pont. Mr. Baker and Mr. Stillman did likewise. This transference was negotiated by Dwight Morrow, who had gained the General's confidence in the old Cedar Street days. It did not simplify the main problem of how the Equitable was to be mutualized. This problem continued to occupy Morrow's mind for a space of two years.

One day in the spring of 1917, Dwight Morrow and Mr. Thomas Cochran,[5] also of J. P. Morgan & Co., had to attend a board meeting up town. They agreed that after the meeting they would lunch together at the Plaza Hotel. As they walked away from the meeting Cochran observed that

[3] George F. Baker, b. Troy, New York, 1840; for many years the chief and moving spirit of the First National Bank of New York; d. 1931.

[4] James Stillman, b. Brownsville, Texas, 1850; president and chairman of the board of the National City Bank of New York until his death in 1918.

[5] Thomas Cochran, b. St. Paul, Minnesota, 1871; Yale 1894; president Liberty National Bank, New York, 1914-17; Morgan partner since 1917; trustee many charitable organizations.

Morrow was in one of his moods of abstraction. He kept edging Cochran off the sidewalk, and when Cochran crossed to his other side, he started, in complete oblivion of his presence, edging him against the shop windows of Fifth Avenue. They entered the Plaza Hotel; they were shown to a table; Cochran ordered luncheon; even when the food was set before him Morrow remained in a trance. Cochran decided to watch just how long this trance would continue. He ate his own meal in silence, motioning to the waiter from time to time to remove from Morrow's place the dishes which accumulated untouched before him. Suddenly, while Cochran was lighting his cigar, Morrow emerged from his stupor. He struck the table with his hand. "That's done it!" he exclaimed. "What," Cochran asked him, "has done what?" "I've mutualized the Equitable! Now, Tom, let's go out somewhere and get something to eat!"

The ingenuity of the scheme which had then occurred to him was such as to be almost incomprehensible to any layman. Its main outlines were as follows: The Society was to transform itself into a mutual life insurance corporation and to purchase from General du Pont the shares that he held. The price of these shares was to be paid in half-annual installments running from November 1, 1917, to May 1, 1937, out of the interest received by the Society upon a mortgage of $20,500,000 given to the Society by the Equitable Office Building Corporation. This involved the surrender to General du Pont of the 9 per cent of the dividends of the Equitable Building Corporation hitherto held by the Equitable Life Assurance Society. It also entailed an extension agreement under which the previous mortgage bond of 1913 was altered so that the mortgage should be paid off, not by November 1935 as previously stipulated, but by May 1974.

The minor adjustments necessitated by this device were of the utmost intricacy; yet, even when these had been agreed to, there remained the problem of how to induce General du Pont to part with his holdings at what would certainly represent a heavy loss. To this day it remains a mystery how Morrow was able to secure his consent. The persuasiveness with which he appealed to his sense of public duty was reënforced by the persistence with which, month after month, he drove him into acquiescence. At such moments Morrow was perfectly capable of adopting third degree methods and wearing down his opponent by actual physical exhaustion. And, as always happened with Morrow's victories, the vanquished felt delighted at their own defeat. When, in July of 1917, the Equitable was finally mutualized and the stock handed over to three trustees for the benefit of the policyholders, Mr. George Baker drove down to Morgan's office and asked to see Dwight Morrow. He went up to him, took him by the lapels of his coat, and scrutinized him with a penetrating stare. "I just wanted," he explained, "to look at you."

4

The mutualization of the Equitable was generally recognized as being one of the most brilliant successes in financial and legal adjustment ever achieved. A less dramatic, more prolonged, but no less complicated problem was that of the Interborough Rapid Transit Company. It must at least be mentioned since it absorbed a great proportion of Morrow's time and energy between the years 1919 and 1927. In the end he became so involved and interested in the New York subway and transit systems that they almost came to represent for him what the "roads of Cephalonia" had represented for Napier. The unification of the whole system was one of his most persistent dreams.

It was Dwight Morrow's custom, as has been seen, to approach a problem cautiously and to study it in all its bearings before reaching a decision. Another characteristic was the persistence with which he pursued a problem during the course of several years. Yet when faced with a crisis, he could work with lightning rapidity and dispatch. A good illustration of his more rapid method is furnished by the rescue of Mr. William C. Durant, founder and president of General Motors.

Mr. Durant was an ingenious but haphazard man. He combined breathless energy, great manufacturing ability, and unbounded self-confidence with a reckless disregard for accountancy and a merry contempt for the old-fashioned methods of more stable financiers. For some weeks, during the fall of 1920, rumors had been circulating that Mr. Durant was in difficulties. It was not, however, until 2 P.M. of Thursday November 18th that Mr. Durant himself became aware that these difficulties called for urgent solution. On that day, at that hour, he telephoned to 23 Wall Street demanding assistance. Dwight Morrow, accompanied by Mr. Cochran and Mr. Whitney,[6] proceeded to the offices of General Motors where they found Mr. Pierre du Pont and Mr. John J. Raskob. It was disclosed to them that the situation was a most serious one, involving brokers' loans for $25,000,000 and that calls for additional margin of a most pressing character

[6] George Whitney, b. Boston, Massachusetts, 1885; on graduating from Harvard in 1907 became associated with the Boston banking house of Kidder, Peabody & Company; partner in J. P. Morgan & Co. since 1920.

had been sent to Mr. Durant and would have to be honored immediately. Morrow took the situation under his control. He asked Mr. Durant to sit down at once and prepare a full statement of his assets and obligations, this statement to be ready not later than 9.30 P.M. that night. At 10 P.M. he returned, accompanied by Mr. Pierre du Pont. Already a broker had ensconced himself in the anteroom demanding checks. The ensuing discussion lasted all night. The following agreement was eventually secured. The du Pont interests were to form a security holding company to purchase 2,500,000 shares of General Motors stock from Mr. Durant. The capital of this new company was to be supplied by a subscription to preferred stock of $7,000,000 by the du Pont interests and a loan of $20,000,000 one year 8 per cent notes on the part of J. P. Morgan & Co. A memorandum of agreement was initialed at a quarter to six in the morning. During the whole of the following Friday, Saturday, and Sunday Dwight Morrow worked upon the contracts and other details. By the opening of the Stock Exchange on Monday morning all arrangements had been completed and Mr. Durant's brokers began delivering General Motors stock to J. P. Morgan & Co. against payment.

"Yes," Morrow remarked to his partners when the crisis was over, "Yes, Durant thanks us humbly now for saving his life, but within a week he will be cursing us for something else."

5

As a background to all this industry was the house on Palisade Avenue and a domestic atmosphere which both stimulated and soothed. Those who visited the Morrow home were conscious of some quality more stirring and more dynamic than the merely sedative happiness of harmonious family life. Behind the love and gaiety, the jokes and shibboleths, which united them into a concentrated clan, were common factors of intelligence, curiosity, wit, independence, energy, and youthfulness.

During the last year of her life his eldest daughter Elisabeth—who of all his children stood closest to him in temperament and humor—was able to recapture and record her childhood's reminiscences. Among these delicate sketches is one entitled "Reading," some extracts from which will convey, better than any commentary, the relations between these six gifted people:

"One of the best spell-binders of all was *Ben-Hur*. It was so real to us, especially the scenes in the leper colony, that we were terrified of catching leprosy. Anne made a solemn compact that if she caught it she would immediately touch Elisabeth, and Elisabeth promised to do the same for Anne, so that if they had to be sent away, at least they could go together. When the book was read to Constance several years later she wrote to one of her sisters—'At last we have finished the chariot race. All night the cry "A hundred sestertii on the Jew!" rang in my ears. It was so thrilling that even Daddy listened. . . .'

" 'Even Daddy listened'—what does this not recall to all our minds? In the living room in his old Morris chair our father sits reading. He has pulled up another chair for his feet and all about him on the floor are strewn newspapers, not to mention his countless and famous little curlicues of scrap paper.[7] He is so deep in his book that it doesn't matter if Elisabeth and Anne are playing chop-sticks on the piano, or Dwight and Constance are

[7] This refers to a strange habit, or nervous trick. Morrow would tear off the corner of a sheet of paper and twist it into a small spill. He would then screw this spill into his ear, throw it on the ground, and shortly afterwards repeat the

having a noisy game of slap-jack together. Nothing disturbs him. Occasionally when our mother has gathered us together for reading and it is something really exciting, he will look over the top of his book. He may even put his book down and come over to join us by the fireplace. But such times were rare and when they occurred they were considered news. It was usually impossible to tear him away from his reading even for dinner. Finally Elisabeth, who was becoming interested in modern education, hit upon the idea of taking his glasses off his nose and putting them beside his place in the dining room. 'Now-a-days,' she told him, 'we make the child *want* to do something else. . . .'

"For us children part of our father's charm lay in the fact that we never could be sure just what kind of book he would be reading. It might be one of the Cambridge Histories or on the other hand it might very easily be the latest Oppenheim thriller. He delighted in a good detective story and we were always glad to catch him in this particular mood, to have him step down from the Olympian Heights and play with us for a little while. When traveling we always carried a book bag as well as a book trunk, and what a mixture! Thucydides, Bryce, side by side with Edgar Wallace and Agatha Christie. Stacks of cheap magazines filled with thrillers would be bought at every station. Our mother did not wholly approve of these orgies in which all of us indulged, but she almost always gave in to our father. His logic as well as his charm was irresistible. Why, he argued smiling, if she had been so careful for ten or fifteen years to have us read only the best books, should she mind a little trash once in a while?

"It is true that he hardly ever read a modern novel. Once, however, having run out of detective fiction and wanting something not too heavy to read, one of his daughters handed him Somerset Maugham's *Cakes and Ale*. After several chapters on Rosie, the

operation with a fresh spill. These spills would litter the floor around his chair. This was a relic of a childhood habit acquired during the period when the Allegheny household were encouraged to make spills to save the cost of matches.

prostitute, he turned to our mother and said, bewildered, 'Betty, this is a hell of a book. Do you think the girls should be allowed to read things like that?' Our mother refrained from answering, but remembering those many half hours before supper which had been devoted to our reading, and realizing that with our tastes formed there was no need to worry any longer, how could she help smiling a little to herself?"

An equally vivid picture of the Morrow home life has been furnished by his second daughter, Anne:

"Breakfast was for a long time the only meal, in fact the only time, we saw Daddy. I realize now, looking back on it, that it was the only time we felt ourselves as a family.

"Breakfast was at quarter to eight. . . . We were always well started on our breakfast before Daddy came down. Mother came first. We could hardly hear her coming—just the creak of the last step as she reached the bottom of the stairs and the click of her heel on the bare place between the rugs. (There were thin yellow silk curtains on the glass doors between the dining room and the hall, but you could see right through them—though you pretended not to—when someone came in the front door to call during meals.)

"Mother was already neatly spreading marmalade on toast when Daddy came down. We could hear him coming, long before we could see him through the curtains, whistling a tune upstairs as he went along the hall with brisk, determined, short little steps— the determined *stomp, stomp, stomp,* down the stairs—the tune getting louder and more abandoned.

"He could not keep a tune—at least he could not keep any conventional tune the way it was written; but that tune of Daddy's was always the same. It was not recognizable to an outsider, though, as he began, you always thought it was going to be— 'O—oh—*Paddy* dear, an' *did* you hear—' and then again, somewhere in the middle, you thought you recognized, 'Three-ee *cheers* for the *red,* white and *blue.'* He was quite consistent about it. It was always the same; and never, as with most people who cannot keep a tune, was there the slightest hesitation or wavering. There was no doubt in his mind as to what note to take next. It might be blatantly inaccurate, but it was always arrogantly positive.

"When he came down like this, he would break into the room, beaming, and like a child who expects you to stop everything to welcome him. We children would all get up to kiss him. Sometimes it was a 'Foursome'—terrible game—all three of us kissing at once. There was a good deal of competition and many complaints—'I didn't get *you* at *all,* Daddy—I just got *Elisabeth!'* 'Well, now, we'll try again!' (And all the time Mother was quietly patting marmalade on to a dry corner of toast or slitting letters with a butter knife.) Sometimes he would come around the room and kiss us, and Mother too. He would make us come to him, too, often several times during the meal. 'You haven't given your father a morning kiss,' he would insist. 'Come up here!' (At first we took all this kissing for granted. But then it became very embarrassing—especially such hearty kisses that we promptly 'rubbed off.' We much preferred the delicate Cutter kiss, that was hardly more than a brush of the cheek, to the loud Morrow smack. Daddy teased us about rubbing the kisses off, and did not like a cheek held up to him. 'No cheek-y! No cheek-y,' he would say.)

"Some mornings, in fine form, he would come down, approach the table sedately, and back away. Then he would make three low bows and say, in sonorous singing tones, 'Making in *all— three* kowtows!'—which simply delighted all of us.

"Sometimes, of course, he would come down without the whistle, preoccupied and serious, and hardly notice us. A fumble with the handle of the glass door and he was in the room, looking straight ahead, not seeing anyone, his lips sometimes moving inaudibly as though he were talking to himself. He might go through the whole meal like this, although it was very seldom that he did not wake up at least once and say, 'Come over here and give your poor old father a kiss—Snippy!' (meaning that we were snippy not to have kissed him before). Or he would put out his hand to the child on either side of him. Very often, though, Mother would speak to him three times before he heard (*we* never tried to interrupt him). 'Dwight—do you hear me? What are we going to do about the Thacher dinner?'

"Once in a while he would come down to breakfast with his hair all mussed and Mother would say, as she might to one of us, '*Dwight*—you haven't brushed your hair!' Then he would put his hand over his head and twinkle in a shamefaced, small-boy way, hesitate, and then perhaps appeal to us. 'Now, Elisabeth, do you think I have to go back and brush my hair?'

"Elisabeth would usually say firmly, 'Yes, Daddy, I think Mother is right.' I would say, trying very hard not to hurt his feelings and yet be loyal to Mother, 'We-ell, I think it would look a little better.' Dwight might quote one of Daddy's own phrases, as 'When Mother lifts her little finger, you know, Daddy—we all tremble!'

"Then he would turn, like a naughty boy caught in some act of disobedience, and go back upstairs.

"After he sat down, the rest of the meal, up to the eggs, was spent behind the newspapers. With the poached eggs he would put his paper down (as he had to use both hands) or let it drop, rather, and he would 'set to' in a very determined manner. With knife and fork he would carve across the eggs in the most ruthless and militant manner, as though it were a steak, the gore oozing all over the plate. Then he would plunge the cut quarters into his mouth.

"With the eggs would come conversation, for he had put the paper down. The conversation was usually to his children, in the form of well worn jokes or teasing. One of the most familiar was the question, given rather roguishly and with a twinkle, 'Who do you like best—your Mother or your Father, Elisabeth? (Anne, or

Dwight—as it might be.)' This was always agony. I could see the question coming to me next, like a bad dream, and I was never well prepared. Elisabeth was asked first and always answered honestly and courageously—perfectly frankly (which delighted him). 'I like Mother best—and *next* to Mother I like Daddy.' Then he would turn to me. I can remember the torture of trying to be honest, yet not to hurt his feelings. First I would say, evading and embarrassed, 'I like you both the same.' But Daddy would persist, 'Now, Anne, tell me the truth—Who do you love best?' Then I would protest— 'But I like you—*differently!*' 'Now, Anne—' He enjoyed very much teasing me and would insist on my explaining myself, going on and on. But I never admitted liking Mother most.

" 'Well—come here and give me a kiss—anyway,' it would usually end."

IX. War Finance 1914–1917

THE WAR WAS UNEXPECTED. WALL STREET UNPREPARED FOR
SUDDEN EXCHANGE PROBLEMS THEREBY CREATED. MOMENTARY
COLLAPSE OF THE FINANCIAL MACHINE. A TYPICAL PROBLEM
WAS PAYMENT OF DEBTS OF CITY OF NEW YORK MATURING IM-
MEDIATELY IN LONDON AND PARIS. METHODS BY WHICH J. P.
MORGAN DEALT WITH THIS SITUATION AND SAVED THE CITY'S
CREDIT. BY 1915 THE POSITION IS REVERSED. EUROPE FINDS IT
DIFFICULT TO OBTAIN CREDITS IN THE UNITED STATES. J. P.
MORGAN & CO. APPOINTED AGENTS FOR THE FRENCH AND BRITISH
GOVERNMENTS. THE MAGNITUDE OF THEIR OPERATIONS. THE
ANGLO-FRENCH LOAN OF 1915. THE 1916 ISSUES. MORROW'S OWN
PART IN THESE OPERATIONS. EDWARD STETTINIUS AND THE "EX-
PORT DEPARTMENT." AMERICAN CRITICISM OF MORGAN'S AS PUR-
CHASING AGENTS FOR BRITISH GOVERNMENT. MORROW'S ATTI-
TUDE TOWARDS THIS CRITICISM.

THE outbreak of hostilities found Wall Street unprepared.
Even in England, even in France, the bankers (having been
trained in habits of reason) considered a war "unthinkable";
they predicted, when the unthinkable occurred, that the
laws of high finance would bring it to an end within six
weeks. The bankers of Wall Street were even more sensible.
They could not believe that men as gifted as William II, as
experienced as Franz Josef, as gentle as the Tsar, could fail
to compose their differences. It seemed to them inconceivable
that the French nation, being the most practical and the most
civilized on earth, would risk the devastation of their country
in what was evidently but an Austro-Russian dispute. It
appeared to them beyond the bounds of possibility that Great
Britain, under the guidance of a Liberal cabinet, preoccupied
as she then was by an acute stage in the Irish controversy,
governed by a humanist such as Asquith and a humanitarian
such as Grey, would risk the life of a single British marine

in order to rescue M. Isvolsky from a personal predicament. They could not bring themselves to believe that the cosmopolitanism to which they were accustomed in their own business was not based upon an equally pacific internationalism among the peoples of the world.

By all the rules of reason they were correct in these assumptions. Yet the structure of European peace was not, in that July of 1914, cemented by reason: it maintained itself by the thrust and counter-thrust of great monoliths of power; that balance had already shifted its equilibrium in 1909 and again in 1911; it required but the loosening of a single pebble to bring the whole edifice to the ground.

On Tuesday July 28th Austria declared war on Serbia. Russia began her mobilization on Wednesday July 29th and declared a general mobilization on Thursday July 30th. Not till then did New York realize that a general war was imminent. On Friday July 31st the New York Stock Exchange was closed for the first time since 1873.

Ten years later Dwight Morrow sent to Thomas Lamont (who was at that time engaged upon his monograph of Henry P. Davison) a memorandum embodying his own recollection of those irresolute days:

"Harry [1] was most positive the day before the Stock Exchange closed that there would be no general European war. As you know, when he was positive he was very positive. In view of all the nonsense that is talked about banks making wars and knowing when they happen, I do not think there is any harm in stressing this point. The evening before the Stock Exchange closed the news from London for the first time began to be very serious. Harry tried to get a meeting of four or five important bankers

[1] Henry P. Davison.

that evening. I recall that Vanderlip had gone home early and could not be reached. The next morning Harry called me up and asked me to come to the office early. He and Jack [2] and I sat down in our office with Vanderlip, Ben Strong, Frank Hine, and, I think, Gates McGarrah. The meeting took place about nine o'clock, with Vanderlip coming in late. About 9.45 the President of the Stock Exchange, with another member of their central committee, came over to our office which was then, as you will recall, in the Mills Building. There had been no funds available for loans on Stock Exchange securities at the close the day before, and there had been a violent decline. The Stock Exchange authorities wanted to know whether to open or not, and nobody knew what to tell them. It got down to about five minutes of ten, and the President of the Stock Exchange called up the Exchange and told them to announce that the Exchange would be closed. He did not get any instructions from anybody to do this, but he did it because he could not get any instructions from anybody not to do it. It was in my very early days in a banking firm and I can remember that I was impressed with how little anybody knew what he was doing. I have always thought that if we had had a little more time the Stock Exchange would have been kept open, as it should have been. I was particularly impressed by Harry's vigor during this period. Although he was fully unprepared for the war, as were we all, still when it did come it presented a brand new problem for him, and he was eager to be doing something every minute."

This "brand new problem" developed within a few hours into a situation unprecedented in the history of finance. There was in the first place the question of exchange. The floating indebtedness of the United States in London was, on that August 1, 1914, no less than $150,000,000. [3] Immedi-

---

[2] J. P. Morgan.

[3] The normal pre-war rate of exchange was dollars 4.8665 to the pound sterling, and dollars 0.193 for the franc. Throughout this book, which is not a

ate payment of these obligations was demanded, with the result that sterling exchange at once rose to dangerous heights in New York. It required, by August 1st, as much as seven dollars to buy a single English pound. The whole mechanism of exchange failed to operate because the export of commodities to Europe was, in those early days, interrupted, owing to the fear of German commerce-raiders. The situation became so fantastic that the United States Government was obliged to dispatch the cruiser *Tennessee,* under guarantee of immunity from each belligerent, with $35,-000,000 in gold for the relief of American tourists stranded in Europe. The leading New York banks agreed, as a transitory measure, to fix among themselves the purely arbitrary rate of $5.00 for the pound sterling. A more scientific scheme, known as the "gold pool," was later devised, under which a fund of $100,000,000 in gold was guaranteed by a number of national and state banks to cover payment of American debts in London. Of this sum 10 per cent was deposited in Ottawa, to the credit of the Bank of England, and sums so deposited were credited in the depositor's London account at the agreed rate of $4.90. The tension was in this manner relieved, and by December 1914 sterling had returned to its normal level in New York.

Before the bankers had been able thus to repair and readjust the dislocated machinery of international exchange, several acute situations had, however, arisen. Of the many problems in which J. P. Morgan & Co. took a lead during those days of crisis, the most important was that of the indebtedness of the City of New York.

Early in August 1914, Comptroller Prendergast called

financial history, the arbitrary rate has been taken of $5.00 to the pound sterling, and 20 cents to the French franc.

upon Mr. J. P. Morgan and disclosed to him that the City of New York had outstanding short-term notes payable in London and Paris in monthly installments to a total respectively of $67,943,940 and $12,300,000. These notes had been issued (at a time when money was cheaper in London and Paris than in New York) in anticipation of the taxes which would be paid to the municipality in the autumn and of the sale of short-term bonds on the home market. In the panic prevailing, there seemed no prospect of selling any such bonds, and even if the necessary dollars were collected in the United States it was impossible, at the then fantastic rate of exchange, to turn these dollars into sterling and francs. Mayor Mitchel of New York was inclined to default, at least upon the earlier installments. Comptroller Prendergast, before consenting to so extreme a step, appealed to Mr. Morgan for his counsel and assistance.

Default, in those days, was still unfashionable. Mr. Morgan determined to do everything in his power to save the credit of the City of New York. In the account of the subsequent operations which he contributed to Thomas W. Lamont's biography of Henry P. Davison, Dwight Morrow gives to the latter the whole credit for the achievement. The honors are, in fact, divided. Mr. J. P. Morgan supplied imagination, knowledge, and, above all, determination. Henry Davison devised the strategy. Dwight Morrow and Arthur M. Anderson [4] executed the tactics.

"Jack, of course," wrote Morrow subsequently, "with his knowledge of foreign exchange, was very keen about the plan and very helpful in blocking it out. Harry, however, was the one who organized the banks. At first we did not get much help. Vanderlip

[4] Arthur M. Anderson, b. East Orange, New Jersey, 1880; banker since 1904; partner in L. von Hoffman & Company 1912-14; Morgan partner since 1926

was luke warm. If, when the notes fell due, we could pay them we would do it, but if we could not we could not. The younger men like Strong, McGarrah, Wiggin, Prosser, *et al,* were as usual ready to follow Harry. Of course *we* did all the work, Kuhn, Loeb going along much as in the Japanese business. It seemed desirable to have them in at that time in order to have an entirely united front. Anderson, who had just come into the office, was invaluable on the whole thing. I signed the contract on behalf of the firm at two or three in the morning at the City Club. . . . I recall distinctly the feeling that I had of the very great power that the House had in leadership. Without this power they would have been unable to do the thing at all."

It was in fact an operation calling for such authority, confidence, and daring as only the house of Morgan could command. Mr. J. P. Morgan himself, at his first conference with Comptroller Prendergast, denied that the situation was irretrievable; in his opinion, City of New York short-term notes could, if properly handled, be absorbed by the home market in spite of the panic which still prevailed. He felt also that, for the purpose of rescuing the repute of their own city, the New York bankers could successfully be asked to surrender gold. One of his first steps was to approach the Secretary of the Treasury. On August 21st he wrote to Mr. McAdoo informing him that his own firm was prepared to organize a syndicate to purchase notes of the City of New York to a possible total of $120,000,000 "upon the understanding that the finances of the city are to be conducted upon a policy different from that followed during many years." He added that if the credit of the city were to be saved it might be necessary for the banks to deplete their gold reserves to a point where they were unwilling to go without the approval of the Treasury and the Comptroller of Currency. Official sanction having been obtained, Mr. Davison, with Morrow as his lieutenant, set about interviewing the directors of one hundred and twenty-six different New York banks, with a view to forming an all-powerful syndicate. It was calculated that a sum of $80,243,940 would be required to meet the maturities in London and Paris. If the dollar fell before the dates of these maturities, then the participating banks would themselves have to shoulder very heavy losses. If it rose, which then seemed most unlikely, then their profits were to be shared with the Municipality of New York. It required all Morrow's powers of persuasion to convince the bankers that the scheme was anything but quixotic.

The contract was signed on September 10th. Under this contract the banks undertook to purchase $100,000,000 in one, two, and three-year notes of the City of New York and to pay, if required, approximately 80 per cent of the purchase price in gold. The first installment of the city's obligations fell due in London on September 28th. J. P. Morgan & Co. had already, on their own account, shipped gold to Ottawa to meet this installment. During the next two months a further amount of $35,000,000 was, under arrangement with the Bank of England, sent in gold across the frontier. The notes, meanwhile, were offered to public subscription and went to an early premium. The exchange situation, at the time of the later maturities, had already righted itself. It had by then become cheaper to buy exchange than to ship sterling; the gold reserves of the New York banks remained undepleted. In the end, instead of the $80,243,940 at first estimated as necessary to meet these City debts, only $78,167,352 were required. The operation thus showed a profit of $2,076,588, which was shared between the City of New York and the bankers' syndicate. Of this profit J. P. Morgan &

Co. received $11,121. The participating banks refused to accept any commission for these services. "I am certain," wrote Comptroller Prendergast, "that the people of the city will, as they should, appreciate the fine spirit of civic interest in which these gentlemen have undertaken their tremendous task."

Dwight Morrow loved tremendous tasks. It was this great battle for the credit of New York which first convinced him of the creative scope of his new functions.

2

Slowly the tide began to turn. A few figures will suffice, better than any verbal explanation, to indicate the extent of that reversal. In July 1914 Great Britain and France were creditor nations. In 1913 the trade balance in favor of Great Britain had been as much as $670,000,000. British investments in the United States alone were estimated at $3,500,-000,000, and their total foreign investments at the figure of $20,000,000,000. The trade balance in favor of the United States was in July 1914 $470,653,000, in 1915 $1,094,419,000, and in 1916 $2,135,600,000.[5] The loss of trade with the Cen-

---

[5] These figures can, for those who believe in figures, be amplified as follows. It should be realized, however, that they take no account of the depreciation of money. Thus although the following table shows a 150 per cent increase, the actual increase was nearer 35.5 per cent.

U. S. TRADE FIGURES 1917-1920 (IN DOLLARS)

	Exports	Imports	Excess of Exports
1917	$6,233,512,597	$2,952,467,955	$3,281,044,642
1918	6,149,087,545	3,031,212,710	3,117,874,835
1919	7,920,425,990	3,904,364,932	4,016,061,058
1920	8,228,759,748	5,279,398,211	2,949,361,537

As a result, the U. S. A., instead of paying Europe $500 million a year ought now to be receiving from Europe $300 million a year. But they are not.

tral Powers was of course important, representing a drop from $344,794,276 in 1914 to $288,899 in 1916; yet it was more than counterbalanced by increased exports to the Allies. Thus, whereas American exports to Great Britain alone had in 1914 been $594,271,863, they increased in 1917 to $2,046,812,678. This enormous expansion in the American export trade was due, of course, to the European demand for war material and food. Such purchases could no longer be paid for in goods and services; only a small proportion could be liquidated in gold; the purchases for 1915 alone were some $700,000,000 in excess of gold capacity; the balance had to be financed by credit.

How could such vast credits be obtained?

Three separate systems were adopted. The first was the export of gold; a billion dollars of gold were transferred to the United States between 1914 and 1917. The second method was to commandeer the American securities held by British and French nationals. This method was first put into operation in January 1916, and in the end provided the British Government with a collateral of $2,425,000,000 and the French Government with a collateral of $51,000,000. The third method was just confidence.

It was J. P. Morgan & Co. who rendered that confidence effective.

In the late autumn of 1914 Henry Davison crossed the Atlantic. On arriving in London he interviewed Lord Kitchener and Mr. Lloyd George. The former assured him that the British Government would require no assistance from any American banker. They had already bought or contracted for all the supplies which they were likely to need from the United States. On December 16th Mr. Davison lunched with Lloyd George. The latter was less optimistic than Lord Kitchener. He asked Davison whether, if need arose, J. P. Morgan & Co. would assist the British Government in financing further purchases in the United States. Mr. Davison assured him that such assistance would be at the disposal of the British Government, and he then crossed to Paris, where he interviewed M. Ribot and M. de Margerie. He advised them that, if much wastage were to be avoided, some concentration of the financing and placing of French and British orders in the United States was essential. They agreed with this opinion. Henry Davison then returned to New York.

It was not long before the French and British Governments came to realize that they would be unable either to pay for purchases already ordered, or to maintain their own exchange, without a large American loan. In June of 1915 Henry Davison again crossed to Europe and discussed the possibility of floating a large Anglo-French loan upon the American market. He pointed out that conditions were not at the moment favorable. The American investor was temperamentally addicted, not to foreign investments, but to speculation in his own Golden West. The people of the United States, moreover, had been told to be neutral in thought and deed. There would thus be both moral and material objections to any large absorption of Allied loans, especially as the cause of the Allies did not, at that date, seem very promising. In September of 1915 Lord Reading was sent on a financial mission to New York and many discussions took place between him and the Morgan partners in his apartment at the Biltmore Hotel or at 23 Wall Street. Dwight Morrow was frequently present at these discussions and established relations of warm friendship with Lord Reading. "I shall always," wrote the latter in 1930, "count my acquaintance with you during the troublous war years as a treasured experience of my life."

Their subsequent meetings were frequent and auspicious. At a dinner party given, in later years, in the house of Thomas Lamont, an incident occurred which is illustrative of Morrow's habits of abstraction. At the outset of this dinner, Dwight Morrow helped himself to a large green olive. He held this olive, as conversation developed, between his thumb and forefinger; soup turned into fish and fish in its turn gave place to entrée; still did Dwight Morrow wave that olive in the air. From time to time he would pass it from his right to his left hand. The other guests, as Morrow continued his rapt monologue, became fascinated by that olive with which he punctuated his remarks; he made sweeping gestures with that olive indicative of the extent of British collateral or of the vast era of the American investing public; he made precise dabs with that olive when distinguishing between different methods of discounting; he pawed the air with that olive when assuring Lord Reading that the situation was not as yet beyond control. Coffee had arrived and the men rose to pass into the smoking room. Morrow was still explaining, holding his olive (by now a dried object with one bite in it) triumphantly aloft. It was then that Metcalfe, the Lamont butler, felt that it was time to intervene. He advanced towards Morrow with a plate extended. "Your olive, Mr. Morrow"—it was only then that Morrow, still unconscious, put it down.

As a result of their discussions with the French and British Missions the firm of J. P. Morgan & Co. agreed to obtain underwriting, without compensation for their services, for a loan of $500,000,000, which was to be a joint obligation of the French and British Governments. A syndicate was to be constituted to underwrite this issue at 96 and to offer it to the public at 98. The bonds were to bear 5 per cent interest and to mature in five years. The whole of this issue has now been paid off.

In order to dispose of this first loan, the firm of J. P. Morgan & Co. created a huge organization, consisting of 1570 members, for the distribution of bonds. The managers of this organization represented sixty-one banks, trust companies, and investment houses in New York City. At the time of the signing of the bond contract, agreements and participations aggregating about $162,000,000 were not actually in hand. "The firm," pronounced Mr. J. P. Morgan himself, "must commit itself to this task regardless of the risk." The house of Morgan therefore signed an agreement for the amount outstanding. The debt which the French and British nations owe personally to Mr. Morgan is one which, as other more material debts, can never be discharged.

An attack upon the loan was at this stage engineered by the German and Irish elements. They threatened to withdraw their deposits from any bank which supported the issue. This campaign was particularly virulent in Chicago, and Charles Dawes,[6] who fought it with courageous violence, invited Lord Reading to visit the city in person. The speech which Lord Reading made on that occasion was one of the most daring and brilliant of his whole career. Yet in spite of this effective counterattack the Anglo-French loan of 1915 was one of the most difficult that the house of Morgan ever attempted to place.

[6] Charles Gates Dawes, b. Marietta, Ohio, 1865; Comptroller of the Currency 1897-1901, General Purchasing Agent A.E.F., member Military Board of Allied Supply, Director U. S. Bureau of the Budget; Reparations Commission 1923-24; Vice President of the United States 1925-29; Ambassador to Great Britain 1929-32; Chicago banker.

3

By 1916 the situation, from the point of view of the Allies, had become even more serious. In the autumn of that year Henry Davison again crossed to London and J. P. Morgan went with him. They were invited to breakfast by Lloyd George, who informed them that the British Government would require in America a credit of three hundred million dollars a month for the next five months. If this credit were not forthcoming the Allies would have to suspend their war purchases in the United States. Could the firm of J. P. Morgan assist them in obtaining $1,500,000,000 immediately? Henry Davison was in no way numbed by this fantastic figure. He made no promises. Mr. Morgan made no promises. "We cannot tell," they said. And then they added—"But proceed with your purchasing program as if the money were there."

In August 1916 a collateral loan was issued for $250,-000,000 and in October of the same year a second collateral loan for $300,000,000. In November an unexpected difficulty arose. Messrs. J. P. Morgan & Co. had evolved the idea of issuing French and British short-term bills for the day-to-day financing of purchases, and published a statement to that effect. On November 27, 1916, the Federal Reserve Board replied that "they did not regard it in the interests of the country that member banks should at this time invest in foreign treasury bills of this character."

This statement filled both No. 23 Wall Street and Nos. 10 and 11 Downing Street with alarm. It was feared that not only would it put an end to the sale of treasury bills, but that it might also throw upon the market the public holdings of other Allied paper. Mr. Reginald McKenna, at that time Chancellor of the Exchequer, took immediate steps to counter this danger. He at once stopped the sale of all further treasury bills and dispatched several cruisers to Canada, transferring thereby, in a period of four months, as much as $422,000,000 in gold. Gold was also transported on Japanese warships to Vancouver. A crisis by these methods was for the moment averted. But the situation remained precarious in the extreme.

Meanwhile, owing to the sensational provocations of German submarine policy, American opinion was veering rapidly in favor of the Allies. On January 22, 1917, a third collateral loan (i.e., a loan secured on private British assets in the United States which had been taken over by the Government) was floated to the total of $250,000,000 and was readily absorbed by the public. In March of the same year a French loan of $100,000,000 was also successfully launched. The demands of the Allies were by then reaching a point beyond the capacity of their own credit facilities. And at that moment, on April 6, 1917, the United States entered the war. From then onward the provision of credit became largely an inter-governmental business and vast governmental debts were incurred, and subsequently repudiated. Messrs. J. P. Morgan & Co. continued none the less their own financing operations and were particularly active during the reconstruction period after the war.[7]

[7] Some conception of the immense area of their activities can be conveyed by the following table of loans issued under their auspices between 1915 and 1925:
Sept. 17, 1914, $100,000,000. City of New York 6% Corporate Stock, dated
   Sept. 1, 1914:
      $57,000,000. 1-Year Notes, due Sept. 1, 1915
      18,000,000. 2-Year Notes, due Sept. 1, 1916
      25,000,000. 3-Year Notes, due Sept. 1, 1917
(Continued on p. 178.)

It should be added that, in spite of the variety and magnitude of the loans issued under the auspices of J. P. Morgan, the investors in such loans were only in one instance exposed to loss. Until Dr. Schacht, in 1935, announced a partial default on the German external loan of 1924, interest on all these loans had regularly been paid. Some 90 per cent have already been fully liquidated.

Feb. 10, 1915, $100,000,000. New York Central R. R. Co. 20-Year 6% Convertible Debenture Bonds, due May 1, 1935

Oct. 14, 1915, $500,000,000. Anglo-French 5-Year 5% External Loan, dated Oct. 15, 1915, due Oct. 15, 1920

July 18, 1916, $94,500,000. American Foreign Securities Co. 3-Year 5% Gold Notes, dated Aug. 1, 1916, due Aug. 1, 1919

Aug. 23, 1916, $250,000,000. United Kingdom of Great Britain and Ireland 2-Year 5% Secured Loan, Gold Notes, dated Sept. 1, 1916, due Sept. 1, 1918

Oct. 30, 1916, $300,000,000. United Kingdom of Great Britain and Ireland 3- and 5-Year 5½% Secured Loan Gold Notes, dated Nov. 1, 1916:
$150,000,000 due Nov. 1, 1919
150,000,000 due Nov. 1, 1921

Jan. 22, 1917, $250,000,000. United Kingdom of Great Britain and Ireland 1-Year and 2-Year 5½% Secured Loan Convertible Gold Notes, dated Feb. 1, 1917:
$100,000,000 due Feb. 1, 1918
150,000,000 due Feb. 1, 1919

March 19, 1917, $100,000,000. Government of the French Republic 2-Year 5½% Secured Loan Convertible Gold Notes, dated April 1, 1917, due April 1, 1919

July 30, 1917, $100,000,000. Government of the Dominion of Canada 2-Year 5% Gold Notes, dated Aug. 1, 1917, due Aug. 1, 1919

Aug. 23, 1917, $150,000,000. United Kingdom of Great Britain and Ireland (90-day) Treasury Bills

Oct. 23, 1919, $250,000,000. United Kingdom of Great Britain and Ireland 10-Year 5½% Convertible Gold Bonds, due Aug. 1, 1929, and 3-Year 5½% Convertible Gold Notes due Nov. 1, 1922

Sept. 3, 1920, $100,000,000. Government of the French Republic 25-Year External Gold Loan 8% Sinking Fund Bonds, due Sept. 15, 1945

April 25, 1921, $230,000,000. Northern Pacific-Great Northern Joint 15-Year 6½% Convertible Gold Bonds (C. B. Q. collateral) due July 1, 1936

May 21, 1921, $100,000,000. Government of the French Republic 20-Year External Gold Loan 7½% Bonds, due June 1, 1941

April 24, 1922, $100,000,000. Government of the Dominion of Canada 30-Year 5% Gold Bonds, due May 1, 1952

Nov. 3, 1923, $100,000,000. American Telephone and Telegraph Co. 20-Year 5½% Sinking Fund Gold Debenture Bonds, due Nov. 1, 1943

(Continued on p. 179.)

4

It is impossible to define the exact part played by Dwight Morrow in these gigantic operations. He was in constant touch with several Allied missions, forming enduring friendships with Lord Reading, Sir Basil Blackett of the British Treasury, and General Wilfrid Ellershaw of the War Office.[8] He was particularly active in organizing the syndi-

Feb. 11, 1924, $150,000,000. Imperial Japanese Government External Loan of 1924, 30-Year Sinking Fund 6½% Gold Bonds, due Feb. 1, 1954

Oct. 14, 1924, $110,000,000. German External Loan 1924 7% Gold Bonds, due Oct. 15, 1949

Nov. 24, 1924, $100,000,000. Government of the French Republic External Loan 1924, 25-Year Sinking Fund 7% Gold Bonds, due Dec. 1, 1949

Jan. 8, 1925, $125,000,000. American Telephone & Telegraph Co. 35-Year Sinking Fund 5% Gold Debentures, due Jan. 1, 1960

Nov. 20, 1925, $100,000,000. Kingdom of Italy External Loan Sinking Fund 7% Gold Bonds, due Dec. 1, 1951

These figures can only be apprehended in anything approaching their correct proportions if the cost of the European War is compared schematically with the cost of other wars. A rough comparison can be made as follows (the figures are based upon Professor E. L. Bogart's "War Costs and Their Financing," p. 85. But they do not follow these figures exactly):

	Duration	Loss of Life	Direct Monetary Cost (in dollars)
Napoleonic Wars, 1790-1815	9,000 days	2,100,000	3,070,000,000
Crimean War, 1853-56	730 "	785,000	1,700,000,000
Franco-Prussian War, 1870-71 ...	210 "	184,000	3,210,000,000
Boer War, 1899-1902	995 "	9,774	1,250,000,000
Russo-Japanese War, 1904-05	548 "	160,000	2,100,000,000
European War, 1914-18	1,562 "	12,991,000	186,333,637,097

The total given above for the cost of the European War represents an estimate of its gross direct cost, and takes no account of such indirect costs as loss of life, property, and production, or the expenses entailed by war relief and on neutral countries. A more detailed estimate of cost has been given as follows:

Net direct costs $186,333,637,097
Indirect costs 151,612,542,560
Total $337,946,179,657

[8] General Ellershaw was drowned in the *Hampshire* when accompanying Lord Kitchener to Russia, leaving a widow and four children. Dwight Morrow was instrumental in organizing among his American friends an "Ellershaw Memorial Fund" of over £6,000 ($30,000.00).

cate which floated the first Anglo-French loan in 1915; and it was he who contrived with Sir Edward Holden the system by which book-credits in favor of the Allies were opened under this loan throughout the United States. He was also instrumental in creating the "American Foreign Securities Company" which launched the French loan of July 1916. And in the post-war period, as will be seen, he was actively interested in those series of reconstruction loans with which J. P. Morgan & Co. endeavored to restore the health of Europe.

The operations of the firm were not, during those years, confined entirely to sponsoring Allied loans. In the early weeks of the war Mr. Morgan and his partners were appalled to observe that the several Allied Governments were competing against each other in the American market. Not only did this competition raise prices to an unnatural level, but the whole system was rapidly demoralizing American industry. Mr. Morgan therefore offered his services to Great Britain as purchasing agent in the United States. This offer was accepted, and an "Export Department" was organized under the control of Edward R. Stettinius.[9] J. P. Morgan & Co. undertook to inform the British Government whenever a contract was accepted by a firm in which any Morgan partner held an interest. Of the hundreds of firms dealt with, the Morgan partners, it was stated, held shares in only eleven, and these shares never amounted to more than three per cent. Inevitably, however, much jealousy and criticism were aroused.

[9] Edward R. Stettinius, b. St. Louis, Missouri, 1865; engaged by J. P. Morgan & Co. to organize department for the purchase of munitions and other supplies for the Allies, partner 1916; 2nd Asst. Secretary of War 1918, member Inter-allied Munitions Council July 1918; partner in J. P. Morgan & Co. from 1916 until his death in 1925.

It had been expected, when the agreement was first entered into, that such centralization would only be required for a few weeks and that within a short time the British Government would establish a purchasing commission of their own. Lord Rhondda was, in fact, dispatched to New York to inquire into the position, but on his return he informed the British Government that J. P. Morgan & Co. were doing the work better than any commission that could possibly be devised. The whole supervision of British, and to some extent of French, purchases in the United States remained, therefore, in the hands of J. P. Morgan & Co. from 1915 until the United States entered the war, when a Purchasing Commission was created in Washington to take over their responsibilities.

The magnitude of this enterprise was so enormous that it absorbed the best energies of the firm and almost eclipsed the banking side. The manufacture of munitions was at that time practically a novelty to American industry; a whole series of new industries had to be organized; and immense labor had to be expended upon discriminating between bidders, inquiring into the capacity of the several firms, and fixing the various tenders. The odium entailed upon J. P. Morgan & Co. by this task was extreme.

Dwight Morrow, who was active in assisting Stettinius in his appalling and invidious duties, remained comparatively indifferent to the criticism which it aroused. He knew that it was both unjustified and inevitable; he maintained a philosophic calm. Patiently he would explain to critics the actual system that was being followed and how unavoidable it was that this system should arouse suspicion and resentment. A letter to his brother-in-law, dated May 6, 1915, illustrates this general attitude:

"With reference to the war contracts, the situation insofar as we know it, is as follows: The firm of J. P. Morgan & Co. represents the British Government in making any purchases that that Government is making in the United States. We are, of course, acting solely in the interests of the British Government, and are trying to get the best prices obtainable and the materials desired within the time that they are needed. Hundreds of middlemen, including lawyers, bankers, commission merchants and others, flock to us with statements that they have this thing or that thing to sell. We decline to deal with brokers unless they disclose their principal and unless their principal is of responsible character and qualified to do the work sought to be done within the time that it is desired. The majority of the people that come to us want to get a war contract of some kind so that they can shop it around amongst the manufacturers. With such people we, of course, decline to deal, and they promptly go out and talk about how we deal only with our friends. Of this latter sort of talk you will of course hear much within the next few months, but if it does not disturb anybody more than it does us no harm will be done."

U. S. ISOLATION. BRITISH BLOCKADE NOT ONLY VIOLATES INTER-
NATIONAL LAW BUT IS AN AFFRONT TO AMERICAN PRIDE. GER-
MANY, HOWEVER, BY HER SUBMARINE CAMPAIGN DRAWS
WHOLE ODIUM ON HERSELF. YET DURING 1915 THERE IS STILL
A DANGER OF AMERICAN INTERVENTION AGAINST THE ALLIED
BLOCKADE, AND J. P. MORGAN THEREFORE SHOWED COURAGE
IN SUPPORTING EARLY LOANS. THE FIRM WAS NEVER NEUTRAL.
MORROW, WHILE PRO-ALLY IN SENTIMENT, REMAINS UNPREJU-
DICED. HE OBJECTS TO ALLIED PROPAGANDA AND TO ATTACKS
ON GERMAN-AMERICANS. HE DISTRUSTS WAR PROSPERITY AND
FEARS THAT STRAIN OF NEUTRALITY MAY DEMORALIZE THE
COUNTRY. AMERICA DECLARES WAR, APRIL 6, 1917. THE NEW
JERSEY PRISON INQUIRY AS A SPECIMEN OF MORROW'S METHOD.
THE WAR SAVINGS CAMPAIGN. MORROW LEAVES FOR EUROPE.

IT would be beyond the scope of this monograph to examine
in any detail the causes which led to the intervention of the
United States upon the side of the Allies. The stages by
which the American people passed from contemptuous indifference, through indignation against all the belligerents
alike, towards their final decision of April 1917, provide important areas of study. Yet the subject is too intricate and
too serious to be dealt with parenthetically.[1] Certain indi-
cations must, however, be given, if the attitude of J. P. Morgan & Co., as well as that of Dwight Morrow himself, is to
be appreciated in correct proportions.

Foreign historians, when endeavoring to analyze the conflict of opinion which arose in the United States between
1914 and 1917, are apt to attach undue importance to material symptoms. They observe a clash of interest between
industry and agriculture; a division of sympathy between

---

[1] An extremely reliable and interesting account is given in Professor Charles
Seymour's "American Diplomacy During the World War."

the English, the Irish, and the German sections of the population; a political cleavage between Republicans and Democrats; a geographical cleavage between East and West; a personal cleavage between those who admired Woodrow Wilson and those who did not. Such divisions were indeed sharp and, on occasions, embittered. The essential conflict, however, was one which took place within the American soul. The American Idea was forced in the end to express itself in terms of power: it did so, most gradually, most unwillingly. It remained an Idea none the less. The conflict can best be understood if it be approached as one between isolation and pride. On the one hand there was the potent tradition of "no entanglements." On the other hand there was an equally potent determination to defend American rights. These rights were attacked "in a spot historically tender—commercial goings and comings on the high seas." [2] And in the earliest stages of the war they were attacked, not by Germany, but by Great Britain.

The blockade established by the British Empire violated the accepted theories of International Law in three vital respects. Commodities, such as copper and cotton, which ought to have been treated as conditional contraband were treated as absolute contraband, whereas foodstuffs, which ought to have been exempt, were seized or rationed. The right of visit and search ought, under established practice, only to have been exercised on the high seas; under the British blockade regulations, neutral shipping was diverted for examination to British harbors. Under the Reprisals Order in Council of March 11, 1915, the doctrine of "continuous voyage" was applied and the most arbitrary restrictions were placed on neutral trade. The British blockade, in fact, was not a block-

[2] Seymour's "American Diplomacy During the World War," p. 11.

ade in the legal sense of the term; it was an economic campaign waged against the Central Powers to the severe detriment of neutrals. "The Allied command of the Sea," writes Charles Seymour, "on the whole was not exercised in a way seriously to injure American pockets. But it did injure American pride." [3] How came it that the Germans were unable to exploit to their own advantage the indignation aroused thereby in the United States?

Germany, on the face of it, held all the cards in her hand. She did not ask the United States to break with their tradition of isolation. All she asked was that the American people should defend their rights as neutrals. She thus reconciled the two major preoccupations of the American soul. Her aim was to induce President Wilson to forbid the export of munitions to the Allied Powers and to break the illegal British blockade by convoying with cruisers of the United States Navy those American vessels which wished to trade with neutral ports. Had she succeeded in this object, she might have won the war. She failed because the German Admiralty were less obedient than the British Admiralty, because Downing Street was more intelligent, and, above all, more authoritative, than the Wilhelmstrasse.

From this aspect, the year 1915 was the most important of the whole war. During that year the Germans might, by abandoning their submarine warfare in overt deference to Woodrow Wilson, have forced the latter to break the blockade even at the risk of war between Great Britain and the United States. Conversely, they might have concentrated upon forcing Great Britain, and therefore the Allies, to surrender by an intensive submarine blockade, executed at a time when American opinion was still uncertain and before

[3] "American Diplomacy During the World War," p. 44.

the victory of the Allies had established itself as a vested interest in the United States. They missed this opportunity. They employed their submarines in such a manner as to outrage American opinion without seriously weakening the Allies. The affronts which they administered to American pride and conscience were greater even than those inflicted by the British Navy. The Allies were violating neutral rights but were at the same time bringing great prosperity to American industry; the Germans were violating the laws of humanity and providing no compensation whatsoever. In 1917, as in 1812, it became inevitable that America would defend her wounded pride against those of her aggressors who had done most harm not only to her rights, but also to her feelings. Yet in 1915 it was still uncertain against which of the two aggressors these rights would be defended. Even if we admit that the American people would not actually have declared war against England or France, they might well, in defense of their own rights and dignity, have created a situation in which a German victory would have become an alarming likelihood. Such a situation would have ruined the financial credit of the Western Powers. It was thus an act of daring on the part of J. P. Morgan & Co. to identify themselves, at this moment of indecision, with the cause of the Allies.

2

"Those were the days," wrote Thomas Lamont in 1920, "when American citizens were urged to remain neutral in action, in word, and even in thought. But our firm had never for one moment been neutral; we didn't know how to be. From the very start we did everything we could to contribute to the cause of the Allies.[4] Mr. J. P. Morgan himself never attempted to be neutral in feeling. He spoke his mind, with shy frankness, both in and out of season. His courage, as we have seen, was of enormous benefit to the Allies during the most critical period of Anglo-American relations. It was also physical. Mr. Morgan nearly paid for it with his life; in July of 1915 he was shot at, and severely wounded, by a fanatic.

Dwight Morrow, during those years of profitable energy, of battered pride, of bewildered passion, of triumphant acquisitiveness, retained his reason unimpaired. His sympathies were from the outset on the side of the Allied Powers. He contributed lavishly but anonymously to the British and French Red Cross funds and he placed himself, as has been seen, unreservedly at the disposal of the Allied missions dispatched to the United States. "Your country," he wrote to Sir William Allardyce [5] in 1916, "is doing a great work for the world. It is a pity that we are not helping her." Yet Morrow, above everything, was an American. Through all those fevered years he was predominantly concerned with the effect which these unnatural excitements would have upon the moral, political, and economic health of his own country.

He loathed intolerance, even as he hated untruth. The unreliability of the war news published in the English and French papers disgusted him; the hysterical futility of their editorial comments filled him with dismay. He turned with relief to the more balanced, if heavier, pages of *The Round Table*. "In fact," he wrote in 1915, "the editors of this magazine seem to me to have a clearer idea of what is going on

[4] Letter to *The Manchester Guardian*, January 27, 1920.
[5] Sir William Allardyce, G.C.M.G., born 1861; Governor of the Bahamas from 1915 to 1920, where he and Dwight Morrow became friends; d. 1930.

in the world today than anybody else who has the temerity to write."

The sanity of his mind is illustrated again by his unwillingness to see the firm of J. P. Morgan & Co. identified with Allied propaganda. Henry Davison and Paul Cravath,[6] those staunch if impulsive friends of the Western Powers, were anxious to form a committee which should educate American opinion regarding the democratic principles for which Great Britain and France were fighting. "I told Mr. Cravath," recorded Mr. Morrow in a memorandum to his partners, "that J. P. Morgan & Co. would not be interested in pro-Ally propaganda, especially as it might well take the shape of criticism against President Wilson. . . . It was against our policy to do anything secretly which we were not willing to do openly."

It saddened him to observe that the nervous passions of the time were setting one good American citizen against another. Such personal prejudices grated cruelly upon his sense of tolerance. On one dramatic occasion he was able, with characteristic gentleness, to salve a wound. It was the morning on which the news of the sinking of the *Lusitania* reached New York. Mr. Jacob Schiff, of Kuhn, Loeb & Co., came round to 23 Wall Street and entered the main partners' room. Mr. J. P. Morgan himself was standing in the room. Mr. Schiff approached him with some timidity, murmuring regrets at this most unfortunate outrage. Mr. Morgan was completely ungracious; he made some cutting rejoinder and turned on his heel. Crestfallen and crushed, old Mr. Schiff walked sadly from the building. An awkward

[6] Paul D. Cravath, lawyer, born Ohio 1861; Columbia Law School 1886; U. S. Treasury representative on the "House Mission" to the Inter-Allied War Conference, Paris, 1917.

silence followed. "I suppose," said Mr. Morgan to his partners, "that I went a little far. I suppose I ought to apologize?" The silence remained both awkward and prolonged. Dwight Morrow drew a writing pad towards him and scribbled these words: "Not for thy sake, but for thy name's sake, O House of Israel!" He tore off the sheet and passed it across to Mr. Morgan. The latter read the message, nodded in complete acquiescence, reached for his hat, and hurried across to Kuhn, Loeb & Co. to apologize to Mr. Schiff.

3

These were but incidental manifestations of Dwight Morrow's distaste for all unqualified opinions. What distressed him to the depths of his soul was the effect which the war might have upon the character of his own countrymen. He dreaded that their fibre might become both fleshy and obtuse.

He viewed with grave suspicion the artificial stimulus given to American industry by the European demand for war material. To him it was no matter for rejoicing that steel should have risen from $19.00 a ton to $44.00, that flax should have jumped from $400.00 a ton to $1,300.00, or that even his beloved copper should be selling at 37 instead of 11 cents a pound. "I have a feeling," he wrote in October 1916, "that sooner or later the enormous production of copper that is going on will produce overproduction. But this will not come till the end of the war. At the end of the war, or some time thereafter, the day of judgment for all that has been done within the last two years will arrive." He was saddened to observe that so few of his compatriots shared with him this vision of judgment.

He deplored the self-satisfaction which the material rewards of neutrality were producing throughout the country. He resented the unthinking arrogance with which some of his compatriots hailed the war as an opportunity whereby the United States could establish their financial and commercial supremacy. Such theories grated, not only upon his gentleness, but upon his conceptions of philosophy, history, and economics. He wrote as follows, on January 3, 1916, to his old mentor, Professor Anson Morse:

"We hear it said here constantly that Europe is to be destroyed by this war and that we are to become the financial centre of the world. It is assumed rather than stated that this will be a good thing for us. What a sorry triumph it would be if this were so! And is there not much in history to make us think such a result unlikely? In the sixteenth and seventeenth centuries the little nation of Holland was hacked to pieces for almost three generations; but she lived. She was much helped by the change in the world's commerce, occasioned by the new trade routes. Was not, however, some of the energy and boldness of her commercial men due to the release of heroic qualities by Spain's oppression? When you consider the situation in England, industrially, before the Napoleonic Wars, can we really say that England was helped or hurt by those wars? Do not misunderstand me! I do not think that a war has ever brought anything that could not have been brought much better without the war. With human nature as it is, however, is it likely that the same progress would have come without the wars? The world tragedy is that progress is bought so dearly, when it could be attained without the cost if we were only different. Are not we in America the ones that are in danger? Not the danger of military invasion, but of having something given to us now

too easily; of meeting the other nations of the world at the end
of the war, they made sturdy by their suffering, we heavy from
our feasting.

"If it turns out that the rich are to bear the taxation burdens
of this war, as I conceive they will be required to do, will the
redistribution of wealth in foreign countries, the rendering necessary of a more spartan life, the specialization of industries, present to us a stronger commercial trade rivalry than we have here-
tofore felt? Can we practice the lessons which they will have
to practice without paying their price? Or shall we fail to keep
up with them because of the difficulty of finding in our life a
substitute for their suffering and discipline. These are questions
to which I haven't got the answers. Won't you come down some
night and give them to me?"

Nor did he restrict the expression of such unusual sentiments to private correspondence with his personal friends.
He had the courage to proclaim them openly. But a fortnight after the date of the above letter to Anson Morse he
addressed the N. Y. State Bankers Association in almost
identical terms. His concluding sentences struck a note
which had not, as yet, been heard from Wall Street:

"But for our own conduct, for our own purposes, we alone
must be responsible. With what spirit will the people of America
approach the new era? Can we keep easy prosperity from dull-
ing the fine edge of endeavor? Can we acquire, without paying
the great price of the warring nations, the unity which the fires
of war are burning into the peoples abroad? Can we go into the
markets of the world with a real coöperation of government
and business men? Shall we be able to assume our new international burdens free from the delusion that has done so much
to bring about the European cataclysm, the delusion that successful trade abroad necessarily means the deprivation of some
other nation of that trade? Can we learn from the European

tragedy that leadership in world trade is not a thing to be sought by any nation to the exclusion of all others? Can we base our plans for foreign trade not upon the weakness of stricken rivals but upon a more intelligent farming of our own lands, the creation of new and better machinery and a more skillful use of that machinery, a greater breadth in our extensions of credit, a better understanding of our domestic problems, a fairer adjustment of our relations one to another? And finally, will we have the unity and the courage to do our part in the great task of bringing the world a little nearer to a dependable international guaranty of the territorial and political integrity of all nations, large or small?"

This address he repeated, a few months later, to a large audience in Kansas City.

It was not only the economic fallacies of America that disquieted him during these years: he was anxious regarding the effect of a long period of nervous tension upon the American character. His views were exactly reflected in an article entitled "Uneasy America" contributed to the *New Republic* by Walter Lippmann on December 25, 1915:

"To feel and feel and feel and never to use that feeling is to grow distracted and worrisome and to no end. We Americans have been witnessing supreme drama, clenching our fists, talking, yet unable to fasten any reaction to realities. Ferment without issue, gestation without birth, is making us sullen and self-conscious and ashamed. . . . When a nation becomes petty and quarrelsome it is because no one has succeeded in holding its attention to a national purpose."

Morrow was so impressed by this article that he sent copies to several friends. "What you say," he wrote to Walter Lippmann, "is exactly right. It will do much good."

His feelings with regard to Woodrow Wilson were sor-

rowful and mixed. On the one hand, he felt for him that
instinctive respect which he entertained for all members of
the teaching profession, while sympathizing deeply with the
obscurities and complexities of the President's task. On the
other hand, he was firmly of opinion that the duty of a
president in time of crisis was a duty of guidance. He feared
that in the absence of such leadership the nerves of the
people would become frayed by uncertainty and dissension.
In a letter dated June 24, 1915, he conveyed his apprehensions with great subtlety to Mr. Lansing, the Secretary of
State:

"Might it not be a very helpful thing to the President if—
without the slightest criticism of Mr. Bryan, and perhaps with
praise for that portion of Mr. Bryan's work that properly may
be praised—you could call the attention of a college audience to
the President's position as a scholar and the advantage to the
country at this time of having a scholar at the head of its affairs?
When I use the word 'scholar,' I mean the scholar as defined
in George William Curtis's oration on 'The Duty of the American Scholar':

" '. . . the scholar is the representative of thought among men,
and his duty to society is the effort to introduce thought and
the sense of justice into human affairs. He was not made a
scholar to satisfy the newspapers or the parish beadles, but to
serve God and man. While other men pursue what is expedient
and watch with alarm the flickering of the funds, he is to pursue
the truth and watch the eternal law of justice.'

"The scholarship that Curtis had in mind was not the scholarship which 'begins in a dictionary and ends in a grammar,' but
the scholarship of Milton, the citizen, which 'began in literature
and ended in life.' "

4

It was on April 6, 1917, that the United States declared war on the German Empire. Dwight Morrow was anxious to obtain some chance of war service. This opportunity did not occur till the autumn, when he was appointed director for New Jersey of the National War Savings Committee. During the early months of 1917 he was engaged upon a task which, although not connected with the war, was at least a diversion. He was plunged in the problem of the penal system in New Jersey.

This task is of interest to a biographer, not so much for its intrinsic importance, but because it furnishes a perfect specimen of Dwight Morrow's methods of work. There is the usual cautious approach, fortified by an intensive study of the present elements and whole life history of the subject. There is the lavish expenditure of private income upon securing the advice and coöperation of experts and scholars. There is the phenomenon, so frequently repeated in later years, of Dwight Morrow entering a committee as a junior member, becoming at once the directing influence in that committee, and ending as its chairman. And there is that patient modesty which aimed, not at the unrealities of dramatic or personal success, but at the realities of careful preparation for ultimately useful ends. A more sensational report could have been issued, had Morrow recorded on paper all the reforms which, after careful investigation, he considered necessary. He refrained from such generalizations owing to his belief that the attainable is always preferable to the unattainable. Instead, therefore, of sketching an ideal program, he concentrated upon providing the machinery by which ideal reforms might, by other people, gradually be evolved. Here is an instance of his "then inquire again" method, of his constant conviction that only across the bridge of the immediately practicable can one reach to the territory of the desired.

For some time articles had been appearing in the newspapers criticizing the penal system in New Jersey and making specific allegations regarding the brutal treatment accorded to the inmates of the State jail at Trenton. Walter E. Edge,[7] Governor of New Jersey, decided that an inquiry was called for. On January 26, 1917, he appointed a commission of five persons to examine the administration of the prisons and to make recommendations for reform.

Dwight Morrow spent the first three days after his appointment to this commission studying the documents in the case. He then, on January 30th, wrote as follows to the chairman of the commission, Mr. William B. Dickson:

"We will have a better chance to get through a large constructive program, and it will be a better program when we get it through, if we can first get a real history of the legislation of the past, of the causes which led to it, of the motives and desires of the people who furthered the legislation, and of the reasons why it has not worked out as was expected."

Such an exhaustive study would inevitably take some months; the State Legislature would in the interval become impatient. Morrow suggested that the commission should first concentrate upon preparing an interim report on immediate abuses and then ask the Legislature to extend their mandate in order to give time for a considered recommen-

[7] Walter E. Edge, b. Philadelphia, Pennsylvania, 1874; in succession Governor of New Jersey 1917-19, U. S. Senator from New Jersey 1919-29, Ambassador to France 1929-33.

dation. The commission agreed with this procedure, but it was not long before Mr. Dickson resigned the chairmanship and Morrow took his place. He then, at his own expense, engaged the services of an expert and a student to act as his personal assistants. The first was Dr. George Kirchwey,[8] who had once been warden of Sing Sing Prison and had been lecturer at Columbia Law School; it was in Dr. Kirchwey's company that Morrow visited the several prisons and institutions of the State. As his historical assistant he employed Harry Elmer Barnes,[9] who, after several months spent in studying the history of penal legislation in New Jersey, produced a volume of 638 pages. This compilation was printed and bound at Dwight Morrow's expense (it cost him $3,319.55), and was attached as Volume 2 to the final report. Having by these means assured himself that their eventual recommendations would be based on expert knowledge, Dwight Morrow concentrated the attention of his colleagues on the presentation of an interim report.

With characteristic vigor he forced them to examine, not merely such temporary abuses as their inquiry might disclose, but the fundamental principles of penal legislation. "On what basis," he asked, "has society the right to punish at all?" He convinced them that the purpose of any penal system must be neither vindictive, nor protective, nor punitive, but reformatory. Their report, if it was to be of any social value, must not merely assign responsibility for past delinquencies, but provide the machinery for "the improve-

[8] George W. Kirchwey, criminologist, b. Detroit, Michigan, 1855; Yale 1879; dean Albany Law School 1889-91; professor of law, Dean of School of Law, Kent Professor of Law, Columbia University, 1891-1916; commissioner on prison reform, New York, 1913-14; warden Sing Sing Prison 1915-16; N. Y. School of Social Work 1917-33; counsel N. J. prison inquiry commission, 1917.

[9] Harry Elmer Barnes, educator and author; editorial writer for the Scripps-Howard newspapers.

ment of the prisoner in character and capacity." Their investigations must therefore proceed from a scientific, rather
than from a political, basis. For this purpose a horde of
experts was let loose upon the New Jersey prisons. Evidence was called upon such problems as juvenile offenders,
the pardon and parole systems, medical examination of inmates, the segregation of habitual from incidental criminals,
and self-government in prisons as a "humanizing influence."
A careful study was made of the penal systems in other states
and countries, and experts were consulted as to the various
experiments that had been attempted from Dartmoor to the
Philippines. Morrow himself went so far as to dine with
several ex-inmates of Sing Sing in order to obtain their views
on the prospect of some form of self-government by the
prisoners themselves. No detail was too small for his esurient
appetite. He was far less interested in the immediate controversy, on which the newspapers were insistent, than in the
errors of method which had rendered possible the abuses
which were disclosed. As always, he twisted the gimlet of
his inquiry towards first principles.

The preliminary report was issued in February 1917 and
provided for certain immediate reforms in Trenton jail and
for the prolongation of the life of the commission itself.
The immediate improvements that were advocated comprised such subjects as more elaborate medical inspection,
better food, increased educational facilities, segregation by
classification, and a system of rewards as supplanting the old
system of punishments. The former dungeons, in which re-
fractory prisoners had been immured, were to be bricked up.
Certain changes were to be made in the prison staff. "The
system of discipline," the report stated, "is marred by the
presence among the officials of men who have, in the course

of their service, become so hardened in temper and routine as to be practically unfitted to exercise authority over the men under their charge." And in fact, while the commission was still sitting, a prisoner died from injuries received in an argument with his warders.

The final report was not issued till January 1918. It called attention to recent investigations in criminology and cited particularly the opinion of Dr. Bernard Glueck to the effect that 80 per cent of the inmates of Sing Sing Prison were mentally abnormal and as such not fit subjects for corrective discipline. It examined the problem of convict labor and suggested a compromise by which prisoners could be usefully employed without raising protests on the part of the trades unions. It drew attention to the deplorable conditions existing in the New Jersey county jails and urged that immediate steps should be taken to segregate "the decent from the depraved," and that in no circumstances should children under sixteen be confined to prison. It condemned Trenton prison as an "evil inheritance from the past" and criticized the "disastrous effects of the disciplinary system and its ineffectiveness to produce even the most elementary order or decency, with its inhuman cruelties and the consequent brutalizing of inmates and keepers alike." It drew attention to the lack of proper identification or care of the mentally deficient, to the shortage of opportunities for educational or vocational training, and to the absence of all central coördination. It recommended therefore that a central board of control should be created, consisting of eight members appointed by the Governor. The members of this board were to be "public-spirited citizens" and were to serve without compensation, and therefore not as politicians. This board was in turn to nominate a "Commissioner of Correction," who would be assisted by six deputies, including two doctors. All further problems were to be considered by the board itself, "aided by its expert advisers, after full consultation with judges and others possessing a wide experience of penal administration."

As a result of this report the New Jersey legislature created a State Board of Institutions and Agencies to supervise and reform, not only the penal, but also the correctional institutions. Dwight Morrow was appointed chairman of this board, but he was soon overwhelmed with other duties and was obliged to resign. His analysis of the defects of the New Jersey system, and the machinery which he provided for an evolutionary improvement, independent of political influences, was, however, so scholarly, so conclusive, so detached, that it served as the pattern for penal reform in many States other than New Jersey. Governor Edge was delighted. He wrote to Morrow thanking him for "the tremendous amount of study and energy" which he had devoted to his task, and expressing his "deep and lasting appreciation of the great work you have accomplished for the State."

And in fact his examination of the penal system of New Jersey had been a masterly combination of sense and vision, of study and imagination, of realism and philosophy, of idealism and practicality.

5

In November 1917 Dwight Morrow was appointed by the Secretary of the Treasury as Director of the National War Savings Committee for the State of New Jersey. Similar committees were established in each of the States with the function of persuading the people to invest in war loans, to save their money for this investment, and, by the exercise of self-denial, to release labor and materials for war purposes. In most of the States these committees competed with each other in a campaign to sell "war savings stamps" and to obtain the highest total of investment in Government loans. Dwight Morrow approached the problem from an economic and educational, rather than from a competitive, angle. He was careful not to overlap the activities of the Liberty Loan committees and he explained to the people of New Jersey that so long as they saved money it was immaterial to the purpose of the war whether they invested such savings in Liberty Loans, in insurance policies, or in the savings banks. As a result, the ostensible contributions of New Jersey to actual war loans was not so high as in some other States. But, as an educative influence, the campaign conducted by Dwight Morrow was far more valuable.

He flung himself into this campaign with meticulous enthusiasm, with excited wariness. He first created his organization with headquarters at Newark and with branch committees in each county. An office was obtained in the building of the Prudential Insurance Company at Newark and a staff of five volunteers was engaged, with Vernon Munroe [10] as secretary, and George B. Mallon as director of propaganda. A bi-monthly paper, entitled "War Thrift," was issued and many pamphlets were circulated throughout the State. Having thus created his organization, Dwight Morrow, from October 1917 to February 1918, toured the State, supervising drives and rallies and speaking in every town.

[10] Vernon Munroe, b. Englewood, New Jersey, 1874; Harvard 1896; Mayor of Englewood; executive secretary and later vice director of National War Savings Committee, N. J.; president International Motor Company; with J. P. Morgan & Co. since 1920; secretary International Committee of Bankers on Mexico.

By these means he hoped to be able, within a short period, to educate the people of New Jersey in the elements of wartime economics.

His theories on the subject were derived from Basil Blackett of the British Treasury, who had himself, in the earlier stages of the war, been concerned with a war savings campaign in England. Morrow's first aim was to remove from the minds of his compatriots the unhelpful, and indeed idiotic, theory of "business as usual." He tried to show them that in times of war business was not usual in the very least, and he therefore preached to them what he called the "Gospel of Goods and Services." He explained to them that goods and services applicable to the prosecution of the war must come from one of two sources: the first was greater production: the second was less consumption. The vital economic aim of a nation at war was to increase its supplies of goods and services usable against the enemy. Anything that contributed to that end might be considered helpful; anything that retarded that end must be considered harmful. "Every time," he said to them, "that you buy anything, you make somebody work for you; but everybody today has to work, not for you, but for the war. It is not a question of what you individually can afford to spend, it is a question of what the nation can afford to allow you to spend."

Having thus indicated to them the vices of spending, he proceeded to preach to them the virtues of thrift. "If," he said, "each of the hundred million people in the United States could save twenty cents a day for three hundred days a year, the capital fund of the United States would be increased by six billion dollars." This simple illustration caught the imagination of his audiences and was repeated by other speakers in every State throughout the Union. It was this chance phrase which first rendered Morrow's name known outside the orbit of New York City.

Morrow much enjoyed his work on the National War Savings Committee. It represented a change from Wall Street. It brought him into touch with the average man. It forced him to move about. And above all, it enabled him to indulge in the simple exposition of intricate problems—an art which appealed to the teaching tendencies which were in his blood.

The War Savings Committee was not, however, the war. Ship after ship put out from New York harbor on the way to Flanders. Morrow turned his gaze wistfully towards the east. Here, in all truth, was the larger adventure. It was inevitable that he should grasp the first available opportunity for work in Europe. His choice, when it came, was almost accidental. Yet it was a choice which accorded strangely with the mental habits which he had by then acquired; a choice which strangely influenced his future approach to national and international affairs.

THE GENESIS OF THE ALLIED MARITIME TRANSPORT COUNCIL.
MORROW IS ATTACHED TO THE EXECUTIVE OF THAT COUNCIL.
HE REACHES LONDON IN FEBRUARY 1918. THE ORIGINS AND
FUNCTIONING OF THE ALLIED MARITIME TRANSPORT COUNCIL
EXECUTIVE. THE SUBMARINE MENACE. THE SHORTAGE OF SHIP-
PING. ENFORCED COÖRDINATION. SIR ARTHUR SALTER AND JEAN
MONNET. CIRCUMSTANCES WHICH RENDERED THEIR EXECUTIVE
A NEW EXPERIMENT IN INTERNATIONAL COÖPERATION. DWIGHT
MORROW'S INTEREST IN THE WORK AND THE NATURE OF HIS
CONTRIBUTION. FALSE POSITION OF THE AMERICAN DELEGATES.
MORROW AT GENERAL PERSHING'S HEADQUARTERS. VALUE OF
HIS SERVICES AT CHAUMONT. HIS PARTNERS ANXIOUS FOR HIS
RETURN. HIS VIEWS ON THE BASIC JUSTIFICATION OF THE AL-
LIED CAUSE. HIS WAR WORK AS AN EXPRESSION OF HIS HIGH-
EST CAPACITIES. "RULE SIX." A VISIT TO LILLE. THE ARMISTICE.
HIS FORECAST OF THE DISILLUSIONS OF THE POST-WAR PERIOD.

IT had required two and a half years of dangerous experience to convince the Allied Governments of the need of
coördination. It was scarcely to be expected that America,
with her isolationist tradition, would learn that lesson within
a few short weeks. The several coördinating missions which
the Allies sent to Washington were not wholly successful.
To the Allies, exhausted by prolonged battle, the word "co-
ordination" meant that America should ease their immediate
burden. To the Americans, who were now providing fresh
sinews of war, "coördination" meant that the supply problem should be concentrated under American management.
The Administration at Washington wished to devote their
whole resources to placing the United States upon a war
footing; the Allies claimed that large portions of these resources should be assigned to the equipment and maintenance of the Allied Armies already in the field. When

President Wilson did, in fact, suggest the creation of a Supreme Financial Council, Great Britain and France rejected this proposal in fear that it might lead to dollar domination. Fortunately two men, and two disasters, intervened to prevent the wastage of effort which such disunion threatened. Mr. Lloyd George and Colonel House were agreed that coördination must be attained. Caporetto and the Russian Revolution proved that this coördination must be immediate. In November 1917 Colonel House crossed to Europe at the head of a mission of military, naval, financial, and shipping experts. A conference of the Principal Allied and Associated Powers was held at Versailles. Important principles of coördination were laid down, affecting such requirements as man-power, food, the blockade, finance, war-purchases, and shipping. Several inter-allied commissions were constituted to assure coördination in these branches; among them was one known as the Allied Maritime Transport Council.

It was to this Council, which will henceforward be referred to as the A.M.T.C., that Dwight Morrow became attached.

As has already been said, it was almost by chance that this opportunity came to him. The Administration at Washington, and especially the Shipping Board, had at first been unwilling to participate directly in the A.M.T.C. and had only been persuaded to do so by Commander Lewis B. McBride,[1] who, as the representative of Admiral Sims on the House

[1] Lewis B. McBride, now Captain, U. S. Navy; b. Columbia, Pennsylvania, 1880; U. S. Naval Academy 1901; Massachusetts Institute of Technology 1905; Assistant Naval Attaché, London, 1914-15; on Staff of Admiral Sims 1917-19; Technical Adviser to A.M.T.C. 1918, his first association with Dwight Morrow; Naval Attaché Mexico 1928-31, working chiefly on questions of public finance and debt; Department of Economics and Government, U. S. Naval Academy, Annapolis, since 1931.

Mission at Versailles, was well aware of the confusion to which American isolation would lead. Mr. Raymond B. Stevens [2] was therefore appointed as American representative on the A.M.T.C. and was asked himself to suggest the names of his assistants. He selected Mr. George Rublee, and it was the latter who advised him to approach Dwight Morrow, although at the time they were scarcely acquainted. Morrow agreed to accompany the commission to Europe, but only on a temporary basis and without any definite function. When Mr. Stevens submitted to Woodrow Wilson the list of his suggested assistants, the President winced when he came to Morrow's name. He did not see why a Morgan partner should be included even in so subordinate a capacity. Mr. Stevens persisted, and the list was passed. The Morrows sailed for Europe, through a torpedo-infested ocean, in the first week of February 1918. The following extracts from Mrs. Morrow's diary throw a light upon the comparative degrees of alarm inspired respectively by submarines and air-raids:

February 17. Berkeley Hotel, London. *Safe* in London! We left New York February 8th and reached Liverpool late last night. Tonight an air-raid. Guns booming over our heads.
February 18. Another raid tonight.
February 19. No real raid tonight. The guns boomed a warning but no aeroplanes got through.

Three days later the Morrows exchanged the relative safety of London for the greater insecurity of Paris. It was considered necessary that Mr. Stevens, Mr. Shearman and Mr. Rublee should establish early contact with such French Ministers as M. Clémentel and M. Loucheur. Morrow joined this

[2] Raymond B. Stevens, b. Binghamton, New York, 1874; Harvard; Vice Chairman U. S. Shipping Board 1917-20; American representative A.M.T.C. 1917-18; adviser on foreign affairs to Siamese Government.

expedition; he was taken on a hurried visit to the front and lunched with General Pershing at Chaumont. He returned to London in the first days of March and entered upon his functions as an adviser attached to the American section of the A.M.T.C. Executive. He lived at the Berkeley Hotel and worked in Lancaster House, among the pictures and show cases of the London Museum. He was introduced to Arthur Salter,[3] Secretary to the Council, to Jean Monnet[4] of the French section, and to Professor B. D. Attolico[5] of the Italian section. With these men he founded friendships based upon mutual respect and an identity of final purpose. They remained his intimate friends throughout the remainder of his life. The influence which they exerted upon him was a valuable influence. Through them he learned how much can be attained in the way of international coöperation by the constant association of experts intent upon a specific task. And from him they learnt that the American Idea, when sensibly conceived, can (without ceasing to be American) become a formative factor in that disheartening process which is the construction of the barriers of peace.

They were gloomy days for those whose hearts were set upon the victory of the Allied and Associated Powers. The memories of Jutland, of Caporetto, of the Russian Revolution, were still active memories; the German offensive in the

[3] Sir Arthur Salter, economist and writer, b. Oxford, England, 1881; Brasenose College, Oxford; Secretary A.M.T.C. Council and Chairman of Executive 1918; special shipping mission to America 1918; Secretary Reparation Commission 1920-22; Director Economic and Finance Section League of Nations 1919-20 and 1922-30.

[4] Jean Monnet, banker, b. Cognac, France, 1888; French representative A.M.T.C. Executive; Deputy Secretary General League of Nations 1919-23; active in the financial reorganization of Austria, Poland, Rumania, etc.

[5] Professor B. D. Attolico, b. Canneto, Italy, 1880; University of Rome; Italian Member A.M.T.C. Council 1917-19; now Ambassador from Italy to the Soviet Republic.

spring of 1918 seemed likely, for some days, to justify their theory that the French and British Armies might be vanquished before the man-power of America could be effectively applied. Morrow was always an optimist; not for one moment did he question our eventual victory. A week before he sailed for Europe he delivered in New Jersey a speech which reflects that almost religious conviction with which he inspired and comforted those with whom he came into contact. He spoke, on that occasion, of the inevitability of reverses and the certainty of triumph:

". . . We are met this evening at a time when we are hearing much about our faults. We hear much about the things in which we have failed. We hear little about the trials of Germany and Austria. Who are we that we should expect uninterrupted success? One needs only to read the surface of history to appreciate that a big part of all wars is made up of delays and disappointments. War is not sunshine: war means rain and sleet and mud. War means the making of plans by finite and fallible men and the standing by helplessly while those plans crumble. War means the making of plans again and again and again, and the frustration of those plans again and again and again. War means a Gallipoli and perhaps another Gallipoli; it means a Rumanian disaster and an Italian disaster. War means hope deferred until all but the stoutest hearts are sick. War means endurance—endurance unto the end. And, finally, war means victory—victory to the nation with the stoutest heart. The nation with the stoutest heart! Does that mean America? Can we match ourselves by the side of Belgium and France and England and Italy and our other Allies, who have endured so much and so long? Can we go through the Valley and be unafraid? . . ."

Morrow throughout those anxious weeks was completely unafraid. As usual, he concentrated upon his immediate task in such a manner as to create around it ever-widening circles of illumination and trust. Yet if we are correctly to estimate the importance of his work upon the A.M.T.C. Executive, we must examine how that organization originated, what were its functions, how it operated, and what effect it had upon Morrow's future conception of the art and science of negotiation.

2

To those who are interested in the machinery of international coöperation there can be few more educative studies than that of the growth, functioning, and method of the A.M.T.C. The story has been authoritatively told in Sir Arthur Salter's "Allied Shipping Control" published by the Carnegie Endowment among its monographs upon the social and economic history of the war. In this volume Sir Arthur Salter shows that the Allied Maritime Transport Council and its Executive did not derive from any academic theory, but were inductively evolved from experience. The fact that the A.M.T.C. Executive became in the end "the most advanced experiment yet made in international coöperation" was due to no preconceived plan but to the pressure of immediate emergencies and the presence of certain compelling factors.

Until 1917 the adjustment between the supply of shipping and the demand for shipping had been regulated in each country upon a system of national controls, with but slight international coördination. In January 1917, however, the German Government embarked on unrestricted submarine warfare. By April the position had become one of the utmost gravity. "The situation," writes Sir Arthur Salter, "was im-

mediately and dramatically altered by the new form of warfare. The whole war effort of the Allies was soon threatened
by disaster; and all the main European Allies were in imminent danger of starvation. If no successful answer had been
found, the whole course of the later military struggle, and
probably the issue of the war itself, must have been pro-
foundly different." [6]

The losses inflicted on Allied tonnage during those early
months of unrestricted submarine warfare were in fact
appalling. In the first three months as many as 1,000 ships
were sunk, and in April 1917 the losses were such that, of
every four ships which took to sea, only one returned. "It
was," writes Sir Arthur Salter, "like hearing the tapping of
the sappers constructing a hostile mine which the rest of
those who were threatened failed to detect—and waiting for
the last ominous silence before the explosion." [7] By May of
1917 the convoy system had been introduced and the situation, though still precarious, ceased to be desperate. It was at
this stage that the entry of America into the war threw upon
the transport requirements of the Allies a new, though welcome, responsibility. Owing to an unfortunate controversy
between the Chairman of the American Shipping Board and
the President of the Emergency Fleet Corporation on the subject of steel versus wooden ships, the gigantic ship-building
program of the United States was not put into operation
for several months. Some time was also wasted in persuading
the Administration at Washington to employ the neutral
and enemy ships sheltering or interned in American waters
and to divert to war purposes the vessels employed in South
American trade. In the end, the assistance furnished by

[6] Arthur Salter, "Allied Shipping Control," p. 77.
[7] Ibid., p. 158.

United States shipping was tremendous, and the American shipyards were able to provide the tonnage which helped to place two million men in France by the date of the Armistice. Yet until the summer of 1918 the Allies had to rely almost wholly upon their own ships, not merely to feed their civilian populations, not merely to supply their armies, but to transport and maintain the United States units in Europe. The magnitude of this problem necessitated drastic measures. It was thus from dire necessity that the Allied Maritime Transport Council, and its Executive, were established by the Allied and Associated Conference held at Versailles in November 1917.

The above account gives some information as to why the A.M.T.C. was necessary. It does not, however, explain how it functioned, or why Morrow's own experience of that functioning became so important a contribution to his diplomatic and political theory.

It should be realized that the Council itself only met four times. In practice, the work was done by the Executive. That Executive was composed of a main committee, and of subsidiary committees dealing with tonnage, imports, programs, and chartering. The operations of the Executive had to be related to those of analogous bodies also functioning under the direction of the Supreme War Council. Such bodies were the War Purchases and Finance Council, the Food Council, the Munitions Council, the Blockade Council, and the Interallied Commission at Versailles. Subject to these were such subordinate interallied organizations as the Wheat Executive, the Meats and Fats Executive, the Petroleum Commissions and the Sugar Program Committees. This catalogue suffices to give some idea of the many competitive interests which the Executive of the A.M.T.C. had to con-

sider. Nor were these the only complications. The members
of the main Executive Committee (Sir Arthur Salter, M. Jean
Monnet, Professor B. D. Attolico and Mr. George Rublee)
possessed a dual function. On the one hand they represented
their Governments and were expected to justify the several
requirements of those Governments. On the other hand, they
represented an ideal standard of coördination and were thus
forced to adjust their national demands for tonnage to the
international supply. The supply, as has been noted, was
never equal to the demand; the process of adjustment thus
entailed upon the several members of the Committee complete confidence in each other's judgment. Unless the Executive as a whole could trust its four members not to make
national demands without convincing themselves that these
demands were really essential, the whole system and purpose
of the Committee would have been stultified. Sir Arthur
Salter, in an interesting passage in his book, analyzes the delicate position in which the officials of the Executive were
thereby placed. He deduces from his own experience of the
workings of the Executive the conclusion that "under conditions of personal confidence and long personal association" a balance can in fact be struck between national and
international loyalty. In his judgment an association of experts such as that to which (in circumstances of acute international competition) he himself belonged, can by constant
experiment adjust regional interests to the interests of the
whole. The Secretariat of the League of Nations has since
demonstrated that this theory is not fantastic.

The circumstances in which the A.M.T.C. functioned
were, of course, exceptional. International action always im-
plies the sacrifice of immediate national advantage. If democ-
racies are to be induced to make such sacrifices, there must

be both motive and discipline. In inducing Governments to subordinate national to international advantage, the A.M.T.C. possessed each of these two requirements. The motive was supplied by fear of starvation. The discipline was furnished by the fact that Great Britain possessed most of the tonnage and could thus dictate her terms. That these terms were not selfish terms was due largely to the high purpose which animated every member of the Executive.

Although, therefore, the Executive was peculiarly favored by the conditions in which it operated, it must be noted that the actual machinery of its functioning was scientifically contrived. Realizing that many conflicting interests would be antagonized, the A.M.T.C. was so devised as to control the action, without displacing the authority, of the national Governments. The inevitable conflict between expert opinion and executive authority was solved by placing on the supervisory Council those Ministers who would be actually responsible for the action demanded. By the principle of "direct contact between specialists" the coöperation between the Allies was thus shifted from a diplomatic to an administrative basis. By this means "the just solution" became a more important objective than any "diplomatic triumph," and policy was taken away from a few over-strained centres of excessive power and treated in the more scientific atmosphere of technical examination.

From this experiment in international coöperation, Dwight Morrow derived many lessons. It suggested to him a possible solution of what he called the "fundamental problem of Government," namely, "how to get the order that goes with unity and still retain that freedom of action that goes with independent units." It emphasized for him "the value of common counsel and the examination of *facts* in international affairs as contrasted with the unsatisfactory form of advocacy usually known as diplomacy" [8] and it convinced him of the significance of the Civil Service.

"I'll tell you," he would often say in later years, "who won the war! The war was won by the Civil Servant of the type of Sir Arthur Salter." This was an exaggeration, induced by Morrow's own respect for integrity, tolerance, and precision. Yet it is a fact that the war might well have been lost had not the Allied Civil Servants been so imperturbable, so gifted, so independent, and so incorruptible. The German Civil Servant possessed similar virtues: he did not possess an authority equally established, or equally unquestioned.

3

In theory, Dwight Morrow was merely the American expert attached to the Imports sub-Committee of the Executive of the A.M.T.C. and Adviser to the United States Delegates. In practice, he was an ubiquitous man who inspired everybody else to do his own job a little better. He became a symbol of the sort of international utility which the United States could offer. By this alone, he became a valuable symbol.

"My part of the work," he wrote to Thomas Lamont in May 1918, "has been to try and get classified in the briefest possible form what tonnage there is to go around and what the demands are against those assets. Such value as I have been able to show over here has been in grouping the various

[8] These quotations come from a chapter jointly contributed by Dwight W. Morrow and Joseph P. Cotton to a book edited in 1919 by Stephen Pierce under the title "The League of Nations."

phases of the problem." A more vivid picture of the difficulties of the task is conveyed in a letter which at the same date he wrote to Edward Stettinius:

". . . I cannot tell you how difficult it is to get people to see that there is *one* tonnage problem, instead of *four* tonnage problems. It is as though you were trying to cover a bed with a coverlet that would not go all the way around. If you pull it over on one side, of course you leave the other side bare. For instance—before you have received this letter America will have had a demand for some tonnage for Belgian Relief. The Versailles Conference, held November last, voted that Belgium should have priority over every other need up to a certain number of cargoes of cereals. Belgium is now very short of food and the French, who have a peculiar interest in that situation because of the portion of northern France which is within the German lines, are insisting that boats be set aside for this purpose. Monsieur Loucheur, at the last meeting of the Council, said that France would give up some boats for Belgian relief. If it were not so serious it would be humorous. France offers to give up one of her wheat-carrying boats for Belgian relief. At the same time she is very short of boats for coal. If she gives the boat up for Belgian relief, she will, as it were, demand two boats for coal instead of one. If the coal need is imperative, she will get the extra boat for coal, however uneconomical or wasteful it is to stop something that is half done in order to give her that boat. The coverlet, having been pulled rapidly from one side of the bed, will be pulled rapidly back to the other side, with strong recriminations.

"What I have been trying to make people see ever since I got over here is that the tonnage situation is all right. Unless the Germans have something new to spring on us, I think the submarine danger is over. What we lack now is not so much boats as intelligent coöperation. We ought to find out what our

214

cloth is and make our programs fit the cloth. If we could make a budget for the next four months and have a 10% margin on the right side, instead of a 10% margin on the wrong side, the tonnage difficulty would disappear. If we do not do this, we will go on making fateful decisions at the eleventh hour—because the Italian or French railways are about to stop, or because somebody is out of nitrates, etc. Meanwhile the Prime Ministers are given an impossible task. When I was in France last week I got a vivid picture of the situation from one of the Ministers. He says a very large part of the Prime Minister's time is spent in listening to the several ministers explaining the terrible calamity that will befall if this, that, or the other thing is not forthcoming at once. Both the Prime Minister that asks for help and the Prime Minister that gives the help are required to guess at the intensity and seriousness of this particular panic, compared to other panics that are also pressing. The result is that, to an amazing degree, the fateful decisions of the war are made not by intelligence—not even by pretended intelligence—but by competitive panic.

"I have set out all the foregoing to give you the picture. I am not a bit discouraged. I think if it had been intended that Germany was to win this war, she would have won it long ago."

The position of the American Members of the Executive was not an easy position. For whereas Sir Arthur Salter could rely on the support of Lord Robert Cecil, Sir Joseph Maclay, and the Prime Minister; whereas M. Jean Monnet was trusted by M. Clémentel and M. Loucheur; whereas Signor Crespi would in the end honor the checks drawn by Professor Attolico; it was never certain whether the Administration at Washington would pay any attention whatsoever to the recommendations of Raymond Stevens, George Rublee, or Dwight Morrow. "It must be remembered," writes Sir Arthur Salter, "that America's association with the organization was always somewhat tentative and provisional. The part taken by American representatives in the allied work was throughout considerable. . . . For many obvious reasons, however, they had a less direct and decisive influence with their national administrations than had their colleagues." [9]

Rublee and Morrow were acutely sensitive to the falsity of this position. Day after day they witnessed sacrifices made by their colleagues; they were depressingly aware that any sacrifices that they themselves might offer would entail a protracted negotiation with Washington. They both returned to America in the hope of convincing the Administration that some form of coördination of tonnage requirements was in fact essential. They exchanged their impressions. "I did everything," wrote Rublee to Morrow, "in Washington that I could. I think it was well for me to leave. Else I might have outstayed my welcome and run the risk of boring people and being too officious. I went rather far on that road as it was. I hope not too far."

"I had," wrote Morrow to Rublee after a similar attempt, "a most satisfactory trip to Washington. I saw General March, General Goethals, Justice Brandeis, and Mr. Baruch, in addition to Stettinius, Perkins, and Joe Cotton. I won't attempt to go into details, but I thought all the conferences most satisfactory. Baruch says he now understands the plan of the program committees and that he is in hearty favor of it. Stettinius thinks that you or I should see Colonel House before we go back."

Neither Morrow nor Rublee need have been so diffident about their efficacy. In the first place, they comforted their associates in London with the assurance that two Americans at least, sympathized and understood. This was a not unimportant consolation. There were many Europeans, at that date, who were obsessed by the fear that the word "coöperation" did not exist in the American vocabulary. In the second place, they induced Mr. Newton D. Baker, Secretary of War, to visit Europe and examine the transport situation for himself. This produced a sensible improvement. And in the third place, Morrow was able to secure the confidence and support of General Pershing.

During the valuable weeks he spent at Chaumont, Dwight Morrow had been able to explain to General Pershing that existing transport difficulties were not due to any selfishness on the part of the Associated Powers, but to actual shortage of supply. Conversely, he was able to provide the A.M.T.C. with a reliable statement of the real transport requirements of the American Army.[10] The main opposition came, not from the A.M.T.C., but from the British War Office who were convinced that American Headquarters had fixed their requirements at an exaggerated figure. It was the Morrow tables and his explanation of them which showed the British military authorities that General Pershing was in the right and which led them to consent at the September meeting of the Transport Council to the diversion of 500,000 tons of British ships for American Army purposes. Morrow's services in this respect were so valuable that they earned him the

[10] He was accompanied to Chaumont by Mr. L. H. Shearman, a very able and experienced member of the firm of Grace & Co., who had been appointed shipping expert to the U. S. delegation. Whereas it was Morrow who convinced General Pershing that American requirements could not be met by American tonnage alone, and who induced the military authorities at Chaumont to work out a definite schedule of requirements for the next twelve months, it was Mr. Shearman who converted these requirements into tonnage terms and calculated the exact amount of shipping that would be required. Without Shearman's expert assistance, Morrow could have accomplished little.

D.S.M. In his citation General Pershing wrote as follows: "He was responsible for the first intelligent epitomization of the allied tonnage situation and his able presentation of the situation to the allied countries materially affected the tonnage policy, resulting in all possible economy. By his tact and good judgment in matters affecting the Maritime Board of Allied Supply he helped materially in the splendid results obtained by that organization."

Morrow became so indispensable to General Pershing that the latter was most unwilling to let him go. He even offered to give him a commission in the United States Army, an honor which Dwight Morrow, who had an affection for his little derby hat, refused.

General Charles G. Dawes, who had been appointed purchasing agent for the United States Army in Europe, had, after consultation with Morrow, conceived the idea of unifying all the Allied Supply services. An account of this negotiation is furnished in General Dawes' own war memoirs. He therein suggests that Sir John Cowans, the British Quartermaster General, was bitterly opposed to the whole scheme, but was in the end defeated by the force, righteousness, and brilliance of Charles Dawes. This account is not accurate in every particular. General Cowans was not, in fact, opposed to the scheme; what he objected to were the manners of General Dawes. It needed all the tact of Dwight Morrow and Paul Cravath to assuage the wounded feelings of this most amiable of generals. Between Dawes and Morrow a warm friendship was thereafter established. The former regarded Morrow with admiring devotion. And Morrow was one of the few who were able to appreciate at their true worth the high qualities of heart and mind possessed by Charles Dawes.

Meanwhile the house of J. P. Morgan & Co. were becoming uneasy at the protracted absence of one of their most valued partners. They began to inquire when they might expect to see Morrow back. The protests aroused by such a suggestion are indicative of the influence which Dwight Morrow had acquired in the councils of the Allies. Paul Cravath, at the time attached to the inter-Allied Finance Council, wrote to Thomas Lamont in despair. His letter is dated June 15, 1918:

". . . Morrow would, of course, be effective anywhere, but it happens that a combination of circumstances has given him an opportunity of doing most effective service in just the quarter where the influence and help of a man of his type is most needed, and that is on the business side of the Army. Morrow has had an opportunity of creating good relations with General Pershing and several members of his staff, of which his happy combination of tact and force has enabled him to take the fullest advantage. What he is really able to do is to help several men in important positions to do very much better work than they would have been capable of doing if they relied solely on their own experience and ability. I believe there may even be an opportunity for his influence to count in the decisions of what might ordinarily be considered purely military questions. It is a pity that a man like Morrow cannot have an opportunity of applying his energy and intelligence directly to the accomplishment of results. Perhaps eventually the opportunity will come. In the meantime, he can do an incalculable service in guiding and inspiring those by whom, or rather through whom, results are now being accomplished.

"Apart from the peculiar work which Morrow can do in connection with the Army, the Shipping Mission would be incomplete without his help; and its work will become increasingly important."

Messrs. J. P. Morgan & Co., who at the time were seriously overworked, were not immensely impressed by this appeal. They again cabled to Morrow inquiring his intentions. He replied that he would of course return if he were essentially required. The suggestion of an impending departure filled his colleagues on the A.M.T.C. with dismay. The rumor of it reached Paris. Through the Paris associates of J. P. Morgan & Co. the French Minister of Commerce addressed a further appeal:

"Minister of Commerce, M. Clémentel, has just personally asked me to cable you that, speaking as President of the Inter-Allied Shipping Board sitting in Paris, and also in the name of all his colleagues, he wished to emphasize in the very strongest manner the great assistance which Dwight W. Morrow represented in the situation and the absolute necessity of his presence in Europe. The Minister said he could not find words strong enough to express his appreciation of what Dwight W. Morrow had accomplished and what a real and effective link he was in the whole Allied shipping coöperation arrangements, and he was exceedingly anxious to impress upon you the need of his presence and the certainty of his return here. Please cable your reply."

It was mainly in order to consult further with his partners that Morrow returned to America at the end of June. In July he sailed again for Europe.

4

Dwight Morrow was not a militarist. "The whole business," he wrote, "of war looks more stupid and more silly the closer you get to it"; he was distressed by the "enormous amount of stupidity and folly and misunderstanding" which war entails.[11] On the other hand he was a firm believer in an integral victory. On July 11, 1918, he set out his views upon the subject in a long letter to Mrs. Thomas W. Lamont—one of the friends with whom he most enjoyed arguing. His contention was that the Allies were fighting in order to demonstrate that "the way of force, the way of the Roman Empire," was not the way by which to achieve the union of mankind. "We are fighting," he wrote, "to end the Roman method of world consolidation and to substitute in place therefor the method of consolidation by agreement. We're fighting, not necessarily to beat Germany, certainly not to crush Germany . . . but to make it clear to anyone who reads history hereafter that the Roman method no longer pays."

He was glad, meanwhile, to return to Lancaster House, being conscious that his work upon the A.M.T.C. Executive was attuned to all that was most efficacious in himself. He was able in this function to extract the greatest value from his capacity for mastering detail, from his peculiar talent for the lucid exposition of relevant facts. He was able, also, to illumine the dry schedules of tonnage and import figures with the glow of his imagination and vision. And he had ample occasion to soften the asperities of competition with the gentleness of his sweet friendliness and humor. Morrow, as has been said, was the most coöperative statesman that ever lived. He was able, in any argument, to state the case for his opponents better than they could state it for themselves. And he was always willing that others should reap the credit for work that he had done himself. His hatred of competition and self-seeking was based, not only upon his ethical system, but upon the actual quality of his humor. He

11 Letter to Vernon Munroe, dated June 2, 1918.

was always amused when any individual imagined that he could personally contribute something important to progressive evolution. On such occasions he would tell the story of "Rule Six." That story, which is a counterpart to the "ask again" story, needs to be explained.

One afternoon in 1918 Morrow entered the room of Sir Joseph Maclay, the British Minister of Shipping. He found this Scottish veteran engaged with one of the officials of the Ministry who was expounding the dreadful results which would ensue if that official's suggestions were not adopted. "Be careful," murmured Sir Joseph, "you are violating Rule Six." The official flushed at this remark, gathered his papers together and left the room. "And what," Morrow asked when the door was again closed, "what is Rule Six?" "Rule Six," Sir Joseph answered, "is 'Do not take yourself too seriously.'" "That," said Morrow, "sounds like a good rule. What are the other rules?" "There are no other rules," answered Sir Joseph.

The war, meanwhile, was drawing to its conclusion. Early in November, Dwight Morrow crossed to France for the purpose of adjusting certain difficulties which had arisen regarding the use of French harbors by the American Army. On the way to Paris he visited the town of Lille, which had only just been evacuated by the German forces. He became detached from the rest of his party, and eventually Sir Arthur Salter came upon him standing disheveled in the town square, clasping in either hand the hand of a small French child. A crowd had gathered to view this strange spectacle and Morrow was facing them with his eyes half closed. "Vive la France!" he was repeating in earnest, almost apostolic accents, "Vive la France!" It was as if an incantation. The crowd were too bewildered, too impressed, to smile.

Two days later Morrow was engaged in conference with French experts at the Ministry of Commerce. Their discussions were interrupted by the thunder of artillery announcing that the Armistice was signed.

He lingered on for three weeks longer, since there was some suggestion that the A.M.T.C. Executive might be perpetuated in the form of a relief organization charged with feeding the starving populations of Central Europe. This scheme was opposed by Mr. Herbert Hoover, who insisted that any such relief must be carried out as a purely American enterprise, and not under any inter-allied control. Dwight Morrow did not, at that time, appreciate Mr. Hoover's attitude. It was many years before he was able to rid himself of the prejudice then created. In the end he came to appreciate Mr. Hoover at what he was worth.

Dwight Morrow was not among those who imagined that the signature of the Armistice had put an end to the sufferings of humanity. A curious incident is related by M. Pierre Comert, at that time in the French Foreign Service, who, at the end of October, visited Morrow in London to inform him of the collapse of Turkey, Bulgaria, and Austria, and of the integral victory which would thereby be assured. He found Morrow in his sitting room at the Berkeley Hotel. "The war is finished!" exclaimed Comert. "It is now all over!" Morrow puffed quietly at his cigar. "And now," he said after a few moments, "America will go home. You will see, my dear Comert. She will leave Europe and not come back for a long time: perhaps never. America will henceforward live alone. There will now be a long period of trouble and much misunderstanding and much bickering. The whole world will be set apart again and not together as it should be. For a long time we shall have neither coöperation nor understanding."

Dwight Morrow returned to the United States in December 1918. He took no part in the deliberations of the Paris Peace Conference.

XII. Reconstruction 1919–1921

IN the early days of January 1919, Dwight Morrow found
himself back at his desk in No. 23 Wall Street. After the
excitements of the last ten months, the uses of that workaday
world appeared to him, if not unprofitable, then assuredly
stale. Having helped to organize the transport of two million
armed men across the Atlantic, it seemed a far less advantageous service to continue organizing the Interborough
Rapid Transit corporation. His experiences in Europe had
given him a deep interest in "diplomacy"—a word which he
rightly interpreted as the art of securing reasonable co-
operation between the peoples of the world.

His energies, during the years that followed, were by no
means confined to the interests of J. P. Morgan & Co. It has
always been a tradition of No. 23 Wall Street that the partners should engage in all forms of public and charitable
activity. Morrow became, at different periods, Chairman of
the Finance Committee of the New York Association for
Improving the Condition of the Poor, a member of the

Board of Trustees of the Russell Sage Foundation, a director of the National Bureau of Economic Research, a member of the New York Committee on Reëmployment of returning soldiers and sailors, and a member of the committee appointed under the Russell Sage Foundation to consider the future industrial and housing development of New York City. The labors of the latter committee were continued over many years and there were those who considered that time and money were being wasted upon purely Utopian schemes. On one occasion a member of the committee pushed a whole bundle of plans and blue-prints impatiently aside. "Those," he exclaimed, "are merely thoughts on paper." "Yes," said Morrow, "but you see, the idea is more important than carrying it out."

Nor were these his only extraneous employments. He became a trustee of the Carnegie Endowment for International Peace, a trustee of the Union Theological Seminary, and a member of the Board of Regents of the Smithsonian Institution at Washington. He became a director of the Bankers Trust Company and of the General Electric Company. As an incidental barometer of the increase in his public reputation from 1920 onwards, it is convenient here to record the honorary degrees conferred upon him by American universities: Rochester (1920), Princeton (1925), Williams (1926), Pennsylvania (1926), Yale (1927), Harvard (1928), Brown (1928), Marshall College (1928), Syracuse (1931), Amherst (1931), Bowdoin (1931), and Dartmouth (1931).

Then there was always Englewood. That warm neighborliness, so congenial in the Americans, was in his case intensified by his protective instincts. He enjoyed expending energy to the advantage of his own community; he believed that the course of human progress was in the end determined by the thoughts and feelings of the ordinary man and woman; he thus was careful to prevent his contact with extraordinary people from blunting the edge of his sympathy with those who happened to live round the corner. There were moments, it is true, when he felt that he and his wife had outgrown the narrow limits of the Englewood circle. Such a moment had first occurred in 1916 when he spent a few days with the H. P. Davisons in Vermont. "He came back," records Mrs. Morrow in her diary, "full of reasons why we should live in New York—not that he wants to, but the Davisons are full of it. 'What a mistake we are making for ourselves and our children, living here.' 'J. P. Morgan & Co. are making history and we are not in New York to enjoy it.' —Talking about it has made me perfectly wretched." This mood of restlessness recurred in 1922. "The truth is," records Mrs. Morrow, "that we have outgrown Englewood and yet cling to it. We don't know what we want." Mrs. Morrow knew very well what she wanted. She wanted to build a house of her own at Englewood, molded exactly to her heart's desire. It was not till 1927 that she was able to persuade her husband to consent to such a luxury.

Meanwhile, as President of the Civic Association of Englewood, Dwight Morrow was enabled to put the affairs of his small community in better order. He was able, by the fusion that he had effected, to administer the local charities by more economical and practical methods. He enlarged the Free Library and it was under his leadership that over one million dollars were raised for the expansion of the hospital. Morrow thus became for his neighbors the dominant citizen in the whole county.

In New York also he extended the area of his acquaintance. He joined several clubs and became a member of a dining club known as the "Heterogenes," where he reopened contact with such men as Arthur W. Page,[1] the Reverend Howard C. Robbins,[2] and Joseph P. Cotton.[3]

These, perhaps, were little things, yet, being entirely devoid of self-importance, he liked handling little things with the same thoroughness with which he handled great things. To him, the local garage proprietor was as interesting as Aristide Briand; he treated them both the same. The influence which in later years he was able to exercise over the tired statesmen of Europe was largely due to this "small town" habit; to that twinkling humanity which enabled him to restore to autumnal politicians something of the April of their youth; to that utter simplicity of good will which stirred in them tremors of their own early idealisms. He brought sunshine into the very cellars of diplomacy; he gave a touch of dawn to the graying lights of European afternoons.

2

Dwight Morrow, as has been said, was intensely interested in national politics. Some account has been given in Chapter VI of his support of Taft in the campaign of 1912. Immediately on his return from Europe he embarked upon a more

[1] Arthur Wilson Page, b. Aberdeen, North Carolina, 1883; Harvard 1905; vice president Doubleday, Page & Co. and editor of *World's Work* 1913-26; vice president American Telephone & Telegraph Co. since 1927; adviser to American Delegation, London Naval Conference, 1930.

[2] Reverend Howard C. Robbins, b. Philadelphia, Pennsylvania, 1876; Yale 1899; rector St. Paul's Church, Englewood, 1905-11; dean Cathedral of St. John the Divine, New York, 1917-29; professor of pastoral theology, General Theological Seminary, New York, since 1929.

[3] Joseph P. Cotton, lawyer, b. Newport, Rhode Island, 1875; Harvard 1896; LL.B. 1900; European representative U. S. Food Administration 1918; Under Secretary of State 1929-31; d. 1931.

personal adventure. His old Amherst friend Calvin Coolidge had, by dint of quiet application—first as a lawyer in North-ampton and later in the Legislature at Boston—become Gov-ernor of the State of Massachusetts and had acquired a national reputation owing to his firm handling of the Boston police strike. Dwight Morrow joined with a small group of friends—notably with Frank W. Stearns, James R. Reynolds, and Thomas Cochran—in running Coolidge for presidential nomination at the Republican National Convention of 1920. "I did not plan for it," records Coolidge in his *Autobiography*. "It came." Dwight Morrow, for his part, planned very hard.

Attention has already been drawn to his loyalty to the Republican Party, a feeling which arose, not only from his strong corporate instincts, but from a studiously considered belief in the party system. He was not unaware of the de-fects of party politics, but he considered those defects were outweighed by other advantages. "How hard it is—" he wrote to Professor Morse in 1914, on the occasion of Wood-row Wilson's speech at Indianapolis—"how hard it is to draw exactly the line up to which a man is justified in going for the sake of party success, without which success his ulti-mate aims cannot be carried out!" Yet he agreed with Profes-sor Morse in thinking that the party system, and particularly the two-party system, is, in our present stage of social devel-opment, the only alternative to revolution. His political phi-losophy is embodied in the long and scholarly introduction which he wrote in 1922 to a posthumous edition of Professor Morse's essays entitled "Parties and Party Leaders." Upon this introduction Dwight Morrow spent two years of inces-sant labor, reading all the authorities from John of Salisbury to Merriam, from Halifax to Bagehot. Professor Morse's own studies of English history had convinced him that the British Parliament only became really effective once it had organized itself into opposing parties. Dwight Morrow fully endorsed this contention. Not only was the party system the sole alternative to revolution, it was the "beginning of tolerance," it was "the first step in the long and difficult problem of organization." His adherence to the Republican Party was not, therefore, a gesture either of partisanship or convenience; it was a deliberate interpretation of his own political creed.

For all his loyalty to the party, as a necessity in the existing political machine, Morrow was not blind to its defects. He referred in 1919 to the "complete intellectual bankruptcy of the Republican Party in New Jersey." He bitterly criticized the existing method of collecting campaign funds, feeling that it gave too powerful an influence to the monied class. And what is perhaps more interesting, he endeavored to educate Calvin Coolidge in his own theories of Liberalism and free-trade.

He embarked upon this tentative mission with a certain wariness. Only a few days after his return from Europe he addressed the following guileful letter to F. W. Stearns, Calvin Coolidge's manager and friend:

". . . I want to have a very long talk with him about his work. You may look upon me, because of my associations, as a conservative, but I really think I have been all my life something of a radical. I have tried, of course, to be radical along lines that would help instead of along lines that would simply throw the existing machinery out of gear. That is what I liked about Calvin's fine aphorism when he was made President of the Massachusetts Senate: 'Be as revolutionary as science; be as reactionary as the multiplication table.'

"Now this has a bearing on the next two years, or ten years, of Calvin's life. I wish he might think carefully about the first part of his maxim. I should like to see him 'as revolutionary as science.' I should like to see him get the real facts with reference to some of the things that are wrong in the world and take a bold stand in making them right.

"For the last year I have been abroad dealing with all sorts of government officials. Some of them have been Socialists like Thomas, the great Socialist leader in France. Some of them have come from old conservative families, like Lord Robert Cecil, son of the Marquis of Salisbury. I have about come to the conclusion that the division of the people of the world is not really between conservative and radical, but between people that are real people and people that are not. Calvin is one of the fellows who is real. He really wants to make things better, not to pretend to make them better. . . ."

Morrow was none the less a trifle perplexed by the astringent realism of his old classmate. "The business of America," Coolidge had said, "is business." Dwight Morrow was not certain that he liked that sort of remark. We find him sending to Coolidge four volumes of William Graham Sumner's works. "Throughout these volumes," he wrote, "you will notice the strong predilection of Sumner for free trade." Coolidge's reply to this gift is dated from the State House at Boston on March 10, 1920:

". . . I have read most of the four volumes of Sumner. I regard his arguments on the whole as sound. I do not think that human existence is quite so much on the basis of dollars and cents as he puts it. He argues in one place that the enunciation of great principles has had little to do with human development; that America became democratic through economic reasons rather than the reasons that came from the teachings of philosophy and religion. He nowhere enunciates the principle of service.

That principle so far as I know has never been applied to protection. My observation of protection is that it has been successful in practice, however unsound it may appear to be in theory. That must mean that the theories have not taken account of all the facts. If I am poor and need the assistance of a protective tariff, why does not the law of service require others to furnish it for me? Or, if I am powerful, why is it not my duty to use my power for the protection of less fortunate industries or people? There must have been something in our country besides an abundance of land to draw the population of Europe here for there was an abundance of land in Russia and in Africa, less convenient of access and so of use. . . ."

Meanwhile the Coolidge campaign was organized with skill and thoroughness. Fearing lest their association with Wall Street might prejudice the cause, Morrow and Thomas Cochran, although moving spirits in the whole drive, remained in the background. The foreground was filled by the large, the devoted, the imperturbable figure of Frank Stearns. Offices were opened in Washington and New York and every one of the Amherst alumni was appealed to with true college spirit. A collection of Coolidge's speeches and addresses was published under the title, "Have Faith in Massachusetts," and some 40,000 copies were circulated to Republicans in every State and to every single delegate to the 1920 Convention. Although the campaign had been instituted, not with the hope of obtaining immediate success, but with the desire to gain experience for the Convention of 1924, Morrow became, as it proceeded, convinced by his own enthusiasm. We find him, on May 25, 1920, writing optimistically to Thomas Lamont:

". . . I have not changed my opinion that I had before you went away. I think it is a miracle that a man of Coolidge's type has been produced for this emergency. Moreover, I think he is going to be nominated and elected. The people that are for him are for him intensely, and they are for him because of a fundamental belief in his character. In looking ahead in the next four or eight years I think what America needs more than anything else is a man who will in himself be a demonstration of character. I think Coolidge comes more nearly being that man than any other man in either party."

A few weeks later he and Cochran traveled to Chicago and plunged into the heated excitements of the Convention. Morrow's room at the hotel became the centre of intensive lobbying. He expounded, he argued, he cajoled. He would seize delegates and senators by their coat lapels and force them almost by physical pressure to believe how essential to the great soul of America was the nomination of Calvin Coolidge. His exhortations were continued even when he was in his bath, and there is a curious picture of Morrow following a delegate out into the hotel corridor with only a small towel around his waist. The cigarette stubs upon the bedroom floor were thick as autumn leaves. At one moment it seemed as if Coolidge would really be nominated. The vote went to Senator Warren G. Harding; and almost by chance, almost by mistake, Calvin Coolidge was nominated for the vice presidency.

Morrow was disappointed with this result.

"The whole show," he wrote on June 28th, "at Chicago was a terrible jumble. Coolidge did not want the Vice Presidency, and there was absolutely no plan on the part of anybody that he should have had it. But the convention just ran away with that idea. Whether or no they would have done the same thing with the Presidency, if the proper conditions had arisen, we never will know. Many of us feel, however, that if Senator Lodge had stood by him in Massachusetts, he would have had a very real chance for the nomination.

"I did not like the nomination of Senator Harding at first any better than you evidently did. Nevertheless I feel that there is nothing against him, and that there is very much in his favor. If he carries on a dignified campaign I should expect to see him elected."

3

It should be realized that Morrow's interest in national politics was part of his wider interest in the politics of the world. Although, during those years 1919 and 1920, he flung himself into the "Coolidge for President" campaign, he was more deeply preoccupied with the problem of post-war reconstruction.

He foresaw from the very moment of the Armistice that the coming of peace would produce in the American people a strong reaction towards isolation. He feared that this reaction might take unworthy forms. In the month following his return to America he sounded a note of warning in a speech which he made, on February 20, 1919, at a banquet of the Trust Companies of the United States. His remarks on that occasion were courageous, unpopular, and wise:

"It seems to me that the United States at the present time has before it a different type of problem, with reference to the relationships of all of us to each other, than it has ever had before. We are going to go through a very critical six months. I am not speaking about business, I am thinking more of the position that this nation is to take in the world in the future. I am thinking of the character that this nation is to establish for itself, for a very long time, by reason of the attitude that it takes toward the war that has just ended. You are going to have a great many men come back from Europe; you are going to have a great many men in this country talk about this war. Why, gentlemen, as long as we live, men will be talking about this war, about what the various nations did, about who won it, about the contribution, the great contribution, that America made, and it is going to be a severe test of America to get the right sense of proportion. You are going to hear stories that range from one end to the other, you are going to hear that America won this war, with an occasional Englishman and Frenchman coming up and patting them on the back to encourage them. . . . It isn't going to be enough to judge this European war from the American point of view as a whole; every real American has got to judge the effort of our Allies, the Allies and ourselves as a whole. . . .

"I hear people today in America, and we will hear more of it, complaining about what was paid for things in France, complaining about what they charged the American nation. Why, you can fasten your minds upon those things and feel a sort of hatred for France. I never begrudge a cent to that French peasant woman whose husband has died at the front for us; I never begrudge a cent that a French peasant woman gets from this country.

"There is hardly a man in this room who hasn't a relative in France today; there is hardly a man in this room who isn't expecting home some time within the next year a boy who is over there, perhaps a son, perhaps a brother, perhaps a nephew. My friends, if on the day the Armistice was signed, every American in France had been put to death, the whole two million of them, from the top to the bottom, if every one of them had been put to death, the price that America had paid indeed would have been much less in comparison to its population than the price that France has paid. And whatever we may think about the price of meat or food in Paris, whatever we may think about

235

the mistakes that some of the French people may have made, those of us who recognize the dignity of death must appreciate from the bottom of our hearts that whatever we do, we will not have paid our ancient debt to France, we will have added to our debt to France, when this war is over.

"Now I want to say just a word about England. It is not easy to talk about England after you have talked about France. England has a wonderful facility for concealing her virtues. A wonderful capacity to avoid telling what she is doing. England goes on indifferent to praise, indifferent to blame, but carrying generally the heavy end of the log, and the part that is not spectacular. Right down to the very end of this war, right down to the very end, when there was something disagreeable to be done, when there was something hard to be done, it was the general opinion that Lloyd George should do it. And he always did do it. I use his name as they do, as a symbol for that ancient people who fight today as they fought a thousand years ago.

"I am not going to speak of their fleet, I am not going to speak of the wonderful contribution that they made to the economic strength of this alliance, I am not going to speak of the great, though perhaps stupid way at times they had of attributing to anybody else the credit of doing things, I am not going to speak of the way they worked with their thumbs when they might have worked with their fingers and antagonized even their friends, but there was one dramatic incident at the end of this war. On the eleventh day of November, when the Armistice went into effect, do not forget that the British Army got back to the place from which they had taken the 'contemptible little army,' or a part of it, and put it off the train in 1914 and started the retreat. The retreat started from Mons, and on the eleventh day of November the British Army got back to Mons and a Frenchman said to me, the day after the Armistice was signed, 'These British are a strange people; they never win any battle but the last.'"

It was indeed an act of boldness as of vision thus to address a New York audience in February 1919. Among the letters of congratulation which he received was one from Arthur Page, the son of the great Ambassador. "I thank you very much," Morrow answered, "for the kind things you say about my very informal and rambling talk. I had a deep feeling of regret when I got down as I had intended to say something about your father, and to use his attitude toward the English as a lesson for other Americans. As a matter of fact, I said considerably more about the Americans and the French than I had intended to say, and I was left at the end with very little time for the English."

4

Inevitably Morrow took a fervent interest in the controversy regarding the American ratification of the Treaty of Versailles and more particularly the future attitude of the United States towards the League of Nations. He was among the first to realize the force of the opposition which was developing against the League Covenant. His partner, Thomas Lamont, was at that time one of the Treasury Representatives attached to the United States Delegation at the Paris Peace Conference, and was one of the few among that admirable body of experts to whom President Wilson lent a willing ear. Lamont was trying to induce the President to strengthen Republican representation on the Delegation by the inclusion of Elihu Root, if not as a delegate, then at least as legal counselor. Morrow, in New York, did all that was possible to further this project and was in frequent consultation with Senator Root. As early as April 1919 he warned

Lamont that the Senatorial opposition to the Covenant was far more serious than the President seemed to realize. "There will," he wrote to him on May 17, 1919, "be a great temptation for the President to make a popular campaign, which may get the country with him, but will render the present Senate even firmer against him than it is now." In a later letter he drew attention to the bitter and justifiable criticism which would be aroused in the United States by those articles of the Covenant which provided for annexations under the specious guise of "mandates," and in order to emphasize the sincerity of the feeling which would be created he suggested, half seriously, that "the only way to bring reality to the colonial aims of the League of Nations" would be if Great Britain transferred the West Indies to the United States under the mandatory system.

Meanwhile he devoted his own efforts to educating American opinion, and between February and March 1919 he contributed a series of articles to the New York *Evening Post* which was subsequently published in book form under the title, "The Society of Free States." The general purpose of these articles was to show that the League of Nations would "do neither the good that its friends say, nor the harm that its enemies say," but that it was essential as "a step towards coöperative organization." The course of his argument was characteristic. He began by a historical summary of the many efforts that had been made in the past to substitute agreement by consent for the old Roman theory of discipline by force. He traced these efforts and theories from La Nouvelle Cynée of Emeric Crucé, through the Great Design of Henri IV, via William Penn, the Abbé de St. Pierre, Leibnitz, Kant, and Alexander I, to the House of Lords debate of May 19, 1918. He showed that these schemes and theories, however

Utopian at the time, had in fact produced International Law; and he contended that from these ideas had evolved such practical experiments in international coöperation as Postal, Sanitary, and Transport Conventions, culminating in a model "fact-finding organization" such as the A.M.T.C. "In the history of a race," he wrote, "a century is a short time." The Covenant of the League of Nations was obviously a step in the right direction. The only question was whether the step was too hurried or too wide.

In answering this question Morrow displayed his accustomed realism. "All advances," he wrote, "in international coöperation come slowly. Those parchment agreements which go beyond the general desires of the people who are expected to observe them may do more harm than good." He frankly admitted that the Covenant, as then drafted, went beyond the desires of the people of the United States. He suggested therefore that it might be rendered more acceptable if the United States were made primarily responsible for its execution in the Western Hemisphere, and the European Powers were to be charged with carrying it out in so far only as the Eastern Hemisphere was concerned. He objected also to Article X under which the frontiers established by the Peace Treaties were mutually to be guaranteed. "The justice," he wrote, "of the territorial boundaries of the New States, however well the Peace Conference may do their work, must remain problematical until experience proves the wisdom of the work of this generation." He feared that the jurists and diplomatists in Paris, viewing human nature as it ought to be rather than as it was, had made upon public opinion too exacting a demand. In an address which he delivered at Columbia University in June 1919, he again returned to his favorite thesis that small practicable idealisms are preferable to large impracticable idealisms. "If," he said, "international good faith is to be promoted in this world, if the plighted word of a nation is to remain a sacred thing, it is very important that nations should not promise more than they can reasonably be expected to perform. A slight promise may tend to keep the peace more than an onerous promise." Thus, while hoping that the Covenant would be adopted, he urged that the Senate should add to it an "interpretative declaration of what America understands the document to mean." "I think it vital," he repeated, "that the people of the United States should *understand* their international obligations." And as a final expression of his doctrine of evolutionary idealism, he concluded his articles with an appeal for patience:

"The ambitions of great men, the suspicions of little men, the constant misunderstandings of all men, may undermine any structure that this generation builds. If, however, we build with wisdom, and with courage, and with patience, those that come after us will be helped by our work. Our building may fall, but if we have built aright, some of the foundation stones will remain and become part of the structure that will ultimately abide."

It was with deep regret that Morrow observed the Treaty controversy degenerating into a personal combat between President Wilson and the Senate. He felt that the former was in error in refusing to accept the Knox reservations or even the Lodge reservations. But, with his patient habit of judgment, he did not regard the final abstention of the United States as fatal to the whole League idea. He felt, indeed, that what the League lost in breadth, she would gain in depth. Above all, the progress of the League must be gradual and based mainly upon the efficiency of its Secretariat. "I have," he wrote to Lord Eustace Percy in October 1919, "looked upon the whole idea of the League from the beginning as a fact-finding body. I therefore look upon the Secretariat as a much more important body than either the Assembly or the Council." And to Jean Monnet, his old colleague of the A.M.T.C., who had then joined the Secretariat under Sir Eric Drummond, he furnished in November certain precepts which illustrate his balanced prescience in all international affairs:

". . . The Council should, during the first few years, take up no matters except those which are absolutely essential. If they get going into the rights or wrongs of controversies between Italy and Jugo-Slavia, the whole thing will break apart. Keep the organization a fact-finding body, and let its power grow, and keep in mind that it takes a very long time to accomplish anything that is to be permanent. You and I cannot afford to wait more than fifty or sixty years, but perhaps the world can. Your League of Nations may not get started, or it may get started and it may fail, but men will come back to the work that you did in London during the war and will turn over the precedents that you made, and some of them will be used in the real concert that will last. . . ."

5

Although he was able to appreciate, and therefore to discount, the aversion of the American people from all European entanglements, Dwight Morrow himself was in no sense an isolationist. It was with unqualified vigor that he flung himself, during those post-war years, into the task of reconstruction. It was not merely as a banking house that, between 1920 and 1927, the Morgan partners devoted so much of their time to the reconstruction loans being issued on behalf of France, Italy, Great Britain, Austria, Belgium, and Japan. They approached such problems both as financial experts anxious to restart the machine, and as statesmen intent upon the furtherance of international sanity.

"What do we owe Europe?" said Morrow at Rochester in May 1920. "A generous judgment of her acts." He had little patience with those who preached reconstruction under the guise of philanthropy. "It is difficult enough," he argued, "to kill one bird with one stone, let alone two birds." He was equally irritated by those who regarded post-war stabilization in terms of immediate financial advantage. He protested against the theory that no reconstruction loans should be made except on the condition that the proceeds should be spent solely in the United States. Such a theory seemed to him to be based upon "leaky economics." He disliked the whole pound of flesh treatments of debts and reparation and was especially incensed by the "holier than thou" attitude adopted by some American politicians:

"When it comes," he wrote to Herbert Bayard Swope, "to the actual indemnities paid, I think it will be found to be literally true that America has received a larger percentage of its losses than any country involved in the war. I have always felt that the President would have had much more real influence in Paris in scaling down what I have called the 'paper judgments' of the Allies against Germany if he had been willing to apply as *against the United States* the principles which he set forward so eloquently in his public addresses."

Morrow was too good an economist not to see through the appearances of the post-war situation. He agreed with Gov-

ernor Strong that if German reparation were to be paid at
all, it could be paid only in American money "by robbing
Peter to pay Paul—and we shall be Peter." He foresaw also
that it would be a mistake to rely on gold alone to adjust the
disproportionate trade balance of the United States. As early
as October 1919, he addressed to the International Trade
Conference at Atlantic City the following note of warning:

"No one believes that we can continue indefinitely piling up
an export balance of $4,000,000,000 a year. . . . But if the de-
crease in our export balance is to be gradual and not abrupt, it
means that for some time to come there will be a substantial
export to be settled in gold or covered by foreign credits. . . .
We can rely upon the further importation of gold only to a
limited extent. That is why we are all studying the problem of
international credits."

And it was thus as much with the desire to render American economy less top-heavy, as with the wish to relieve a
stricken Europe, that he played so large a part in inducing
the United States public to invest in foreign bonds.[4]

Two reconstruction loans engaged Morrow's particular attention. The first was the Austrian reconstruction loan issued
under the auspices of the League of Nations in 1922 and
1923. Sir Arthur Salter was the moving spirit in this great
work of reconstruction, which in fact rescued Austria from
collapse. His admiration for this former colleague of the
A.M.T.C. added to Morrow's zest in launching a portion of
the loan in the United States. The issue was in the end successful, and Morrow was delighted to receive from Sir
Arthur Salter a warm letter of congratulation:

[4] Those who are specially interested in Morrow's attitude on the subject of
foreign loans should read an article entitled "Who Buys Foreign Bonds?" which
he contributed to *Foreign Affairs* for January 1927.

League of Nations
May 31, 1923.

My dear Morrow:

Now that, under the lead of Morgan's, an American syndicate has undertaken an issue of the Austrian loan, I want to write to you to say how much we all appreciate the part you have yourself taken in this great decision. This is much the biggest work the League has yet undertaken; it is much the biggest piece of international construction work undertaken anywhere. And it is very pleasant to think that you and Monnet and I should have renewed our association of the war to take part in this most interesting of post-war jobs. . . .

Even more personal and scholarly was the work which Morrow did on behalf of France. The American Army had returned from Europe in a mood of disillusion, which took the form of dispraise of the Allies and created an atmosphere almost of rancor. In particular, the old sentimental feeling for France was succeeded by criticism and distrust. Dwight Morrow was saddened by the injustice of this reaction and was more specifically distressed by the American public's underestimation of France's credit and of her amazing powers of recuperation. In order to correct these false assumptions he crossed to Europe in February 1921, and devoted three months to an intensive study of French conditions. He interviewed such authorities as President Millerand, M. Ribot, and M. Viviani; he toured the country and examined the work of reconstruction on the spot; and he engaged the services of Professor Joseph S. Davis of Harvard University to assist him in the more strictly economic branches of his inquiry. The result of his investigation was embodied on his return in a "Memorandum on the Economic and Financial Condition of France" which he had privately printed and circulated in influential quarters. In this statistical survey Morrow examined the post-war condition of French agriculture, mining, industry, transport, foreign trade, currency, and finance. He described the progress made in the reconstruction of the devastated areas. He indicated the uncertainty from which the French budget would continue to suffer so long as the Debt and Reparation questions remained unsettled—"So long," he wrote, "as the German indemnity question remains in the air it is likely that France will continue to frame unbalanced budgets by sweeping [sic] a great portion of her annual expenditure against a fantastic amount expected one day from Germany." And he concluded that, although the war had cost France physical losses of a serious nature, yet she had gained in powers of organization. "No one," he said, "who knows the French can doubt that their difficulties will be solved."

This survey was valuable, not only for its actual effect upon Wall Street opinion, but because it gave Morrow a profound sympathy for the French point of view. The affection which he thereafter felt for France was not primarily based, as it is with most of us, upon respect for her value to modern civilization, or even upon any conscious delight in her intellectual, artistic, and even culinary distinction. It was based on a clear appreciation of the solid qualities of the French character, of their thrift, industry, and patriotism. And it was fortified by the fact that, having acquired a knowledge of French fiscal and budgetary problems greater than that possessed by any other American, he came to regard these problems as a specialty of his own and thus to extend to them those "protective" feelings which enabled him to give a touch of gentleness even to the most precise statistics.

XIII. Two Protectorates: Amherst
and Cuba 1921–1923

IN January 1921 Dwight Morrow was approached with a
suggestion that he should accept the presidency of Yale. He
was sorely tempted by this proposal. Certain of his friends,
notably ex-President Taft, conveyed to him that it would be a
mistake for a non-Yale man, and one who possessed no
specifically academic training, to exchange his present functions for a position which would certainly be difficult and
might become delicate. Morrow was persuaded by these
arguments to decline.

"I do not think," he wrote to those who had approached
him on behalf of the Yale Trustees,

"that being or not being a Yale man is necessarily a conclusive
reason by itself. I feel quite strongly, however, that although I
have had a very deep interest in educational problems, it has
been the general interest of a trustee—the interest of one anxious
to help in interpreting the outside world and the academic
world to each other. The transition from that position and attitude to the position of titular head of an important constituency

246

like Yale's is so great that anyone without special academic training might well shrink from the responsibility, even though he were a graduate of the college. When to his lack of intimate familiarity with specific academic problems there is added the fact that he would be going into a university with whose traditions he was familiar only as they could be communicated to him, the difficulty seems to me very much greater. This all seems peculiarly true in the case of Yale, which has had such a splendid tradition of close brotherhood amongst its alumni body.

"I am writing this note to you because I want to convey to you that my reasons are to my mind conclusive and I think it is only fair that those who have shown this very great confidence in me should know at once and unequivocally that I am unavailable.

"I do not think I need to say to you that the things that you said to me will always remain very proud possessions in my life. Unconsciously, perhaps, you have set for me a higher standard of conduct in whatever line of work I may hereafter be engaged."

In the months that followed he came to regret this refusal. He felt that the Yale presidency might have offered a valuable transition between Wall Street, which had ceased to satisfy him, and that public life towards which, from now onwards, he increasingly aspired. When passing through London in March 1921, a chance remark of Lord Beaverbrook had increased his restlessness. "Morrow," the latter said to him, "were you an Englishman you would now be a Cabinet Minister." The extent to which he was perturbed by this true but most unsettling remark is shown by an entry in Mrs. Morrow's diary:

March 29. His mind has gone back to it [the Yale offer] so many times that I am worried. Perhaps it *was* a mistake. I

247

reproach myself for not having more fully appreciated what the position would have meant to him, and for not having urged him to consider the offer more carefully. I think I relied too much upon his judgment, his decision, which is always so clear and firm. Perhaps, however, I was just timid and am trying to find an excuse for my timidity. I tried to say to him this morning that I have always felt that what he wanted and what he would do splendidly would be a piece of political work. He says it would have come—the chance for it—at Yale better than where he is now. If a chance for politics comes anywhere in the near future I shall feel that Dwight made no mistake in refusing the Yale presidency. If it does not, I shall feel that he did make a mistake and that I share in the mistake because I did not urge him to consider the thing very carefully. However, as he said this morning, "If I was big enough for the Yale job, I am big enough for something else."

There was always Amherst. In 1916 he had been elected a Life Trustee and in 1920 had become chairman of the Financial Committee. He had taken a leading part in the centennial gift and celebrations of 1921, and was by then generally recognized as being the most effective member of the Board of Trustees. It was thus mainly upon his shoulders that fell the onus and the odium of the controversy which thereafter developed between the Board and Dr. Alexander Meiklejohn, President of the College. This controversy formed one of the most distressing episodes in Morrow's life. It must therefore be examined in some detail.

It will be convenient first to state the elements of the problem; then to explain why the ensuing storm overflowed the Amherst teacup and spread throughout the country; and finally to assess Morrow's own part in the controversy and the impression which it left upon his mind.

248

Alexander Meiklejohn had been born at Rochdale in Yorkshire and possessed many of the virtues, and some of the intractability, of his origin. At the age of eight he had emigrated with his family to America; after graduating from Brown, of which university he was dean from 1901 to 1912, after obtaining his doctor's degree at Cornell, he was appointed President of Amherst in the autumn of 1912; he was then at the age of forty. From the very first he announced that his aim would be to "challenge the young people of America with spiritual enterprise" and to create among the Massachusetts hills the perfected example of "The Liberal College." His efforts and his energy were, during the first few years, universally applauded. "No one," wrote the *New Republic* in later years, "will deny that the educational development of Amherst College under President Meiklejohn was one of the greatest public significance. No other college in America has exhibited in comparable degree the intellectual life which has been stirring in Amherst during President Meiklejohn's régime." He was able, not without Morrow's assistance, to attract to Amherst some of the most brilliant and progressive instructors of the United States, and to obtain as temporary lecturers such eminent English educationalists as Professor Ernest Barker, Professor R. H. Tawney, and Professor Holland Rose. He was adored by the students, who regarded their "Prexy" as the embodiment of progressive idealism. He rendered Amherst a hotbed of new ideas.

Inevitably, as the years progressed, the alumni councils and some of the trustees came to look upon the modernism of Dr. Meiklejohn's methods with a certain disquiet. He would read the New Testament in Johnson Chapel as if it were a story by O. Henry; he allowed the boys to smoke in class;

he wished to deprofessionalize athletics; he was an avowed pacifist; a tinge of socialism, even of atheism, seemed to color his doctrine. In his hands the old New England spirit of Amherst was being transformed into something strange; their college, they felt, was being taken from them.

For many years the Board of Trustees supported Dr. Meiklejohn against all opposition. They continued to accord him their confidence and to allow him to administer the college in his own manner. Largely owing to Morrow's influence they allocated funds to him for the purpose of assisting his educational experiments. By 1921, however, two factors came to disturb the trustful relations between the Board and the President. In the first place it was discovered that Dr. Meiklejohn was totally unable to manage his personal finances. In May 1921 a committee of three trustees, of whom Morrow was one, was appointed to investigate this difficulty under the chairmanship of Judge Arthur Prentice Rugg. Dr. Meiklejohn did not respond to this investigation either with good humor or tact. He accused the trustees of using these minor misunderstandings, in regard to which he was technically in the wrong, as a covert means of attacking his liberal principles. He had, he said, "an obligation to the college which it was his duty to discharge, whatever the trustees might think of him." "It seems strange," wrote Morrow at the time, "that a man can write and speak so well and yet be careless about things which seem fundamental to most of us."

The second factor which disturbed the relations between the Board and the President was the actual inability of Dr. Meiklejohn to maintain even average harmony among the professors. The President was an obstinate man who loved dialectics; his passion for youth rendered him impatient of the elderly, nor could he conceal from the senior members of the faculty that he considered them incompetent, obstructive, and past their work. The professors might well have borne with these insults, had they felt convinced that their President was in fact translating into practical institutions his alarmingly successive ideas regarding a "Liberal College." He would continually be asking them to interrupt their current labors for the purpose of "working out on paper" one or other of his own experimental schemes. They would devote much valuable time to the elaboration of these theories, only to find that some new idea had in the meanwhile taken possession of Dr. Meiklejohn's mind. These constant and inconsequent interruptions produced among the senior members of the faculty the impression that the President was volatile rather than inspired, rude rather than reasonable. By the summer of 1922 the faculty had been split into two combative camps and the whole administration of the college was thereby impeded. A second committee of investigation, under the chairmanship of Arthur Rounds, was appointed in June 1922, and reported in May 1923. It was at this stage that the controversy ceased to be a purely collegiate dispute and became a national issue.

2

The more intelligent and progressive sections of opinion in the United States had for long been concerned with the state of American education. A feeling had for some years been growing that higher education was too much at the mercy of such conservative, and indeed reactionary, elements as the alumni councils and the trustee boards. The Meiklejohn controversy thus became a test case in an important issue. Alexander Meiklejohn was enlarged into a symbol of educational progress; the Amherst trustees were diminished into symbols of educational stagnation. The supporters of the President were quick to exploit this dramatization of the problem. The trustees were appalled at realizing that a domestic dispute had swollen overnight into a national controversy and that their beloved college was being exposed to the full glare of critical publicity.

They acted with comparative determination and rapidity. A meeting of the Board was summoned and a committee of five was appointed, under Morrow's chairmanship, to discover a solution. This committee had before it both the Rugg and the Rounds reports. Dwight Morrow was not overwhelmingly affected by the mismanagement of the President's personal finances. He was unable to deny, however, that the chaos of the Meiklejohn household accounts did suggest a certain lack of authority and care. The Rounds report was far more embarrassing. It disclosed in effect that the senior members of the faculty refused to work in even adequate harmony under Meiklejohn's direction. Morrow might have been able to persuade his fellow trustees to ignore either one of these two reports; he was unable to convince them that the two together did not impose on the Board the necessity of obtaining Alexander Meiklejohn's resignation. The problem was how to secure his removal without rendering him a martyr to his principles. The committee adopted the unusual course of asking each member of the faculty to vote in secret ballot whether he considered the interests of the College required Dr. Meiklejohn's removal. A two-thirds majority voted in the affirmative.

The final scene took place on the night of June 16th, in the philosophy room of the Library. The windows were open to the hot air outside and the lights within blazed upon a tense discussion. The students and the reporters, armed with field glasses, watched from surrounding posts of observation the little drama in the lighted room. They could deduce from the gestures of the participants that the argument was heated in the extreme. President Meiklejohn had in fact accused the trustees of blackmail. They, for their part, had offered to ease his departure by a pension or by some professorship in the College itself. He refused such mitigations. He resigned.

The public criticism to which the trustees were thereafter exposed was impulsive and unjust. Typical of the attacks made upon them was an article published in the New York *American* of June 22, 1923:

"Three years ago a man of Wall Street told me that Meiklejohn was doomed, that financial interests had determined that they must get rid of him at Amherst. It is significant that Dwight Morrow, a member of the firm of J. P. Morgan & Co., should lead in the movement which has caused the intellectual guillotining of one of America's choice spirits—a great educator, a man of vision, of which America is in need."

This criticism was ill-informed. Morrow had been the first of the trustees to support Meiklejohn; he was the last to oppose him. He was supported in his efforts by his friend Professor F. J. E. Woodbridge,[1] a practical and endearing philosopher who exercised both a soothing and a stimulating influence on Morrow's mind.

---

[1] F. J. E. Woodbridge, university professor and writer, b. Canada, 1867; Amherst '89; Union Theological Seminary 1892; studied for several years in Germany; professor of philosophy University of Minnesota 1895-1902; professor of philosophy, Johnsonian professor, and for many years dean of the faculties of political science, philosophy, pure science and fine arts, Columbia University; Roosevelt professor in Berlin 1931-32.

These attacks produced an effect on the College itself. Three out of twenty-nine professors, and five out of fifteen associate professors resigned in protest. At the ensuing Commencement six seniors refused to accept their degrees. Morrow was not unduly perturbed by such incidents. He refused to reply to the attacks made upon him. "I have been brought up," he said, "to believe that a man is only written down by what he writes himself." In the end Professor Olds was nominated President, Dr. Meiklejohn retired to Wisconsin, and the waters of Amherst resumed their wonted placidity.

There was one attack, however, which wounded Morrow to the quick. On July 25, 1923, the *New Republic,* a paper for which he entertained the greatest respect, published "An Open Letter to Dwight Morrow" accusing him of lack of educational idealism. After rejecting the theory that the dismissal of Dr. Meiklejohn was due to his financial embarrassments or to his disagreements with his own faculty, the *New Republic* continued as follows:

"The man in the street surmises that you, as a member of the house of Morgan, could not tolerate Dr. Meiklejohn's liberalism. We cannot accept this surmise. So far as we know, you are as much of a liberal, politically, as Dr. Meiklejohn. It is further surmised that you were displeased with the liberalism of some of Dr. Meiklejohn's appointees. But in recent years lecturers have been brought to Amherst, at your personal expense we believe, who stand much farther to the left than any appointee of Dr. Meiklejohn.

"Was it, after all, something much more fundamental that set you against Dr. Meiklejohn: an irreconcilable antagonism between his educational ideals and your own? On the surface those ideals may have appeared identical through a great part of the eleven years of his incumbency. Both of you believe in scholarship, in the free play of ideas, in the fostering of independent personality. But within that apparent agreement a very wide rift between two educational ideals is conceivable. The one is rationally opportunistic, at home in the world as it is and content with it, self-assertive, ruthless at need, never sentimentally loyal, or revengeful. The other is uncompromisingly idealistic, prepared to take up arms against the world, despising the rewards of the world unless they come on the recipient's own terms, with the humility and unbending pride of the martyr, neither yielding subjection nor accepting obeisance. And as the contrast between your fundamental aims and those of Meiklejohn became more sharply drawn through the successful development of his work, did the antagonism of ideals grow into personal hostility until you were ready to grasp at any means to destroy him?"

This again was a misinterpretation of Morrow's whole attitude. "I came," he wrote to Calvin Coolidge on June 22, 1923, "to the view that President Meiklejohn could not stay at Amherst much more reluctantly than some other members of the Board. It seemed to me that the issue of academic freedom was really an important one, and that as long as the faculty could stand him, we should put up with him. When it became perfectly clear that the faculty could stand him no longer, we certainly were justified in acting."

The main consideration which affected Morrow's judgment was, in fact, one which it was difficult publicly to affirm or ostensibly to justify. He was perfectly prepared to overlook Dr. Meiklejohn's financial muddles, and the dissensions within the faculty might perhaps have been overcome by tact and firmness on the part of the trustees. He had himself labored for many months with this in view. What finally determined Morrow's judgment was a growing doubt as to the quality of Dr. Meiklejohn's intelligence. He observed that behind those billowing clouds of verbiage, uplift, and martyrdom, there was little constructive, or even correct, thinking. The President had a remarkable gift for dramatizing educational issues; he possessed no gift whatsoever for translating those issues into workable educational institutions. What really deprived Dr. Meiklejohn of Dwight Morrow's support was the latter's suspicion of the President's intellectual frivolity.

How far he was justified in this assumption can best be judged by submitting to the reader a specimen of Dr. Meiklejohn's oratory. The following passage is taken, not from any of the President's more incidental allocutions, but from his farewell address at the alumni dinner, an occasion which obviously called for the most considered dignity of expression:

"I think," said President Meiklejohn, "that they [the trustees] are making educationally a very bad mistake. . . . I believe in setting learning apart from life and keeping it there, that it may be pure and true and clean and free. . . . Life today in America is a great tremendous spiritual adventure. . . . American life, with its attempt to live beautifully, sweetly, honestly and courageously, is a glorious, mad, intoxicating thing. I have had a good taste of it and so have you. . . . I differ from most of you on most of the issues of life and I am going to keep it up."

Those who admire the above remarks will feel that Morrow was wrong: those who regard them as foolish will feel that Morrow was right.

He himself always looked back on the Meiklejohn controversy as one of the most unhappy episodes in his life. He was deeply distressed by the personal tragedy of Alexander Meiklejohn; he was disillusioned by the discovery that the teaching profession, which he had since childhood invested with a halo of sanctity, could be as obstinate and as internecine as any other; it was galling for him to consider that Amherst, perhaps owing to some lack of foresight on his own part, had been exposed to the full glare of public criticism; and he felt it unjust that he himself should have been pilloried as a person of illiberal opinions.

Above all he regretted that the dispute should have led to open rupture and that all conciliation should have failed.

Many years afterwards Stanley King—who today rules a happy Amherst in Dr. Meiklejohn's place—was passing through London and visited Morrow in the midst of the roar and rattle of the Naval Conference. He found him buried in tonnage and calibre statistics, pestered by callers of every nationality, buzzed around by secretaries, experts, and reporters, with the telephone shrilling in all corners of the disordered sitting room, and the click of typewriters mingling with the incessant droning of the elevator. "Why, this," said Stanley King, "is hell on earth!" "No, Stanley, it's not so bad as the Meiklejohn business. Besides, in that business we failed to cure." "But, Dwight," protested Stanley King, "an amputation in that case was quite inevitable." "Amputations create wounds: they do not heal them. No, Stanley, we did poorly over that business. We did not do well."

This anecdote is illustrative, not merely of the deep impression left on Morrow by the Meiklejohn incident, but also of his remorseless habits of self-scrutiny. Judged by his own unique standard of conciliation, the whole controversy ended in failure. Yet even he could scarcely have contended that the final decision was either evitable or a mistake.

3

His private affairs, during those years, were prosperous and calm. His partnership in the firm of J. P. Morgan & Co. had brought him a considerable fortune and he invested his savings with shrewd skill. His increasing riches did not, however, tempt him to any ostentatious scale of living. He had always been extravagant about books and this extravagance henceforward became positively reckless. Whenever he read a book that pleased him he would buy several copies and send them to his friends. He was lavish also in his gifts to charitable organizations, stipulating in most cases that the gifts should remain anonymous; thus in the year 1927 his accounts show charitable donations to the total of $145,463. He was generous to his family and friends and was glad to render the last years of his mother's life as comfortable as she would allow. But for the rest, he spent his money upon increasing the efficiency of his own work. He never hesitated to employ experts in collecting historical data for any problem he had on hand; his use, and sometimes his abuse, of the telephone was phenomenal; and he was not in the least economical when undertaking a journey or providing for his own mobility.

The old Packard, however, which they had purchased in 1914 remained for many years a trusted rusted friend. It was in the days before the George Washington Bridge had flung its penciled strand across the Hudson; those of the citizens of Englewood who did not go by train to New York were obliged to cross by ferry. This entailed a congestion of automobiles upon the ferry and much delay in getting off. Morrow, as has been said, had a mathematical mind. He calculated that much time would be saved if he possessed two cars and two drivers. The one car would drive him down to the ferry on the New Jersey shore and the other car would meet him when the said ferry reached New York. He was delighted by this discovery and at once communicated it to his fellow commuters. "I have," he informed them delightedly, "solved the problem. It is perfectly simple. We must all have two cars, one on each side of the river." "But, Dwight," they answered, "we are not all Morgan partners. Most of us cannot afford two cars." There are those who to this day remember the expression of bewildered consternation which then settled upon the features of Dwight Morrow. It was followed by one of his rare moments of embarrassment. "I am sorry," he mumbled contritely. It was always with difficulty that he remembered that he could be different from anybody else.

Then there were those happy winter holidays with his wife and children. Year after year he would go to Nassau in the Bahamas, leasing Everton House, bathing and playing golf. He formed a close friendship with Sir William Allardyce, Governor of the Bahamas, and with Mr. Harcourt Malcolm, the Speaker of the Assembly. In the latter's company he would explore not merely the methods of British colonial administration, not only the local treatment of the color problem, but the records of Bahaman constitutional history. On Saturday nights there would be turtle suppers at the Club. And on occasions the children would arrange a small stage under the breadfruit tree and act plays of their own composition. The title of one of these tragedies has been preserved: it is called "Prince Albert of Montagu; A Drama in Four Acts."

There were other and more extended journeys. In 1922

he went on a visit to Panama, where his brother, General Jay Johnson Morrow, was Governor of the Canal Zone. His mother accompanied him, chuckling with delight at the importance of her soldier and her statesman sons. She died in June 1922. She was buried, beside her husband, in the high graveyard above Allegheny.

There was a ten weeks' visit to England and Scotland. And there were several trips to Cuba undertaken on behalf of the firm. His negotiations with the Cuban Government, which mark a further stage in his development, are of more than banking interest.

4

The Cuban episode is important in that it enabled Dwight Morrow to acquire the experience, and to perfect the technique, which a few years later rendered his Mexican mission an example to all professional diplomatists.

The relations between the United States and Cuba were intricate and perhaps illogical. That lack of definition which causes Anglo-Saxon policy to seem so irrational to Latin observers, can, in the case of America, be explained by the interaction of several conflicting tendencies. There is the tradition of isolation, fortified by a democratic instinct to dislike what is not understood; there is a splendid aversion from all annexations, imperialism, wars, and bullying; there is the pressure of commercial interests expressing itself in an inclination towards dollar diplomacy; there is a justified uneasiness regarding the strategical vulnerability of the Panama Canal and a consequent desire for "security" in the Caribbean zone; there are the ordinary impulses of national

GOVERNOR J. J. MORROW, MRS. J. E. MORROW, DWIGHT MORROW, AT
PANAMA, 1922

conceit which are known as patriotism; and there is that most obstructive of all human documents—the Constitution —and the resultant confusion between the functions of the legislature and those of the executive. The course steered by the Department of State between these hidden reefs, those magnetic rocks, those emotional whirlpools, those hurricanes of righteousness, is, although often skillful, inevitably erratic.

It is not surprising, therefore, that the relations between the United States and the Republic of Cuba should have been exposed to some discrepancy. On the one hand, there was a sincere desire to accord to Cuba that independence which the American nation had won for her by war. On the other hand, there was an equally sincere desire that the sugar trade of Cuba should not injure the sugar trade of the United States. Moreover, it was essential that Cuba should not become so internally chaotic as to constitute a weak link in the Caribbean chain. Thus the resolution of Congress by which, in 1898, the United States decided to liberate Cuba from the domination of Spain, disclaimed "any disposition or intention to exercise sovereignty, jurisdiction, or control over the said island." Whereas the terms which, in 1901, eventually determined the future relations between the two countries provided, under the Platt Amendment, that the United States might intervene in Cuba, or in other words might exercise sovereignty in the island, "for the preservation of Cuban independence or the maintenance of a government adequate for the protection of life, property, and individual liberty." This amendment was embodied in the Cuban Constitution, and thereby established a cat-and-mouse protectorate over the island.

Morrow was far too sensible a man to regard the Platt Amendment as an act either of bad faith or of hypocrisy.

He realized that, in the circumstances, it was salutary and wise. His interpretation of that amendment did, however, represent a gloss upon, and even an extension of, current political theory. He contended that the amendment created, as between the United States and Cuba, the relationship of guardian and ward. "This makes it," he wrote, "highly imperative that the United States, if they assume the rights of guardian, should also assume the duties; and that means that whenever they administer the ward's estate they should administer it in the interests of the ward rather than in the interests of the guardian."

This view was not shared, apparently, by Herbert Hoover, Secretary of Commerce in President Harding's Cabinet. On the occasion, in 1921, of his first visit to Havana, Dwight Morrow called upon President Zayas. He at once won the confidence of that despot by treating him as if he were an honest man. The President was so impressed by the friendliness of Dwight Morrow that he showed him an official note which he had that morning received from the United States Government above the signature of Secretary Hughes. In that note the Cuban Government was informed that they were producing far too much sugar and were instructed to destroy one-third of their crop. The President asked Morrow how he should reply to such a communication. Morrow told him to preface his answer by a textual quotation of the note to which it was a reply, to continue that the sugar crop was a domestic question affecting the Cuban Government's rights of sovereignty, and to conclude by indicating that the correspondence would be published. The State Department was much disturbed by this rejoinder, and when Morrow next visited Secretary Hughes the latter accused him of being its author. "I am certain," he said, "that this impertinent note was not drafted by Zayas." "I was equally certain," Morrow answered, "that the note to which it was a reply was not drafted by Charles Evans Hughes." Mr. Hoover, on hearing of this incident, was much displeased.

The question of Cuban sugar was, it is true, but indirectly the cause of Morrow's interest in the affairs and welfare of the Island Republic. He made no attempt to conceal the fact that the tariff policy of the United States Government would in the end prove disastrous, not only to the sugar industry in Cuba, but to the sugar industry in the United States. The main purpose of his repeated visits was, however, to bring some order into the chaos of Cuban finances.

These finances, in 1921, were in a serious condition. The great sugar boom of the war period had been followed by a sudden slump. The administration of President Zayas had proved itself to be both incompetent and corrupt. The budgetary balance had been dissipated for several years, and the debts owing to the United States Administration and to private American interests seemed irrecoverable except by forcible methods. A powerful campaign had been started in America for "cleaning up" Cuba under the Platt Amendment.

There was some justification for this campaign. The Cubans had been given every chance to govern themselves and had failed to profit by their opportunity. The chaos and confusion which reigned at Havana offered little hope of reform from within. The Banco Nacional had closed its doors and it was impossible to discover the extent of the floating debt or the nature of the Government's commitments. No departmental accounts appeared to be in existence. "But," protested Morrow on entering this Augean stable, "why don't you add up the stubs in your check book?" "There is no check book," answered Secretary Gelabert, "and no stubs." Undeterred by this incompetence, Morrow set himself, with gentle persistence, to inspire the Cubans with at least the rudiments of efficiency and self-respect.

His central purpose was to enable Cuba to emerge from the crisis by her own efforts. Ostensibly he had gone there because of the danger threatening the sinking fund payments on Cuban bonds issued by J. P. Morgan & Co. His real mission was to coöperate with General Enoch H. Crowder, President Harding's representative, in setting Cuba on her feet. Throughout his connection with Cuban affairs he benefited by the firm support of General Crowder and of the State Department at Washington. It is questionable whether, without that support, he could have achieved as much as he did.

General, subsequently Ambassador, Crowder, was the finest type of American administrator, being both visionary and practical. It was Morrow's coöperation with this magnificent pro-consul that saved Cuba from a renewal of American occupation. Their views upon the principle involved were in fact identical. In May of 1922 Morrow wrote to General Crowder as follows:

"From a lifetime of service in the army you realize that the credit does not count; it is the durable results in which real men are interested. . . . Of course the Government of Cuba has been, and is, very bad. It is possible—yes, it is probable—that the United States might run Cuba much better. As I get older, however, I become more and more convinced that good government is not a substitute for self-government. The kind of mistakes that America would make in running Cuba would be different from those that the Cubans themselves make, but they would

probably cause a new kind of trouble and a new kind of suffering."

"We ought not," he wrote again, "to use the Platt Amendment to collect the debts, or to enforce the contracts, of private
individuals."

Morrow arranged two loans for the Cuban Government
during these years of crisis. The first was a loan of $5,000,000
and was made in the early part of 1922 to meet such pressing
emergencies as certain checks already issued, certain postal
order debts to the American Government, and a three
months' service of the external debt. Having thus deferred
any immediate danger of intervention, Morrow settled down
to the study of some more permanent and comprehensive
scheme. He was able, owing to the personal influence which
he had acquired, to induce the Cuban Administration to
accept, as a condition of a further loan, a contract which left
them little latitude in the allocation of its proceeds. This
arrangement provided for the liquidation of past indebtedness, the payment of overdue salaries, and the rapid amorti-
zation and retirement of other internal and external issues.
The Government, in return, was to receive a loan of $50,-
000,000. It is true that, once the loan had been obtained,
the Zayas Administration did its best to evade the contract. Four years later J. P. Morgan & Co. were obliged to
lend a further $9,000,000 to clear up the remainder of the
items the discharge of which had been provided for in the
original contract. Yet Morrow had been able, none the less,
to provide Cuba with the material with which she rescued
herself.

More important, perhaps, from the point of view of his
biography, is the opinion which, during his Cuban ex-

periences, he formed of the Latin American character. He was able to rid himself of all sentiments of superiority. The philosophic angle from which he approached deficiencies is well illustrated by a speech which he delivered in April 1925, on the occasion of a banquet given in New York to Señor Machado, at that time Cuban President Elect:

"All nations," he said, "are prone to judge themselves by the loftiness of their own purposes, and to judge other nations by their failure to attain their high purposes. To judge any nation by its lapses from its standards is to do it an injustice. Nations, like men, are to be judged not alone by what they are but by what they earnestly desire to become. Our belief in democracy rests upon a faith in what humanity can become as well as upon the frank recognition of what humanity is."

These lessons, both in thought and practice, were of the greatest value to him when, in 1927, he embarked upon the Mexican experiment.

XIV. The Man Who Knew
Coolidge   1923–1927

DEATH OF PRESIDENT HARDING. MORROW'S RELATION TOWARDS,
AND OPINION OF, CALVIN COOLIDGE. ALTHOUGH NEW PRESIDENT
OFFERS MORROW NO IMMEDIATE EMPLOYMENT, FACT OF THEIR
INTIMACY INCREASES LATTER'S PRESTIGE. HIS REFUSAL TO EX-
PLOIT THAT INTIMACY. THE REPARATIONS QUESTION. MORROW
HOPES TO BE APPOINTED AGENT GENERAL BUT IS DISAPPOINTED.
FURTHER RECONSTRUCTION LOANS. MORROW ON THE DEBT SET-
TLEMENTS. APPOINTED TO AIRCRAFT BOARD. ORIGINS OF THAT
BOARD. ITS PROCEDURE. ITS RECOMMENDATIONS. COLONEL WIL-
LIAM MITCHELL. THE MORROW REPORT INCREASES HIS PUB-
LIC REPUTATION. HIS NAME MENTIONED AS SECRETARY OF
TREASURY, AMBASSADOR TO MOSCOW, AND MINISTER TO CHINA.
HE IS, HOWEVER, APPOINTED TO MEXICO.

ON the night of August 2, 1923, Dwight Morrow had invited a few friends to dinner at his Englewood home. Robert
Frost, who was present, recalls how in the course of the
evening Morrow was summoned urgently to the telephone.
He returned in a few minutes and stood in the centre of the
room plunged in one of his moods of abstraction. He stood
there, staring at them with unseeing eyes. They roused him
from his trance. "Dwight," they said. "Tell us! What has
happened?" He woke with a start. "Calvin Coolidge," he
announced slowly, "is President of the United States." It
was in this manner that he broke to them the news of
President Harding's death.

Obviously the promotion of his old classmate to the
Presidency affected Dwight Morrow's own prospects of
public employment. They had been friends for nearly thirty
years. Morrow had supported Coolidge at Amherst, he had
supported him in his Massachusetts elections, he had sup-

ported him at the Chicago Convention. True it was that he had always been careful to furnish that support in such a manner as not to wound the dry susceptibility of his friend or to create in him any sense of indebtedness. So long ago as October 1915, when Coolidge was running for election as Lieutenant Governor of Massachusetts, Morrow had written to Frank Stearns as follows: "I shall be very glad to contribute to Coolidge's campaign fund, for I feel about it just as you do, but I do not want to make a contribution which would place Coolidge in the position that he feels under an obligation to anybody." The idea of any such obligation never occurred to Morrow when, with the death of President Harding, Coolidge went to the White House. Nor did it ever occur to Calvin Coolidge.

It may seem strange, none the less, that on his elevation to the presidency Coolidge did not make immediate use of the capacity and faithfulness of his old classmate. Apart from sentimental reasons, Coolidge had an almost mystic belief in the importance of coincidence; it seems never to have occurred to him that one of the most favorable of the many coincidences which had furthered his career was that, on becoming Chief Executive, he could command the services of a loyal friend who was universally recognized as possessing exceptional talent for the conduct of foreign affairs. Even when in March of 1925 Coolidge became President, not only by the grace of God but by the votes of the American people, he hesitated to entrust Morrow with any important administrative function. He contended that Morrow would scarcely wish to abandon the firm of J. P. Morgan & Co. for any public office; he may also have felt that the popular prejudice against Wall Street would render any such appointment subject to public criticism. The fact remains

that during the six long years of President Coolidge's administration Morrow was never called into counsel on general
public affairs. It remained for Herbert Hoover, who in the
past had frequently been on terms of disagreement with
Dwight Morrow, to realize his usefulness. A trivial illustration will point the difference; during the years 1929 and
1930 President Hoover (an inveterate telephonist by nature)
telephoned to Morrow at least three times a week; during
the years 1923 to 1929 Coolidge only telephoned once, and
that was upon a purely domestic matter.

There is no evidence that Dwight Morrow ever resented,
or was even aware of, this failure of the President to recognize his usefulness. His friends were never allowed, even in
jest, to speak disparagingly of Calvin Coolidge. His loyalty
was absolute. Their personal relations remained unclouded
to the end.

The faithfulness which Dwight Morrow maintained towards President Coolidge was compounded of many different elements. Predominantly, there was his own high sense
of public duty and the respect which, as a very excellent
American, he accorded to the office of President. This rever-
ential feeling was enforced by the loyalty which he felt towards all Amherst men of the class of '95. And behind it
all was a very real appreciation of Coolidge's integrity,
shrewdness, and precision of mind. Yet in his many eulogies
of Calvin Coolidge a note of perplexity can often be detected. "Coolidge," he wrote to Howard C. Robbins in
January 1920, "is a very unusual man and a strange combination of transcendental philosopher and a practical politician." A friend contended that Coolidge always seemed to
reach the first place by some stroke of fortune. "Perhaps,"

answered Morrow with one of his twinkling smiles, "but," —and here he dug the critic in the ribs—"he always reaches the second place by sheer merit." "Coolidge," he would sometimes say, "may possibly be overestimated by the public: he is certainly underestimated by the intellectuals." And again and again, when told of some lack of human warmth on the part of the President, "You must remember," he would say, "that Calvin Coolidge is a strange man."

It was generally assumed by outside people that Morrow, in that he was one of the oldest friends and earliest supporters of the new President, possessed enormous influence at the White House. He was pestered by all manner of persons to intervene on their behalf. He invariably refused to do so, pleading an "insurmountable objection against lifting my finger to get any man who is a friend of mine any public office."

"I spend," he wrote to Bruce Barton, "most of my days writing letters to my relatives, my boyhood friends in Allegheny City, my classmates in college, my friends in the legal profession, and my various banking associates, explaining to them that it is not my business to appoint ambassadors to the various courts of Europe or to make Federal Judges. I have also a large pile of unanswered mail dealing with the presentation of young ladies to the Court of St. James'."

To such applications his reply followed an invariable formula. "While," he would answer, "I have known the President for a long time, I have made it a rule not to impose advice upon him either as to personnel or as to policy. He has, of course, his constitutional advisers."

Morrow was too shrewd a realist not to be aware that this public misunderstanding of the real nature of his relations with the President had its advantageous side. "As a matter of fact," he laughingly confessed to a friend in later years, "I seldom write to the President and he hardly ever writes to me. But everybody is convinced that we maintain a constant correspondence and this gives me, I am glad to say, a quite unwarranted reputation and much influence with people unconnected with the White House."

In the six long years of Coolidge's Presidency, Morrow only once volunteered advice and only once asked for a favor. The occasion on which he broke his rule occurred in the very first days of the presidency. On August 4, 1923, while traveling to Chicago, he dictated two letters, the one to Frank Stearns and the other to Coolidge. The favor he then asked was the release of political prisoners undergoing imprisonment for sedition during the war. The advice he then tendered covered the whole field of foreign affairs. He urged the new President, after an interval of cautious reflection, to consider summoning a Conference—"Like the Portsmouth Conference which Roosevelt called between Japan and Russia"—with a view to easing the deadlock which had arisen in Europe over the reparation question and the Ruhr. He urged him to establish a consistent policy towards Latin America and to put an end to the inconsistencies of method entailed by the dual control exercised by the War Department and the State Department. And he suggested that Colonel Harvey should be replaced as Ambassador in London by Elihu Root—"an appointment that should shine by contrast." That was the sole occasion on which he tendered advice on general problems.

During the same journey he wrote a personal letter to the President himself:

En route to Chicago
August 4, 1923

Dear Calvin:

Three years ago in Worcester I told you in all sincerity that I was convinced that you were better equipped in character and in training to serve this nation as its President than any of the other possible candidates that were being discussed. That conviction was based upon your character as I knew it and your long training in public affairs. I have never changed that belief. The greatest responsibility that rests upon any man in the world has now come to you. No former Vice President who succeeded to the Presidency by the death of the President was confronted with responsibilities as great. Your whole life's training fits you for your mighty task; and the faith that you expressed in the closing line of your short statement made in Vermont is the faith that all your real friends will share. May God bless and keep you strong and well!

2

It has already been noted that on the solitary occasion when Dwight Morrow tendered unsolicited advice to the President he had suggested American intervention in the problem of German Reparations. He had for long been cognizant with this question and had kept himself up to date by a careful study of the *Economic Review* and such other publications as dealt informatively with the subject. It was not long before an opportunity was offered to the Coolidge Administration to coöperate usefully in this work of international appeasement.

In December 1922, Secretary Hughes had made his New Haven address in which he had indicated that the United

States Government would not view with disfavor the co-operation of unofficial American experts in the solution of these controversies. The situation in Europe was not at the moment propitious to any general review of Franco-German differences regarding reparation, but in the following year Lord Curzon seized a favorable opportunity to reopen the question of American participation. This suggestion was for a while successfully sidetracked by M. Poincaré, but a few months later, in December 1923, the French Prime Minister agreed that the Reparation Commission might nominate certain independent experts to consider the question of stabilizing the German mark. Morrow may well have hoped that he would himself be chosen to preside over such a Commission, since his name had already been proposed by the Finance Section of the League of Nations as Commissioner General for Austria. In this he was disappointed. General Dawes was selected by the Reparation Commission, and it was Morrow himself who suggested that, in view of the General's lack of experience in European finance, he should be accompanied by Owen D. Young. During the early months of 1924 he had several conferences with General Dawes and Mr. Young and endeavored to convince them of the difficulty of floating a loan in the United States for the sole purpose of enabling Germany to pay France. When the eventual Dawes Report was issued, Morrow contended that it greatly exaggerated Germany's capacity, and that the schedule of payments was more than optimistic. He considered the report to be lacking in "reality" and he feared that the hasty approval given to it by the several governments concerned indicated that they each interpreted it as meaning something different.

It will be remembered that the Dawes Report provided

for the appointment of an Agent General for Reparation who should be vested with wide powers of control and should establish his office in Berlin. The European news-papers at once suggested that Dwight Morrow was the ob-vious person for such a function. They were not alone in this assumption. The Governor of the Bank of England had in fact consulted J. P. Morgan as to who would be the best man for this important office, and Mr. Morgan had replied that Dwight Morrow seemed indicated for the task. Both the President and Mr. Hughes, when sounded unofficially on the point, raised no substantial objection. It seemed cer-tain, by June 1924, that he would be offered the appoint-ment. Mrs. Morrow was distressed:

June 22, 1924. I have been much upset thinking of either Dwight's leaving J. P. M. & Co. to be Agent General for Reparation and go to live three years in Germany!!!—or to accept a professorship at Columbia.

On June 30, 1924, Morrow was informed by the Governor of the Bank of England that his name had been unani-mously chosen by the Reparation Commission, subject to the approval of the United States Government. It was at this stage that a hitch occurred. A member of the American dele-gation attached to the Reparation Commission managed to convey to the State Department that the interested Govern-ments would not approve of the appointment of a member of J. P. Morgan & Co. to such a position. This opinion was confirmed by Ambassador Houghton, who had just reached Washington from Germany, and was verbally conveyed to Morrow by the Secretary of State. Morrow thereupon with-drew his name from the list of candidates and Mr. S. Parker Gilbert was chosen in his place. It subsequently transpired that Ambassador Houghton had derived his information, not from any statement on the part of the German Government, but from the American member of the Reparation Commission already referred to. The British authorities were so distressed by this misunderstanding that they dispatched an emissary to New York in the hope of inducing Morrow to reconsider his withdrawal.[1] He declined to do so; matters, by then, had gone too far. Yet he did not conceal his disappointment. Mrs. Morrow's diary (that charming barometer of all his moods) bears at this date two significant entries:

July 4, 1924. Dwight is so disappointed, though he will not say so. It has all been so fatiguing, his having been worked up for nothing.

July 27, 1924. I have had nothing all week but ugly envious thoughts in my mind.

He was fortunate, had he known it, to escape this function. It was fulfilled by Parker Gilbert with tact, thorough-

---

[1] The British and French experts were far more worried by this unfortunate misunderstanding than were their United States colleagues. Mr. Owen Young, for instance (whom Morrow had introduced to the circles of high finance), seems to have remained wholly unconscious that Morrow's great qualifications were being ignored.

Not so Sir Arthur Salter, who did all in his power to obtain Morrow's assistance. "We needed," wrote Salter at a later date, "someone who combined a knowledge of the higher international finance, of the world credit and money system, and of such problems as Reparations and Allied Debts, with sagacity and soundness of judgment, a position of trust and influence in America, and at the same time a profound understanding of the European position and the specific features of the English and French situation and outlook. . . . Morrow combined all these qualities in a degree that I believe to be unsurpassed, and perhaps unequalled, by any living man." (Article in the *News Chronicle*, October 7, 1931.)

Salter, as all European experts, was so distressed by the failure of the United States administration to employ Morrow upon Reconstruction problems, that he attributed it, perhaps unfairly, to the intrigues of self-seeking men. It was to Morrow's "magnanimity and courage" that Salter dedicated his famous work "Recovery."

ness, and intelligence. But it may be questioned whether an older man, and one who had for so long been connected with Wall Street, could have survived the odium and rancor of so thankless a task.

It was in the autumn of 1924 that the Bank of England begged J. P. Morgan & Co. to float just over one-half ($110,-000,000) of the ensuing Dawes loan upon the American market. Mr. J. P. Morgan and Thomas Lamont, who happened to be spending that summer in England, held several interviews with Mr. Montagu Norman, Dr. Luther, and Dr. Schacht. They pointed out that the American investing public would be unlikely to absorb such a loan unless they were assured that it would in fact reëstablish the economic equilibrium of the Continent, and as a prerequisite of such assurance some pledge would be necessary that the French would evacuate the Ruhr. Would this loan, they asked, really set Germany on her feet again? Could they count on the solidarity of the Allied and neutral countries in sponsoring such a loan? Above all, could Germany be trusted to carry out the provisions of the Dawes loan in perfect good faith? To all these questions they received strong affirmative answers from Mr. Montagu Norman and from Dr. Schacht.

The caution with which J. P. Morgan & Co. entered into this business is shown by a letter addressed by Dwight Morrow on September 18, 1924, to Charles E. Hughes, Secretary of State:

". . . It is the foreign control to which Germany is to be subjected that has made us somewhat fearful about the permanent success of the Dawes Plan. In the public press the plan has from time to time been attributed to our influence. As a matter of fact, if we had been consulted we should have said what we have always believed: that the real security for any governmental loan is the desire of the nation which does the borrowing to obtain the money, the benefit of the loan to that nation, and the probability that the people of that nation, in order to preserve their national *credit,* will have not only the ability but the desire to discharge the obligation upon the terms and conditions to which their Government or its predecessors in power have agreed.

"What really impresses us favorably in Governor Norman's opinion is not the extent of the foreign control upon Germany, but the disposition of the German people at the present time. We have some fear, however, that that disposition may not continue. However desirous Germany is of getting the loan at the moment in order to free the hold which France has upon the industries of the Ruhr, it is almost inevitable that this loan will be unpopular in Germany after a few years. The people of Germany, in our opinion, are almost certain, after sufficient time has elapsed, to think not of the release of the Ruhr but of the extent to which what was once a first-class Power has been subjected to foreign control.

"The opinion of Governor Norman that unless the loan is made Europe will break, is also of great importance to us. Our main reason for going on with the business would be the heavy responsibility that would rest upon us if our failure to proceed caused a breakdown. . . ."

Secretary Hughes replied to this letter to the effect that the Dawes plan furnished a prospect of European recovery and that it would be "most unfortunate" if its failure could be ascribed to the abstention of American bankers.

It was in such circumstances that J. P. Morgan & Co. allowed the prestige of their name to be associated with the Dawes loan. It should again be noted that of all the countless millions of dollars which they induced the American public to invest in foreign bonds, it has been on this loan only that default has occurred.

3

Before we leave the area of high finance it may be well to indicate as shortly as possible certain other operations in which Dwight Morrow became involved before his departure in 1927 for Mexico. Typical of all such operations was the loan of $100,000,000 floated in 1920 on behalf of the French Government under the auspices of 23 Wall Street. The bonds of this loan were purchased outright from the French Government by a group consisting of J. P. Morgan & Co., the First National Bank of New York and the National City Bank of New York. These bonds, which had been purchased at 94, were then sold to a syndicate of thirty-six members at 95. This syndicate, in turn, disposed of them at 96 to a national syndicate of some eight hundred members, who in their turn sold them to the public at 100. This procedure is typical of what followed in other cases, nor would it be of interest to the reader to examine the several operations of this nature which were successfully carried through.[2]

More significant, from the point of view of Morrow's biography, are the personal connections which during the

[2] In 1925 Dwight Morrow was asked to act as arbitrator in the Brady Will Case—a study which was not completed till the actual eve of his departure for Mexico. His handling of this arbitration displayed a masterly fusion of legal caution, financial wisdom, and creative common sense. To deal with it in detail would falsify the proportions of this monograph; to deal with it in summary would be to convey no idea of Morrow's intricate manoeuvres between the extremes of legal correctitude and human understanding. The whole case is urgently recommended as a thesis for some Law School graduate.

course of these negotiations he was able to form, and the consequent increase in his own influence and reputation with the several European Governments. In 1926, for instance, he was much occupied with the Belgian stabilization loan. In 1927 he had several discussions with Montagu Norman, M. Moreau of the Banque de France, and Dr. Schacht of the Reichsbank regarding a stabilization loan for Poland. The French currency crisis in the summer of that year was a problem after Morrow's own heart; he had already when in Paris had two long discussions with M. Poincaré regarding the future of the franc. When in July 1927 the franc fell to 236 to the pound sterling, the house of Morgan inquired whether they could be of service. M. Poincaré, who assumed office on July 23rd, replied that for the moment he could manage without external assistance.

Morrow's own knowledge of French finances naturally led the French funding commissions that came to Washington to seek his aid and counsel. M. Caillaux in 1925 was particularly insistent, and Ambassadors Bérenger and Claudel as well as M. Lacour Gayet, the Financial Agent of the French Government, were continually appealing to him for advice. Morrow discountenanced such advances:

"I think," he wrote to Lacour Gayet, "it is most desirable that in any dealings which the French Government have with the American Government with reference to the debt settlement that the representative of the French Government should deal direct with the Debt Mission through its proper officers and refrain from conferring with outsiders, in which class I include myself. I am sure you sympathize with this idea, but I am not sure that all of the representatives of your Government in the past understood the wisdom of taking and holding such a position."

His own attitude to the debt settlements was skeptical in the extreme. When summoned in June 1926 to give evidence before the Senate Committee on Finance, he was able, during the four hours of his examination, to express some sensible, if obvious, truths. He startled the Senators by drawing a distinction between an "agreement" and an "effective agreement." When asked what he meant by the latter term he answered, "An effective agreement is an agreement that is likely to work." Senator Harrison then asked him whether he considered the debt settlement concluded with Great Britain as an effective agreement. "I thought it," he answered warily, "a very heavy obligation for Great Britain to assume and an act of great courage on her part in assuming it." He then proceeded to explain to the Committee that these debts could ultimately only be paid in goods and services. Senator Jones then asked him whether that meant that France would have to sell goods which would compete with American products. "Presumably," Morrow answered. "There is nothing that any right-minded person with experience should regret in that. . . . Whatever you do you cannot prevent it. I think you are somewhat personifying a nation there without looking at it as it actually occurs. It is quite a common impression that nations trade with nations. As a matter of fact individuals in nations trade with individuals in other nations." And with such simple homilies on economics the Senatorial Committee had to rest content.

4

On Sunday, September 13, 1925, Morrow opened his newspaper to read that he had been appointed a member of a

Board constituted by President Coolidge for the purpose of
reporting on the best means "of developing and applying
aircraft in national defense." His first inclination was to
refuse this service on the ground that he possessed no knowledge of aviation. True it was that he had been for some time
a Trustee of the Guggenheim Foundation for the Promotion of Aeronautics, and that in the previous March he had
received a crisp curt letter from the President vaguely indicating some such area of study. "I have in mind," President
Coolidge had then written, "that I may like to have you
look into the subject of airplanes for me." Nothing further
had been heard of this inspiration on the part of Calvin
Coolidge and Morrow's knowledge of aeronautics remained
that of an intelligent amateur.

During the autumn of 1925, however, the question of air
defense had become a subject of popular interest. The destruction of the dirigible *Shenandoah* had created some
anxiety, and this anxiety had been fanned into flame by
the sensational allegations of Col. William Mitchell, head
of the Army Air Service. This officer possessed a gift for
publicity; he had made the flesh of millions creep by drawing a vivacious picture of the American eagle cowering
under the imminent assault of all the lesser birds of the air
and possessing as its only defense an air force which was
incompetent, decentralized, antiquated, and riven by internal
jealousies and intrigue. It was in order to meet these hysterical surmises that the Board had been nominated. It was
pointed out to Morrow that the President, in selecting him
for a task of such topical and popular interest, might be
hoping to disinfect his old comrade from the contaminations
of Wall Street and thereby to render his name acceptable to
public opinion in the event of some more important public

office becoming available. Whatever hesitations Morrow may have felt in the matter were dispelled by the peremptory wording of the summons which, by the first post on Monday, he received from the White House:

September 12, 1925

My dear Mr. Morrow:

Enclosed is a copy of a communication which you may have seen in the press. I request that you serve in the capacity indicated and I would like you to meet me at the White House on Thursday, September 17th, at 11.00 o'clock in the forenoon, and lunch with me at 1.00 o'clock. . . .

Very truly yours,

Calvin Coolidge

On the receipt of this communication Dwight Morrow left Englewood for Washington, where he engaged a suite at the Wardman Park Hotel.

The Board nominated by the President consisted of nine persons. They were Major General James G. Harbord, retired, Rear Admiral Frank F. Fletcher, retired, Mr. Dwight W. Morrow, Mr. Howard E. Coffin, consulting engineer, Senator Hiram Bingham, Judge Arthur C. Denison, Mr. William F. Durand, President of the American Society of Mechanical Engineers, Congressman Carl Vinson, and Congressman James S. Parker. On the motion of Senator Bingham and General Harbord, Morrow was elected chairman. The Board sat for eight weeks, at first in public session in the Committee Room of the House of Representatives, and later in the privacy of Morrow's rooms. Ninety-nine witnesses were summoned, including the Secretaries of War, Commerce, the Navy, and the Postmaster General. A large number of officers on the active list were also invited to give evidence under a guarantee of immunity. A dramatic figure was Mr. Orville Wright, "the modest gentleman from Dayton." "We have asked you," said Morrow to this witness, "to appear before the Board since in a sense you are responsible for the whole problem. You and your brother taught men to fly." The quiet good sense of Mr. Wright's deposition formed, as Morrow intended, a significant antidote to the exuberance of Colonel Mitchell.

The first problem was how, without allowing the proceedings of the Board to degenerate into a public wrangle, to render clear to the public that the allegations of Colonel Mitchell were grossly exaggerated. By the patient questioning of expert witnesses Morrow was able to show that, in the present condition of aeronautics, America was not menaced by any overseas Power. The result of this line of investigation was to demonstrate, in the words of the final report, the improbability of any invasion "in any future which can be foreseen." The report continued: "To create a defense system based upon a hypothetical attack from Canada, Mexico, or any other of our near neighbors would be wholly unreasonable. For a century we have, under treaty, left the Great Lakes unguarded by a naval force; by mutual consent the long Canadian frontier is free from armament on either side. The result has justified such a course."

Having in this manner disposed of Colonel Mitchell's most sensational premise, Morrow proceeded with great skill to deal with the Colonel's minor grievances. The latter had evidently counted upon being able to dramatize the situation. He arrived on the witness stand carrying an enormous globe. This exhibit, as the long hours of his evidence dragged onwards, became an object of extreme physical embarrassment. He had counted, again, on interruptions, questions, arguments. There were no interruptions.

"Colonel Mitchell," Morrow began, "please give your statement in your own way." The Colonel talked all morning. That afternoon he continued his evidence. "Will you be good enough to proceed, Colonel Mitchell?" The suavity of the chairman was indefatigable. After one hour of the afternoon session even Colonel Mitchell's fluency showed signs of flagging. "Do you," he asked, "not think this is taking too much of your time, Mr. Chairman?" "Not at all, Colonel, go right ahead." During the next half hour it became evident that the Colonel was losing touch, not only with the press correspondents, not only with the great heart of the American people, but even with his own line of argument. He paused in desperation. "Are not you gentlemen of the Board getting tired of this sort of stuff?" "No, please continue, Colonel, we find it very interesting." For another hour Colonel Mitchell continued. He paused again. "How much further do you want me to go?" he bleated hoarsely. Morrow was all consideration. "Go right on, Colonel—we do not wish to put any undue strain on your endurance." Another hour passed, during which Colonel Mitchell became more and more exhausted. Finally he broke down. "I think," he said, "that I will take a little rest."

On the conclusion of their public sessions the Board then met in prolonged private discussions of the report. "I think," Morrow remarked when it was all over, "I never appreciated before that it is no easy task to get nine honest men into an agreement on a subject." The President had been promised the report by a certain Tuesday. On Saturday there seemed no prospect of unanimity. Assisted by Captain Lewis McBride, by J. A. M. de Sanchez and by his own private secretary, Arthur Springer, Morrow worked all through Sunday with the result that the points of difference were narrowed down to the Naval section. Work was resumed on Sunday night and continued until dawn glinted through the curtains. By 1.00 P.M. on Monday unanimity had been secured and the report was hurried off to the printers.

The Morrow report is fully characteristic of its main author. The admission is made in the preamble that the controversy between "the newer and the older arms" had been waged "with some bitterness." "The conflict," the report continues, "is one between the old and the new, emphasized by the sharp adjustments required in a period immediately following a great war. Such conflicts of thought have gone on from the beginning. They will go on until the end. It is in many ways desirable that they should go on. . . . What is needed is a more generous appreciation by each side of the difficulties of the other side. On each side there is need of patience with what seems the unreasonableness of the other side. The fundamental problem may not be settled. It may, however, be understood, if men will approach it with less feeling and more intelligence."

Having thus appealed for patience, Morrow proceeded to apply it to his recommendations. "We aimed," he said later,[3] "to put the problem in process of settlement, in process of a more careful and sustained study. This kind of problem can only be settled by what Secretary Root once called 'the true Anglo-Saxon method of improvement by experiment.'" He was thus opposed to any panic legislation, based upon the theory that the air will henceforward become the only area of military operations. "The next war," comments the report, "may well start in the air but in all probability will wind up, as the last war did, in the mud."

[3] Evidence before the Committee on Military Affairs, January 1926.

After thus warning the public to expect no dramatic proposals, the report makes certain recommendations for mitigating the competition and jealousy existing between the Army, the Navy, and the Air Service, and for achieving better coördination. Assistant Secretaries were to be appointed in the departments of War, Navy, and Commerce, and were to be detailed for aviation. A special aviation section of the General Staff was to be organized. Commercial aviation was to be kept distinct from the fighting services. Certain flying officers were to have temporary rank corresponding to other branches, the name of the Air Service was to be changed to Air Corps, and a flying decoration was to be created for rewards in times of peace or war. Recommendations were also made regarding the development of civil aviation and the carriage of air mails. The whole scheme was to be reviewed within five years' time.

The Morrow report was successful in stilling the uneasiness and agitation which Colonel Mitchell had aroused. It was widely applauded. General Pershing conveyed his congratulations. "That such a Board," he wrote, "could submit a unanimous report is to my mind quite remarkable." "I fear," wrote Morrow to Jean Monnet in December 1925, "that I am in danger of getting out of the class of which my son considers you one of the most conspicuous members —that small group which tries to get things done for which other people get the credit. In this case I have been somewhat praised and somewhat blamed for what a group of nine men did."

It was characteristic of Dwight Morrow that during these congested weeks at Washington he found time for other occupations. He had many talks with the French Debt Commission, with the Italian Debt Commission, and with unofficial representatives of Soviet Russia who had been allowed to enter the United States.

Two years more were to pass, however, before he was offered further public employment.

5

Dwight Morrow's handling of the Aircraft Inquiry had, as was intended, rendered his name familiar in circles wider than those of Wall Street or Washington. It was generally anticipated that he would shortly be offered Cabinet office. As early as November 1925 the *New Republic* had predicted that he was to be appointed Secretary of the Treasury in succession to Mr. Andrew Mellon:

"So far as anyone has suggested there exists but one possible reason why, if and when old Mr. Mellon gets out, young Mr. Morrow should not take his place, and that is a political reason. Not that Mr. Morrow's politics are not all right but because some of the little Massachusetts advisers in the unofficial Cabinet who help to make up the night life of the White House are apprehensive lest the appointment of a partner in the House of Morgan would have a bad political effect on Mr. Coolidge. An absurd idea! In this day and generation, with everybody intent on grabbing for money and everybody getting a little, a connection with the House of Morgan isn't a liability. It is now classed as an asset. As to hurting Mr. Coolidge politically if he put Mr. Morrow in as Secretary of the Treasury, nothing will hurt Mr. Coolidge politically until the people as a whole get a crack over their collective skull that starts their mental machinery moving again."

The astringency of this comment produced no effect upon Mr. Coolidge or his circle. Morrow was well aware that there was little prospect of his being given a Cabinet position and that his main chance of escaping from Wall Street lay in an appointment to some diplomatic post. Even then he did not aspire to one of the more eminent embassies such as Paris or London. "No," he would say when these capitals were suggested, "my relations with Coolidge are such that I cannot accept an honor from him. But I *can* accept a job." This renunciation narrowed down the alternatives to those diplomatic posts which Charles Fay would have described as "the lemons of the Foreign Service." His friends observed during those years that he would frequently be reading books about China, books on Mexico, and reports on Russia. His interest in the latter country dated from 1917 when Thomas D. Thacher had been a member of the American Red Cross Mission during the revolution. It was strengthened by his friendship for Alex Gumberg, who had come to New York as representative of the All-Russian Textile Syndicate. "I have felt," he wrote in May of 1927, "that sooner or later the time would come when something would have to be done for Russia." He was himself active in furthering unofficial relations between Soviet emissaries and the State Department, and he provided M. Litvinoff with a warm letter of recommendation to Sir Arthur Salter at Geneva. Nor was this all. When in Paris in the spring of 1927 he gave a dinner party at Foyot's to which he invited M. Rakovsky and other Soviet representatives. The Russians were unable to account for this sudden solicitude on the part of a member of the house of Morgan. They did not realize that Dwight Morrow had an insatiable appetite for the misunderstood.

Even by that date, however, it was becoming obvious that his diplomatic destination would be neither Moscow nor

Peking but Mexico City, and during that same visit to Paris he talked to Agustin Legorreta, a prominent Mexican banker, in such a manner as to convey the impression that he anticipated an offer of the Mexican Embassy. This offer did not materialize until June 1927 when, on his return from a journey in Spain, he stayed for two nights with President Coolidge at the temporary White House in Dupont Circle:

"The President," notes Mrs. Morrow in her diary for June 9, "talked to him about Mexico and practically offered that place to him—a hard job. I feel Dwight usually does the work and then someone else gets the credit."

Four weeks later the suggestion was renewed in more precise terms. On July 15th he received a letter written in the President's own hand:

> The White House
> Washington
> July 14, 1927

My dear Mr. Morrow:

Ambassador Sheffield says Mexico offers the greatest place for service to the country that he knows. He is entitled to 60 days' leave which I want him to have before his successor is appointed. It expires August 14.

I would prefer to trust you with this place above anyone else I know but I want you to consult your own wishes. You will be greatly serving the country wherever you are. I do not wish you to think of me personally at all but only of yourself, and make your decision without reference to whether I run again or not.

With best wishes to you and your family, I am,

> Cordially yours,
> Calvin Coolidge

The receipt of this letter faced Dwight Morrow with a perplexing decision. Mr. Morgan and the other partners begged him not to abandon them, arguing that Mexico was the grave of all diplomatic reputations. He himself, now that the moment had come, dreaded the loss of all his New York associations. True it was that there had been many occasions during the long years of his membership of J. P. Morgan & Co. when with his usual restless curiosity he had longed for some new range of experience, some fresh combination of problems and personalities. In this moment of retrospect he was able to assess at its true value the immense debt which he owed to his association with 23 Wall Street. It had from the start given him a position of authority and influence such as he could hardly have achieved as a corporation lawyer. It had brought him into contact, both in the United States and in Europe, with the finest minds of his age. It had familiarized him, not merely with the problems of international finance and currency, but with the wider issues of world politics. It had secured him complete financial independence. And it had forged for him some of the deepest and most durable friendships of his life.

For Mrs. Morrow the thought of exile was even more painful. She had by now, in New York and Englewood, created around the family that ideal circle of intimate friends which, in those distant days at Cold Spring Harbor, had seemed so difficult of attainment. Only a few months before, they had entrusted to their friend Chester Aldrich the task of building for them a house at Englewood and a summer home on North Haven Island. These plans would now have to be postponed. This Mexican mission would mean a thankless task for her husband, and for herself severance from all that she held most dear:

"The blow has fallen!" she noted on July 19. "President Coolidge wrote to Dwight today asking him to be Ambassador to Mexico and Dwight is going to do it! It is a hard job, and not much honor, and it comes late— 'No skates or sleds left in my bag!' says Santa Claus, 'but here's a silly little whistle!' Coolidge won't run again, but Dwight goes and does a hard job for him when there is no chance of reward. How characteristic!! It means giving up J. P. Morgan's and New York. It puts off the house. I wish I thought it was an adventure!"

On August 19th, Dwight Morrow visited President Coolidge at Rapid City:

"I had," he wrote to J. P. Morgan, "several hours with the President. He was very interesting and in some ways amusing. What in substance he said to me was that you were probably right that I could do more good where I was than in Mexico. He said, however, that that was not the whole story; that it was not the business of the Government to do good but to prevent harm, that when Governments tried to do good they generally got themselves and other people into trouble, that he felt that I should probably prevent a good deal of harm if I went to Mexico now. The upshot of it was that I told him he was the President and that if he thought I ought to go, I was willing to go.

"All the foregoing sounds rather formal. I cannot tell you how much of a wrench it will mean to me personally to leave you. It is just a little over thirteen years since I left the practice of the law and those thirteen years have been very happy years. The progress that the firm has made under your leadership during those years has been not only an advantage to the country— and the world—but a source of profit and happiness to all of your partners and employees. I want you to know, dear Jack, that I am not doing it without a very real sorrow at leaving, and a very great pride in having been associated with you during these years."

"I have," he wrote to his wife, "a curious feeling of the kind I had when I left Simpson, Thacher & Bartlett. I felt I would be sorry whichever I did. You felt that we would be happy whatever we did. And so it has turned out."

"The President," he continued, "wants me very much to go to Mexico—and I am going—that is to say I am going if you stick to your bargain and go with me. . . . As I talked to him I thought more and more that it was up to us to go and that I and probably you would regret it always if we didn't do it. . . . Anyway, dear heart, this appeals to me more than Yale or the Reparation job or International Law at Columbia—and to borrow a line from the 'Ballad of the White Horse' I must *choose* the risky things rather than the

'slow moons like silver rings,
And the ripening of the plums.'

". . . For your own information, I do not count it a sacrifice to give up either the income or the power, important as they both are. The sacrifice is to give up the intimate association with the friends.

"And for you, dear heart, you are a brick. Who knows? Maybe we will be trying to write the rest of our lives, you poetry and myself history."

This letter dispersed all doubts on the part of Mrs. Morrow. Her diary bears the following entry under August 26th:

"This afternoon such a beautiful letter from Dwight telling about his talk with the President. There is one golden sentence in it—one word of balm so perfect to my heart! 'This appeals to me more than Yale or the Reparation job or International Law at Columbia.' I would go after that—if I had to *crawl* to Mexico!"

Mrs. Morrow was exposed to no such necessity. They left New York from the Grand Central Station by private car.

As I talked to him I thought more and more that it was up to us to go and that I and probably you would regret it always if we didn't do it. By the way I stopped in Chicago and took dinner with Vice President and Mrs, Dawes. Dawes was very keen about my going. He doesn't agree with Tom. He says that it is always true that in political office it looks as though nothing can be accomplished; that when things look worst there is the best opportunity.

Anyway dear heart, This appeals to me more than Yale or the Reparation job or International law at Columbia — and to borrow a line from the Ballad of the White Horse I must choose the risky things rather than the "slow moons like silver rings, and the ripening of the plums"

FACSIMILE OF DWIGHT MORROW'S HANDWRITING

They stood together on the observation platform as the train slid out. The faces of their friends blurred into a rapidly diminishing perspective. And in the memory of those who stayed behind there lingered the picture of Dwight Morrow waving—small, hatless, triumphant. Behind his glasses his eyes flashed their deepest blue. One at least of that large crowd recalls to this day the expression of those eyes. "It was," she records, "an expression of creative benignity."

They reached Mexico City on the morning of October 23rd.

XV. Mexico: The First Approach 1927

IMPORTANCE OF MORROW'S MEXICAN MISSION. NOT ONLY DID HE CREATE A UNIVERSAL PRECEDENT, BUT HE BROUGHT CURRENT THEORIES INTO LINE WITH EXISTING REALITIES. EXAMINATION OF THOSE THEORIES. THE MONROE DOCTRINE AND ITS SUCCESSIVE INTERPRETATIONS. SIMILARITY AND DIFFERENCE BETWEEN MORROW'S CONCEPTION AND WOODROW WILSON'S CONCEPTION OF UNITED STATES POLICY TOWARDS LATIN AMERICA. MEXICAN DISTRUST OF THE UNITED STATES. NATURE OF THE MEXICAN REVOLUTION. THE FORBEARANCE OF THE STATE DEPARTMENT. AMBASSADOR SHEFFIELD. CONDITION OF UNITED STATES' RELATIONS WITH MEXICO AT THE TIME OF MORROW'S ARRIVAL. HIS EARLY STEPS TO WIN MEXICAN SYMPATHIES. THE LINDBERGH FLIGHT. HIS APPROACH TO PRESIDENT CALLES. HIS EARLY INTERVIEWS. THE EXECUTION OF FATHER PRO JUAREZ AND ITS BEARING ON MORROW'S RELATIONS WITH CALLES.

DWIGHT MORROW'S mission to Mexico is often cited by students of international affairs as one of the most instructive episodes in modern diplomatic history.[1] This opinion, if it is to remain anything more than an opinion, must be examined.

His practical achievement in Mexico was not either comprehensive, durable, or complete. The compromise which he contrived between the rights of American capital and the aspirations of Mexican nationalism was neither deep nor lasting. His negotiation of an armistice between Church and State led to no permanent settlement of that unhappy controversy. And he failed to induce the Mexican Government to establish their finances upon a far-seeing program rather than upon contracts of immediate expediency. Why, there-

[1] See particularly Lionel Curtis, "The Capital Question in China," pp. 255-275, and Professor Arnold Toynbee, "A Survey of International Affairs," 1930, pp. 384 ff.

fore, should his mission be regarded as of such historic importance?

It must be realized in the first place that Mexico represented, in that autumn of 1927, a test case for the future policy of the United States towards the whole of Latin America. Morrow's Mexican mission was bound to create a precedent affecting the policy of the Department of State towards the whole southern continent. Nor was this all. Owing to the Monroe Doctrine, the European Powers would also tend to conform their attitude to that of Washington. They also, sooner or later, would follow the Morrow precedent. This precedent, by analogy, would moreover affect the policy of the Great Powers in dealing with other backward but suddenly nationalistic countries. Great Britain, for instance, would in the end find it difficult to adopt in Persia or China a policy essentially different from that to which, in Mexico, she had been committed by the Morrow precedent. It was for this reason that his mission to Mexico City was watched with anxious interest by all the world.

He arrived at a moment when the conflict between imperialism (whether of the territorial or economic variety) and nationalism (whether socialist or militaristic) had reached a bewildered stage. In dealing with the revolt of the backward nations, the capitalist Powers had drifted into a mood of sulky defeatism. On the one hand they were unwilling to defend their vested interests by force; on the other hand they had not arrived at the point where they were prepared to cut their losses, to call a new deal, and to establish with the countries which they had previously disciplined, relations of coöperative confidence. Morrow's handling of the Mexican problem constituted an outstanding experiment in such coöperation. It was not, from the material point of view, a completely successful experiment; yet as a demonstration of a new theory of intercourse between the strong and the weak it was of immense importance.

Morrow started from the axiom that force, or authority, should no longer be regarded as the only policy; he showed that by conciliation something, at least, might be saved from the wreck. Nor was this all. Most Governments had realized by then that a policy of force would not command the ultimate approval of their electorates; they hesitated to reject that policy mainly owing to those ingrained habits of national credit which are called "prestige." Morrow, by inventing and applying the theory of "moral guardianship" exercised by the strong over the weak, provided a spiritual antidote to loss of prestige. He saved the imperialistic face. And since it was the face of his own government that he most demonstrably rescued, his theory can most conveniently be examined in terms of the relations between Mexico and the United States.

It is beyond the range of this biography to enter into any detailed analysis of United States policy towards Latin America in general or Mexico in particular; nor is it intended to diverge into an examination of modern Mexican history.[2] Yet if the reader is to obtain any satisfactory conception of what Morrow actually did in Mexico, it will be essential to describe some of the conflicting ideas and interests which by the year 1927 had rendered the situation one of irritated purposelessness and confused misunderstanding.

[2] The most comprehensive study of modern Mexico is Ernest Gruening's "Mexico and Its Heritage." For the diplomatic relations between the United States and Mexico consult Mr. Frederick S. Dunn's excellent monograph on "Diplomatic Protection of Americans in Mexico," Mr. Charles Wilson Hackett's "The Mexican Revolution and the United States" (World Peace Foundation pamphlets, Vol. IX, No. 5), and Professor James F. Rippy's "The United States and Mexico."

The account which follows describes, in its essence, the impact of a precise but visionary mind upon a situation in which fact and theory had become inextricably entangled. Morrow was able to bring current theories, which were outdated and contradictory, into line with existing realities; and to raise facts to a level where they could be examined in the light, not of national prestige, but of human philosophy. Before we pass to the facts it may be well to consider the theories.

The Monroe Doctrine, as first propounded more than a century ago, was a purely unilateral ordinance; the United States by implication renounced all desire to intervene in Europe provided that Europe renounced all desire to intervene in the Western Hemisphere. By the end of the nineteenth century the Monroe Doctrine had, however, assumed a more objective, and indeed imperialist, form. It had all but become a "power doctrine" justifying itself by such phrases as "manifest destiny" and "security in the Caribbean." During the same period American capitalists had invested huge sums in developing the resources of Latin America. It thus came about that the United States Government had, often insensibly and sometimes unwillingly, drifted into a position of constant interference with the internal affairs of the Caribbean Republics.

This state of things was obnoxious to the conscience of the United States people, the great majority of whom are hostile to all forms of political bullying or capitalist exploitation. The United States Government found themselves, therefore, in a false position. On the one hand they could scarcely refuse to afford protection to American lives and property in cases where these were being flagrantly endangered; on the other hand, such protection entailed intervention and with it the hostility of Latin America and the disapproval of their own electorate. It was Dwight Morrow who led the way out of this blind alley.

President Wilson, it is true, had already refused to allow the Monroe Doctrine to be exploited for purposes either of "manifest destiny" or "dollar diplomacy." Yet although Woodrow Wilson strongly disapproved of intervention for any imperialist or economic purpose, he himself practiced it in support of his own didactic theories and in defense of those "rights" which he regarded as accruing under International Law to United States citizens owning property in Latin America. The Wilsonian system sanctioned, and even sanctified, the use of power for the purposes of "teaching Latin America to elect good men"; as such it perpetuated a dangerous precedent and did little to place relations with Latin America upon a basis acceptable, either to the Latin Americans, or to the great mass of the United States people.

The significance of Morrow's contribution was that he propounded as permanent axioms what Wilson had intermittently advanced as ideas. He was thus the first responsible American to proclaim with complete clarity that forcible intervention, however noble its purpose, was in fact a "power doctrine" and as such in conflict with the conscience of the United States; he was the first to make it clear that the hazy tenets of International Law, while furnishing an admirable basis for controversy, offered no sure ground for settlement; he was the first unwaveringly to support Elihu Root's contention that private debts in foreign countries ought not to be collected by governmental coercion; he was the first to argue that coöperation between the United States and Latin America, however uncertain and disappointing it might momentarily appear, would in the end prove the only practicable policy; and he was the first to demonstrate how much could be achieved by sympathy and confidence as the only possible alternatives either to legal controversy or to menaces and marines.

The criticism made against Morrow (mainly by American and British business men long resident in Mexico) is that he approached the problem from a purely sentimental or idealistic angle and forced himself to see in the Mexicans qualities which they did not, in reality, possess. Such a criticism is a slur upon Morrow's intelligence and sincerity. He was perfectly aware that the virtues and defects of the Mexican character were different from the virtues and defects of the Anglo-Saxon character. Yet he did not attribute these differences to any superiority of civilization; he regarded them merely as symptoms of diverging patterns of culture. He was well aware that if he paused to consider the weaknesses of the Mexicans he would blur his own judgment and achieve nothing: it was only by appealing to all that was best in the Mexican character that he could hope to create any durable improvement. The affection and respect which he felt for the Mexicans was both deliberate and sincere; it was this very sincerity of conviction which enabled him to win the confidence of the Mexicans themselves and to leave behind him a name which, among the Mexican people, will never be forgotten. The Mexicans are far too shrewd a people to have been gulled by any insincerity of approach; it was because they felt there was no affectation in Morrow's attitude that they welcomed it so warmly as something which restored to them their battered self-respect. "I know," Morrow had said before leaving Englewood, "what I can do for the Mexicans. I can *like* them." He was thinking in terms of ultimate rather than of immediate realities; and even his severest critics were silenced by his success.

With this introduction it is possible to pass from an examination of theory to an examination of how far that theory was affected by, and applicable to, the facts.

2

The suspicion with which the United States was, in that year 1927, regarded in Mexico was due to causes, some of which were recent and some of which remote. There was in the first place the indelible memory of the annexation of Texas in 1844, of the war of 1846-1848 (described by General Grant as "one of the most unjust ever waged by a stronger against a weaker nation"), and of the ensuing treaty of Guadalupe Hidalgo, as a result of which the United States took from Mexico more than half her territory, namely, approximately 619,000 square miles represented today by Texas, New Mexico, Arizona, and California. There was in the second place the memory of successive humiliations imposed upon the national dignity of Mexico by a series of United States Ministers, from Joel Poinsett to Henry Lane Wilson, some of whom were merely bewildered and some of whom were "cantankerous and incompetent rascals" of the type of Anthony Butler.[3] There was in the third place the thirty-two years of Díaz dictatorship and the era of economic exploitation from 1884 to 1910.[4] There was the fear lest the

[3] Justin Harvey Smith, "The Annexation of Texas," Vol. I, pp. 62-63.

[4] The Díaz period is here envisaged from the point of view of the Mexican revolutionaries of 1910 who were apt to identify American capitalism with what they regarded as a period of oppression, and who took no account of the immense services rendered to the country both by Díaz and his Finance Minister, José Limantour.

United States might decide to construct an "Isthmian Route" or canal across Tehuantepec. And there were the feelings of wounded pride which had been inflamed by the policy adopted at Washington towards the Mexican revolution, culminating in the bombardment and occupation of Vera Cruz and in the Pershing expedition of 1916.[5]

So much for the remoter causes of misunderstanding; the more immediate causes arose from the nature of the Mexican Revolution of 1910 and from the anti-foreign and anti-capitalist program established by the Constitution of 1917. These two factors must be examined in greater detail.

The Revolution initiated by Francisco Madero in 1910 was in its inception a rising against the political dictatorship of Porfirio Díaz and had as its slogans, "Effective suffrage: no reëlection." So soon, however, as the dictator had left Mexico the revolution lost its political aspect and became nationalist,

[5] The guiding dates in Mexican history are as follows:

1519–1521	Cortés conquers Mexico.
1821	Mexico achieves her independence.
1844	Annexation of Texas.
1846–48	War with the United States.
1848	Treaty of Guadalupe Hidalgo.
1853–61	Civil War. Juárez and Santa Anna.
1861–63	French intervention.
1864	Maximilian Emperor.
1867	Maximilian executed. Juárez President.
1877–80 1884–1911	Díaz President.
1910–11	Revolution. Madero President.
1913	Madero shot. Huerta President. U. S. A. withhold recognition.
1914	Carranza President.
1915–16	Villa and the Pershing Expedition.
1915	Carranza recognized by U. S. A.
1917	Constituent Assembly draws up the Constitution.
1920	Carranza assassinated. Obregón President (December 1).
1923	U. S. A. recognize Obregón.
1924	Calles President (December 1).
1927	Dwight Morrow arrives.
1928	Obregón assassinated.

social, and agrarian. Madero, with his nineteenth century liberalism, was almost immediately outdistanced, and thereafter the revolution became not a struggle for liberalism, but class warfare against the foreigner, the landowner, and the capitalist.

The agrarian problem was, at the outset, the most prominent. Porfirio Díaz, with the ostensible purpose of creating a peasant proprietor class and with a less reputable desire to buy off his political rivals, had in 1890 decreed the expropriation of the village communes or *ejidos*. This decree was enforced with the utmost brutality with the result that some 134,547,885 acres of communal land, the property of an Indian or semi-Indian population of 14,000,000, passed into the hands of the Spanish land-owning class or *hacendados*.[6] These people numbered only 834 and their individual estates comprised, in some cases, *latifundia* containing as many as 6,000,000 acres. The Indians, deprived of their village lands, degenerated into the status of serfs tied to the several *haciendas;* according to the census of 1910 there were some 3,103,402 of such *peones de campo* held in debt service.

It was inevitable that the passions of such people, once they had been released, would not remain satisfied with purely political formulas. Carranza in the north and Zapata in the south headed revolts against Madero for the purpose of obtaining the immediate restoration of the *ejidos*. Their attainment of this object was delayed by a conservative counterrevolution under Victoriano Huerta in February 1913, and on the latter's overthrow in 1914 was still further

---

[6] The 1910 statistics give the following population figures:

  Indians, 6,000,000, i.e., 39%.
  Mestizos or half castes, 8,000,000, i.e., 53%.
  Whites, 1,150,000, i.e., 7.5%.

The figures for the Whites are much exaggerated.

postponed by the civil war which thereafter broke out between Carranza, Villa, and Zapata. Between September 1914 and February 1915, Mexico City changed hands no fewer than six times. It was in order to enlist popular support against his rivals that on January 6, 1915, Carranza issued his famous agrarian decree. Under this decree not only those villages which had been robbed of their *ejidos* were to be accorded full restitution, but even those villages which had never possessed *ejidos* were to be "donated" with lands expropriated from adjoining properties. The execution of this decree was entrusted to local Agrarian Commissions with the result that an authorized *jacquerie* spread throughout the Mexican states.

On October 19, 1915, Carranza was officially recognized by the United States and thereafter set about embodying the results of the Revolution in legislative form. A Constitution was submitted to a Constituent Assembly which met at Querétaro in February 1917 and was promulgated in the following May. It contained 136 articles of an advanced nationalistic character, of which the most important, from the point of view of this narrative, was Article 27. This article provided for the nationalization not only of all land, but also of all subsoil deposits, including minerals and oil. It also placed restrictions upon the acquisition of property by foreigners, and vested in the nation the possessions of "the religious institutions known as churches." It was around this article that the ensuing controversy between Mexico and the United States circled between 1917 and 1927.

It will be observed that the Mexican Revolution of 1910 followed the classic curve of all such outbreaks when they take place in communities where no strong middle class exists as a buffer between rich and poor. Beginning as an

intellectual movement for political liberty, it rapidly overflowed into a struggle for land. The rivalries between the
several leaders led them to outbid each other in promises to
the proletariat, with the result that the revolution swung
further and further to the left until it came to embrace a
complete nationalist and Marxist program of the confiscatory type. By 1926 the revolution had already passed
through its first phase of violent oscillation and, under the
strong control of Plutarco Calles, was steadying down to the
second phase of consolidation. It has sometimes been contended that it was Dwight Morrow who transformed Calles
from a revolutionary into a statesman. Such a contention is
untrue. What happened was that Morrow arrived at the
precise stage in Calles' own evolution when the latter was
most receptive of experience, encouragement, and advice.
Had Morrow arrived a year earlier or three years later, his
Mexican mission would not have been the dramatic triumph
that it became.

3

It would occupy too large a space to examine in detail the
successive phases of indignation and forbearance through
which the United States Government passed during those
bewildering years. The outrages upon the lives and property
of American citizens were flagrant and frequent, and the
pressure brought to bear upon the successive administrations
of Presidents Wilson, Harding, and Coolidge to intervene for
the purpose of "cleaning up Mexico" was, if not very authoritative, occasionally acute. That the State Department were
able to resist this pressure speaks highly for their integrity
of purpose, the underlying motive of which was expressed,

THE GENTLE STATE DEPARTMENT

with his accustomed purity of style, by President Wilson in
an article which he contributed to the *Ladies' Home Journal*
in October 1916:

"The United States can establish permanent peace on her
borders only by a resolute and consistent adoption in action of
the principles which underlie her own life. . . . I can say with
knowledge that most of the suggestions of action come from
those who wish to possess Mexico, who wish to use her, who
regard her people with condescension and a touch of contempt,
who believe that they are fit only to serve and not fit for liberty
of any sort. Such men cannot and will not determine the policy
of the United States. They are not of the true American breed
or motive."

The leaders of the Mexican Revolution were not in the
least grateful to the United States people or to President Wilson and his successors for this magnificent forbearance. They
interpreted it (and correctly) as a proof that the United
States would not, in the last resort, declare war upon Mexico
for the purpose of protecting American capitalists against
the confiscatory policy of the 1917 Constitution. Having dismissed this danger from their minds, they proceeded to regard all attempts of the United States Government to protect
the lives and properties of their citizens as symptoms
of bourgeois fanaticism and as outrages upon Mexican
sovereignty and self-respect. The patient endeavors of the
State Department to achieve by negotiation what they were
too high-minded to obtain by force were not successful; the
endless written protests addressed to the Mexican Government by the United States Embassy, and the occasional out-
bursts of justifiable fury which appeared in the American
press, induced in the Mexican Government a mood of sly

and sulky obstinacy. This mood culminated during the residence in Mexico City of Mr. James R. Sheffield, Morrow's immediate predecessor as Ambassador of the United States.

Attempts have frequently been made to represent the Sheffield and the Morrow systems as completely antithetical, picturing the former as all clouds and thunder and the latter as all sweetness and light. Such a dramatization of differences is neither accurate nor fair. Ambassador Sheffield was a gentleman of integrity and good sense. His endeavor was to interpret in diplomatic, or rather in judicial, terms the instructions of the State Department and the pronouncements of the President and the Secretary of State. These pronouncements had not always been helpful or even wise. President Coolidge had proclaimed that he proposed to protect "American lives and American rights" in accordance with the requirements of International Law.[7] Speaking in New York on April 25, 1927, he had advanced the theory that the "persons and property of a citizen are a part of the domain of the Nation even when abroad" and had proceeded to argue that in allowing foreign citizens to cross its border a country had issued to those visitors a "tacit invitation" and was thereby bound to extend to them the safeguards generally recognized by the law of nations as incumbent on a sovereign Power. Charles Evans Hughes went even further and contended that when a foreign government was unable to perform the "functions of sovereignty and independence" a neighboring country was justified by law in resorting to intervention or, as Mr. Hughes phrased it, "interposition of a temporary character." Secretary Kellogg announced that no United States citizen could, even if he wished, renounce

[7] Speech to the National Republican Club, February 12, 1924.

his right to receive protection from his own Government or absolve that Government from the duty of according such protection. The Secretary of State had been unable, moreover, to refrain from indulging in a regrettable and ignorant outburst against the Mexican Government for its "Bolshevik" tendencies:

"The Bolshevist leaders," he informed the Foreign Relations Committee of the Senate in January 1927, "have had very definite ideas with respect to the rôle which Mexico and Latin America are to play in their program of world revolution. They have set up as one of their fundamental tasks the destruction of what they term American imperialism as a necessary prerequisite to the successful development of the international revolutionary movement in the New World. Thus Latin America and Mexico are conceived as a base for activity against the United States."

The spectre of "a Mexican-fostered Bolshevik hegemony intervening between the United States and the Panama Canal" so foolishly drawn by Mr. Kellogg alarmed the Senate and outraged Mexican opinion. The situation was further embittered by the overt encouragement given by Mexico to those elements in Nicaragua who were resisting American intervention. Renewed rumors of war became current in Mexico City and at Washington; and the notes addressed to the Mexican Foreign Office by Ambassador Sheffield were either returned or answered in a provocative manner. It would not be accurate to say that relations had become strained to the point of rupture; American opinion was anxious not to go to war; all that the State Department desired was to be able to prove that their tolerance was justified in practice as well as in theory. Ambassador Sheffield, patiently, good-humoredly, but wholly unsuccessfully, was endeavoring to provide them with this justification.

It was at this stage that an unfortunate incident occurred. In March of 1927 it became known that the Mexican Government had in their possession copies of certain compromising documents found in the office of the United States Military Attaché. Whatever may have been the truth regarding these documents, it is evident that their authenticity was credited by Calles himself. In his message to the Mexican Congress of September 1, 1927, six weeks before Dwight Morrow's arrival, he vented his spleen in words of direct defiance:

"To speak plainly, our relations with the United States . . . have unfortunately assumed an indeterminate character, which frequently has manifested itself in disagreement and even culminated in controversy. Acts have taken place which are regarded by the Mexican Government as deplorable. . . . I am confident that at the proper time a spirit of good will and a cordial comprehension of our problems will soften the acerbities of this controversy which is still latent."

Such language is unusual on the part of the head of one foreign state in reference to another. True it was that the relations between the United States Embassy and the Mexican Government had come to a deadlock. Ambassador Sheffield had pushed Mr. Kellogg's juridical arguments to a point where they could go no further; a new deal was entailed. Yet had not Mr. Sheffield been so conscientious and so persistent the necessity of a new deal would not have impressed itself, as it certainly did impress itself, upon President Calles. It is thus no exaggeration to say that Ambassador Sheffield, at the cost of great unpleasantness to himself, had prepared the soil. Such an acknowledgment does not in any degree detract from the brilliance with which Dwight Morrow thereafter sowed and reaped.

4

The appointment of a Morgan partner as successor to Ambassador Sheffield was not welcome to Mexican opinion. "After Morrow," wrote one paper, "come the Marines." President Calles himself suspected that the selection of a prominent banker implied some new campaign for the collection of Mexican debts. Nor did any of them understand how a partner of the house of Morgan could exchange the princely revenues of such a function for the exile and intricacies of a Mexican mission.

It was not long before these anxieties were allayed. President Machado of Cuba wrote a personal letter to Calles assuring him that Dwight Morrow was the most sympathetic Anglo-Saxon that had ever lived. Agustin Legorreta, from New York, urged his compatriots to welcome Morrow with open arms. And once his appointment was announced, Morrow himself handled his own publicity with accustomed skill. In interview after interview he proclaimed that he was not going to Mexico as a debt collector but as a sympathetic friend; he would be careful, he said, to respect the dignity of the Mexican nation; he would behave with no less regard for local sovereignty and for diplomatic conventions than that manifested by the British Ambassador in Washington. In this manner a favorable atmosphere was created even before he arrived in Mexico City.

From the first moment of his arrival it became obvious

even to the most nationalistic Mexican that Morrow had
come to placate, to appreciate, and to please. His insatiable
friendliness, his utter simplicity, the very exuberance of his
good will, held them enthralled. He applauded their food,
their climate, their agriculture, their hats, their ancient
monuments, the bamboo cages in which they kept their tame
parrots, their peasant industries, their patriotism, their volcanoes, even their finances. Here at last was a North American who neither patronized nor sneered. His boyish enjoyment of his task was infectious. In the sunshine of his zest,
under the warm breezes of that creative credulity, even the
most morose suspicions melted. There was something about
Morrow's personality and appearance which, at the very first
contact, allayed all feelings of inferiority and elicited both
from the sophisticated and the simple a slow smile of almost
parental affection. He would buy pots in some village market
place, shaking hands delightedly with the Indian by whom
they had been made; yet the very intensity with which he
would examine those same pots gave to his gesture an intention more serious than any demagogic courtesy. His small
size, his untidy clothes, the utter collapse of hat and trousers,
the curious contrast between the slow deliberation of his
walking stick and the upturned scuffle of his little shoes, the
general zest and bustle which he created around him, the
gentle wistfulness of those deep blue eyes, his utter absence
of self-consciousness, aroused delighted feelings such as are
evoked by the spectacle of a happy and bright-mannered
child. Upon the fascinated receptiveness thus induced the
effect of his high qualities of intelligence and character was
overpowering. It was the almost physical affection aroused
by his appearance that enabled people to admire his genius
with wholly unresentful awe. Morrow captured the imagina-

MORROW IN MEXICO

tion, the sympathy, and the complete confidence of the Mexican people within a week.

He was too shrewd a man not to realize that this favorable impression must be confirmed and perpetuated by some dramatic gesture. In the previous June, when staying at the temporary White House in Dupont Circle, Washington, he had made the acquaintance of Charles A. Lindbergh, who had just returned from his trip to Paris. Before leaving the United States, Morrow had suggested to this famous aviator that a flight to Mexico City would be both interesting and useful. The nature of Colonel Lindbergh's response to this invitation is best conveyed in his own words:

"After returning from Europe and completing a flying tour of the United States with the *Spirit of St. Louis* I wanted to make another long distance non-stop flight before retiring the plane from use and placing it in the museum. The plane and engine were practically new and in a number of ways the *Spirit of St. Louis* was better equipped than any other plane for long flights. I was particularly interested in the future possibilities of long distance flying and wanted to make a flight under different conditions than I encountered on the New York-Paris trip. The flight to Mexico was made during the long December nights, under conditions of storm and fog during nearly the entire night, and over country varying from high mountains to low coast line. I wanted to experiment with these conditions and if possible to demonstrate that flying could be made practical under them.

"In addition to the technical side I loved any opportunity to fly, particularly in the *Spirit of St. Louis,* and I was fascinated with the idea of going to Mexico City when Mr. Morrow made the suggestion."

Morrow's own intention had been that Colonel Lindbergh should reach the Mexican capital by easy, although very triumphant, stages. He had never expected a non-stop flight or desired to risk a single feather of the lone eagle for the sake of a little propaganda. Colonel Lindbergh, however, persisted in his intention. "You get me the invitation," he said to Morrow, "and I'll take care of the flying."

Colonel Lindbergh took off from Bolling Field at 12.26 P.M. on December 13th. He records his experiences as follows:

"After crossing the mountains into the valley of Mexico I could not locate my position. There were numerous railroads below but I could not find corresponding ones marked on my maps. I tried unsuccessfully to read the names of railroad stations. I climbed then to high altitude and obtained my approximate position from the direction of watersheds. Later I flew over a city and after coming down to low altitude could read the words 'Hotel Toluca' on the side of a building. I found Toluca on my map to be only a short distance from Mexico City."

The rest of the trip, from his point of view, was plain sailing. But for Dwight Morrow and President Calles, who had been waiting at Valbuena Field since 8.30 A.M., the suspense was trying in the extreme. The excitement of that moment is best conveyed by quoting from Mrs. Morrow's diary:

December 14, 1927. Lindbergh is here, sleeping at the Embassy. It has been a thrilling day. We left at 8.30 for the field, riding out with motor cycle escort. There was an enormous crowd on the field already when we arrived; many had been up all night. I sat in the grandstand next to the President, Dwight on the other side. He was very pleasant but evidently terribly nervous about Lindbergh. We waited and waited and waited! Many false reports on hand and the only report was that he had passed Tampico at 8.50. It got fearfully hot; everybody was nervous; many had had no breakfast. Mrs. Weddell served sandwiches and lemonade from a picnic basket. Finally we heard that Lindbergh was at Toluca and five planes flew off to meet him there. He sailed over our heads a few minutes before three—landed at exactly sixteen minutes of three. It was perfectly thrilling when the plane came to earth. Dwight and Capt. Winslow went over to the plane and brought him back to the grandstand in our open car. Dwight brought him to the President who welcomed him and gave him the keys of the city. Lindbergh only said "thank you" very simply. The throng on the field shouting and screaming with joy was indescribable. As we went to the car our clothes were almost torn off. Dwight, Constance, Lindbergh, General Alvarez, and I were in the car, Burke driving. Ceto and two officers on the running board. Oh! The crowds in the streets on the way to the Embassy!—On trees, on telegraph poles, tops of cars, roofs, even the towers of the Cathedral. Flowers and confetti were flung every moment. We took him to the Chancery and to the balcony to wave to the crowd. He had soup and a bath while the Staff had a buffet lunch. We all drank to him in champagne. Then he came out and met all the Staff, telegraphed to his mother, and saw the reporters. We left him sleeping tonight as we went to the University Club dinner for Will Rogers.

During the next week Mexico City abandoned itself to the cult of Colonel Lindbergh. Ambassador Sheffield, the oil magnates, Porfirio Díaz, even the Treaty of Guadalupe Hidalgo, were forgotten. Having by this dramatic gesture reversed the current of popular feeling, Dwight Morrow settled down to the more serious aspects of his task. He concentrated on winning the confidence and support of President Calles. "I must," he said to his wife, "get the Presidents behind me at each end." On the support of President Coolidge he could already rely. "My only instructions," the latter had said on parting, "are to keep us out of war with Mexico." The problem of President Calles was more intricate and uncertain. Morrow seized upon this problem with delighted zest.

5

General Plutarco Elias Calles was then some fifty years of age, having been born at Guaymas on September 25, 1877. His father belonged to a family which had long been established in the State of Sonora. His mother was of Indian blood. No confirmation can be traced in any official record of that Syrian or Armenian strain which legend has added to his origin and which has earned him the local nickname of *el turco de Guaymas*. It may be a faint physical resemblance to Mustapha Kemal which has caused this legend to originate and to persist.

After a short period as school teacher, farmer, journalist, and saloon keeper, Plutarco Calles obtained a post in the frontier police at Agua Pinta. The Madero revolution gave him his first opportunity and he emerged from the early battles with the rank of general. He subsequently sided with Carranza against Huerta and upon the latter's downfall was appointed Governor of the State of Sonora. He thereafter served as Minister of War, Gobernación and Labor in successive Cabinets, and contracted with General Obregón an alliance which amounted to a duumvirate. In December 1924 he was elected President on a four-year term. Within twelve months he had reformed the whole administration. He discouraged graft and enforced economies. He created schools and an agricultural bank. He was able to pay off fifty million pesos of internal debt and to found a National Bank with a paid-in reserve of sixty million pesos. He was hailed, and is still hailed, as the most forceful statesman whom Mexico has produced since Díaz.

In 1926, however, the triumphs of Calles' first year of office had been dimmed by complications. In trying to enforce the 1917 Constitution on every front at once, he had aroused the simultaneous opposition of the landowners, the Catholics, and the United States. By the end of 1927 he was thus in a mood of retrenchment. It was at this fortunate moment that Dwight Morrow arrived.

The latter had of course realized that his only hope of achieving anything in Mexico was to win the confidence and support of Mexico's President. He was aided in this purpose by the whole-heartedness with which he was able to approach people who were different from himself. He had always been insensitive to the more subtle differences of human character, a defect which his more fastidious friends were apt to resent as a want of social taste. In political and diplomatic life this lack of excessive discrimination is a useful asset. A man more preoccupied than he was with the intricacies of human character might have been distracted in approaching Calles by a consciousness of many cultural differences; Morrow pierced through these differences to the points of essential similarity; he at once recognized in Calles a man of character and intelligence; he confronted the President with the same cheerful confidence with which he would have confronted Mr. Stephen Birch. The simplicity of this approach put President Calles at his ease. To that solemn, sensitive, suspicious man Morrow's almost complete lack of psychological inquisitiveness came as a relief. Here, at last, was an American who trusted him and whom he could therefore trust. Here obviously was a man of the highest integrity and the most brilliant mind who was from the outset willing to treat him as something similar to himself. The actual loneliness of the President was solaced by such an apparition. The confidence which Morrow inspired in that hard, heavy, handsome man was immediate, almost emotional, and complete.

Their first meeting took place on October 29th, when Morrow presented his letters of credence. The address which the new Ambassador delivered departed from the formal phraseology customary on such occasions. "We shall not fail," he said, "to adjust outstanding questions with that dignity and mutual respect which should mark the international relationship of two sovereign and independent States." This statement was much applauded.

On November 2nd Morrow was invited to breakfast with President Calles at the latter's ranch at Santa Barbara, twenty miles east of Mexico City. A trivial incident ministered to the success of this crucial interview. Calles sent a message to the Ambassador asking him to come to the interview unaccompanied by any member of his Staff. Morrow replied that he would be very ready to entrust himself to the President's own interpreter. The latter was Mr. James Smithers, a close friend of Calles, who during the Sheffield régime had not been welcomed at the Embassy. It was obvious that the new Ambassador had no intention of standing on his dignity.

This first private interview proved a complete success. So far from raising such awkward questions as oil, properties, or debts, Morrow displayed an intense interest in, and knowledge of, President Calles' own irrigation schemes. The invitation was renewed for the following week and a second interview took place on November 8th. On this occasion Morrow did in fact discuss oil; but he again displayed so charming a taste for irrigation that Calles invited him to accompany him on a six-day tour of inspection in northern Mexico. They visited the Calles dam in Aguascalientes and the Don Martin dam at Monterrey. Will Rogers was also a guest upon the train and kept the party in constant good humor. Again the new Ambassador refrained from profiting by such propinquity to push American claims. Yet when he returned from the journey the oil question, as will be seen later, was all but settled; and his intimacy with President Calles had been proclaimed to the world.

His impressions of this journey were conveyed in a private letter to Robert E. Olds, Under Secretary at the Department of State:

"On the trip with President Calles I did not seek an opportunity to take up pending questions with him. I rather sought to get fully his point of view. He seemed very desirous that I should see one of the agricultural schools, some of the irrigation works, and one of the land banks. . . .

"The President talked to me a great deal on the trip about the land reforms, and explained how essential a part of the revolutionary program the reform of the land laws had been. I asked him a good many questions, and was struck with his deep interest in the land problem and his firm belief in the efficacy of curing a great evil by governmental interposition of the type that he has under way. One could well understand the divergent stories that come out of Mexico. If an educator comes down here and sees one of these schools, or banks, or irrigation projects, he may easily believe that the whole nation has been transformed. If he went to a ruined hacienda and saw peons out of work, and in deep distress, he could easily believe that the revolution had brought nothing but havoc in its train. As a matter of fact, the truth lies somewhere between. This revolution, like all revolutions, has been frightfully costly. It has started some new things which ultimately may be of great value to the people. These new things are experimental institutions. Some of them may grow into permanent institutions. . . ."

From these dramatic gestures of friendship the American newspapers evolved a moving story. The President and Dwight Morrow returned, locked in a fond embrace, on the very day that the invitation was publicly extended to Colonel Lindbergh. Mexico, from that moment, became front page news. In the interval before Lindbergh's arrival the correspondents stoked the fire of anticipation by stories of this sudden and beautiful friendship between the President and the new Ambassador. Under such streamlines as "Ham and Eggs Diplomacy," the Presidential breakfast party had been broadcast throughout the United States.[8] And when, a few weeks later, the oil controversy was amicably allayed, even serious observers felt that Morrow had won the confidence of Calles with almost miraculous ease. Yet to a certain extent the dramatization of this friendship was a piece of deliberate policy on the part of Plutarco Calles. The publicity which it received became a cause of great embarrassment to Dwight Morrow.

It has already been indicated that Calles had been led by the juristic persistence of Ambassador Sheffield into what he now realized was a blind alley. He welcomed the departure of Mr. Sheffield as furnishing a chance of escaping from this deadlock without loss of face. Yet his motives in inviting Morrow upon that railroad journey to the north were not exclusively due to a desire for the appeasement of tension with the United States. He also wished, during that par-

[8] These captions were inaccurate. Calles' breakfast food is pop corn lightly powdered with chocolate.

ticular week, to demonstrate to the Mexican Catholics that they could look for no assistance from Washington.

On November 13th a bomb had been thrown at General Obregón, who had escaped unscathed. The Government fixed the responsibility for this outrage upon the Catholics and especially upon Father Pro Juarez and two younger members of the League for the Defense of Religious Liberty. The victims were tried and condemned. Father Pro Juarez and his companions were shot on November 23rd. Great indignation was expressed at these executions and it was foreseen that the Knights of Columbus and other Catholic organizations would start an agitation in the United States. It was with the subsidiary purpose of countering this agitation that Calles staged and advertised the trip to Aguascalientes.

Dwight Morrow was much criticized in Catholic and diplomatic circles for lending himself to this manoeuvre. It was felt at the time that he was too simple and too naïve to realize that he was being exploited for political purposes. As a matter of fact he was acutely aware of the implications underlying the President's hospitality. "I went," he wrote to Robert Olds, "with reluctance, because I realized that some Catholics would consider my trip an endorsement of the act of the Government." He argued with his usual realism. Had he declined the invitation he would have sacrificed all hope of gaining the confidence of President Calles, and have rendered no service whatsoever to the Catholic cause. By accompanying the President at that moment he did more than create confidence: he placed the President under an implicit obligation. The decision was one of the most difficult that he was ever called upon to take. He went with Calles, knowing that his action would be misinterpreted. A vainer man would have dreaded the accusation of gullibility; a weaker man would have feared the odium which would result; a less intelligent man would have failed to see that the issue was one of fundamental importance. By thus allowing himself to be momentarily represented as condoning the execution of Father Pro Juarez, Morrow established relations with Calles which, even from the extreme Catholic point of view, were more than justified by results.

XVI. The Mexican Achievement 1927–1929

ALTHOUGH Dwight Morrow possessed long experience of
international negotiation, he had little knowledge of professional diplomacy. He was in fact inclined to regard the
diplomatist with merriment, not untinged with contempt.
He would refer to Embassy attachés as "cookie pushers with
the milk of Groton still wet upon their lips," and from fear
lest his own family might become impressed with his ambassadorial grandeur he invented for them one of the more
nonsensical of his many domestic catechisms:

Question: Do you know what an Embassy is?
Answer: The home of the Dodo.
Question: And who, pray, is the Dodo?
Answer: The Dodo is somebody who is dead but doesn't know
it.

Moreover, in order to facilitate the intensive research work
which was the constant basis of his method, he collected a

private staff of his own. As his advisers on claims commissions, as on the agrarian and oil problems, he brought with him J. Reuben Clark, who, both inside and outside the State Department, had for many years specialized on legal questions. His old colleague on the A.M.T.C., George Rublee, joined him in March 1928 and was of the utmost assistance, at first on labor problems, and later on the Church question. And another collaborator from the old days of Maritime Transport, Captain Lewis B. McBride, was appointed to the Embassy in the guise of Naval Attaché, but for the express purpose of assisting the Ambassador in unraveling the tangle of Mexican finance.

It speaks highly for the public spirit of the career diplomatists serving in the Embassy that they did not resent this covey of private assistants.[1] On becoming closer acquainted with those hard-worked, ill-paid, unrewarded, ridiculed, righteous, much-harassed, and greatly deserving individuals who form the framework of the American Diplomatic Service, Dwight Morrow completely revised his previous criticisms. In return for their loyalty he awarded them his warm friendship and his absolute confidence. He turned over to Arthur Schoenfeld and the junior staff the whole current work of the Embassy. He was thus able to concentrate on specific problems without interruption.

His diplomatic method departed in many important par-

[1] The Staff of the United States Embassy during the first year of Morrow's mission consisted of H. F. Arthur Schoenfeld, Counselor, Arthur Bliss Lane and Alan F. Winslow, First Secretaries, Frederick Hibbard and Stanley Hawks, Second Secretaries, Allan Dawson, Third Secretary. Lieutenant-Commander Donald W. Hamilton was Naval Attaché. Alexander W. Weddell was Consul General. Later E. P. Lowry was attached to the Embassy. Messrs. Williamson S. Howell, Herschel V. Johnson and Joseph Satterthwaite were subsequent additions. The Military Attaché was Colonel Alexander Macnab with Major Harold F. Thompson as Assistant. On Mr. Schoenfeld's departure in 1929, Stokeley W. Morgan was appointed Counselor, a post filled later by Arthur Lane.

ticulars from conventional technique. One of the most stringent principles of diplomacy is that all communications with a foreign government must be recorded in writing. Dwight Morrow, with the example of Mr. Sheffield before him, was determined not to enter into any form of written exegesis with the sophists of the Mexican Foreign Office; practically all his negotiations were conducted orally. A second fundamental principle, which Morrow flagrantly violated, was that of secrecy. His communications with the State Department were to an unwarranted extent conducted on the telephone, a method which was not only expensive but unwise.[2] It was well known that his telephone was tapped and that all his remarks were recorded for the information of the Mexican Government. A mild protest reached him under this heading from the State Department. "If," he replied, "we spend our time feeling that the main object of the Embassy is secrecy we will become the slaves of our suspicions instead of the servants of our governments." A third diplomatic convention which he persisted in disregarding was that according to which a foreign representative can only communicate with a government through the channel of the Foreign Secretary. To this rule Dwight Morrow paid no attention at all. Not only would he go direct to Calles in any important issue, but he would invade the several departments of the Mexican Government and buttonhole the junior officials who dealt with any particular case. This procedure is known in diplomatic terminology as "short circuiting"; it represents a particularly heinous offense.

Dwight Morrow was able to commit with impunity these

[2] His telephone bills were enormous. There is one, covering a period of little more than ten weeks, for as much as $5,000.00. He defrayed these expenses out of his own pocket.

violations of convention, not merely because of his charm and persistence, but because both the Mexican Foreign Office and the State Department were well aware that the two Presidents stood directly behind him. He possessed, more-over, the friendship and confidence of the two Under Secre-taries at Washington, Joseph P. Cotton and Robert Olds. His violations of these established rules are not, however, held up as an example to be followed by other diplomatists, whether young or old. The principles which he violated are not foolish principles: they represent the acquired experience of many centuries. Dwight Morrow could ignore them; yet even he, by the end, came to realize that these conventions were as sensible and serious as those that govern the practice of medicine or the law.

His other innovations in diplomatic practice were more exemplary. He believed in a profound and prolonged study of every problem. He carried truthfulness to a point where it exceeded ordinary veracity and became a scrupulous solici-tude for the correctness of impressions whether received or conveyed. His tolerance was only exceeded by his patience, his energy equaled only by his persistence. He was always sympathetic, always outspoken, and never vain; he would allow the other man to speak without interruption and to claim the full credit for any agreement that might be reached. He seldom argued; he rarely contradicted; if a per-son expressed an opinion that was manifestly silly or extreme, Morrow would put on an expression of pained astonishment, pursing his lips into a rounded "O" of doubt, "which," as one of his victims has subsequently confessed, "was most disconcerting." Behind all this was his rectitude, his intelli-gence, and his force. And in front, there played the dappled sunshine of his charm.

"I have seen," records Montagu Norman, "the potent power of his personality in conference with dull, stupid, mean minds that were determined on making a settlement difficult. Dwight would let his mind play on them. He would be amusing and agreeable. He would talk, and he was a beautiful talker, until the whole atmosphere would be changed and these men who had been so hard and repellent would try to please Dwight by coming to an agreement."

He approached international problems with that gift for simplification which he had acquired during his long years of discipline as a corporation lawyer. His method has been well described by Thomas Lamont:

"A careful study of the history of, and factors in, the situation; a stripping away of all unessentials, and then a rebuilding and presentation of the situation in a way both simple and convincing."

Such was the potent machinery which was applied to the settlement of the tangled differences between the Governments of Mexico and the United States.

2

The four problems with which Morrow had to deal were those of Oil, Land, Claims, and Debts. Of these four the oil question was the most controversial and therefore the most dangerous. It had formed the subject of embittered wrangling between the State Department and the Mexican Foreign Office over a period of ten years. It is unnecessary for our present purpose to examine in detail the arguments and counterarguments which, during this long period of controversy, were advanced on either side.[3] It is proposed only to describe, as simply as possible, what Morrow actually did.

The mining code in force in Mexico from 1783 to 1884 reserved title to minerals in the Sovereign, or in other words the State. In 1884 the Mexican Congress passed the first mining code enacted after the achievement of independence. American capitalists who acquired oil lands contended that this code divested the State of its title to petroleum on privately owned lands and lodged this title in the private owners of the land. Yet Mexico has never conceded that the code granted more than the right to exploit the mineral resources contained in the sub-soil and has insisted that even this right does not vest until the owner of the surface has performed a "positive act" evidencing his intention to exploit. It was inevitable in any case that the leaders of the 1910 revolution, fired as they were with nationalist and even Marxist convictions, should endeavor to restore to the Mexican nation the vast national wealth represented by the oil industry.[4] Accordingly, Article 27 of the Constitution of May 1917 laid down the principle that "in the nation is vested the direct ownership of oil." This principle was embodied in the Petroleum Law of December 26, 1925, which was to become effective on January 1, 1927. Under this law, which declared oil to be the inalienable property of the nation, it was enacted that owners of oil lands who had either begun exploitation

[3] An authoritative and lucid account of the oil controversy was contributed by J. Reuben Clark to *Foreign Affairs* of July 1928.

[4] It should be noted that this industry was of comparatively recent growth. It was only in 1900 that E. L. Doheny prospected at Tampico and purchased his 283,000 acres of land. It was not till 1904 that the first well gushed. In 1901 only 1,465 cubic metres were produced; by 1924 this figure had risen to 20 million. In December 1924 American capital invested in Mexican oil totaled 448,157,836 pesos, British capital 204,408,322 pesos, Dutch capital 88,639,949 pesos, and native Mexican capital 23,519,964 pesos.

before May 1917, or had committed some "positive act" indicating their intention to exploit, were required to obtain the grant of a new right in the form of a concession for fifty years in place of the perpetual right already acquired. Unless such a new concession were applied for within twelve months, the original perpetual right would be regarded as null and void. A further provision required the insertion of the so-called "Calvo Clause" whereby foreigners owning property in Mexico could not claim diplomatic protection from their own governments but must be subjected to Mexican jurisdiction. The Petroleum Law of December 1925 was, on April 8, 1926, embodied in a series of Regulations, giving wide powers of action and interpretation to the Mexican Ministry of Industry and Commerce.

For ten long years the State Department endeavored by every argument in its power to convince the Mexican Government that the Petroleum Law and its derivatory Regulations represented a violation of international law. It claimed that to force holders of fee simple titles to exchange such titles for concessions for a period of only fifty years was in fact to impose legislation which was not only retroactive but confiscatory. It claimed that the Calvo Clause was inadmissible since no Government and no foreign national could ever renounce the duties or the rights of diplomatic protection. It argued with subtlety and at length as to what constituted or did not constitute a "positive act." And it contended that those provisions of the Mexican law and Constitution which forbade foreigners to own land in certain arbitrarily determined frontier and coastal zones were discriminatory in character. These arguments formed the purport of an incessant interchange of notes, interspersed with occasional conferences, with the result that by October

1927 an almost complete deadlock and much bitterness had resulted.

Before leaving for Mexico, Dwight Morrow had studied the oil problem in all its bearings. He had come to two main conclusions. The first was that the State Department would never obtain their desires by threats of intervention, since such threats would not be taken seriously. The second was that, in appealing to International Law, they were allowing themselves to be manoeuvred onto uncertain, and in fact invidious, ground. On the one hand they were asking the Mexican Government to accept the theories of International Law in regard to oil concessions, while themselves rejecting those theories in respect of claims for damage occasioned during the revolution. On the other hand, they were asking the Mexican Government to embody in their oil legislation principles which were not recognized in the analogous sections of United States Law. Moreover, in a purely judicial argument, the Mexicans could answer that by the Eighteenth Amendment, as by the California Land Laws, the United States had themselves passed and enforced legislation which was demonstrably both confiscatory and retroactive.

Morrow decided, therefore, that the only possible method of finding a solution was to seek for that solution not in the debatable precepts of international jurisprudence but within the area of Mexican municipal law. Article XIV of the Constitution of 1917 laid down the principle that no legislation should be retroactive. If, therefore, he could obtain Mexican authority for defining the Petroleum Law as being of a retroactive nature, then that law could be declared unconstitutional by the Mexicans themselves. He hoped, in other words, to achieve his object, not by external pressure or authority, but through the normal operation of existing Mexican insti-

tutions. For this purpose he availed himself or the thin end
of a very ingenious wedge.

3

It will be remembered that under the Petroleum Law of
1925 owners of oil properties who had not applied for a
"renewal of their concessions" before January 1, 1927, were
to forfeit these concessions. Only a small proportion of the
foreign oil companies had complied with this regulation,
with the result that on January 2, 1927, the concessions of
several important American companies were legally null and
void. The Mexican Government hesitated to proceed to the
extreme course of actually declaring such concessions for-
feited; they adopted the middle course of penalizing re-
calcitrant companies by allowing the Department of Industry, Commerce, and Labor to cancel drilling permits.
Certain of the companies thereupon filed suits *"in amparo"*
before the local courts demanding a stay of execution on the
ground that the relevant articles of the law were unconstitutional. The local courts decided in favor of the companies
and against the Department of Commerce. The latter lodged
an appeal with the Supreme Court. Morrow realized that
if the Supreme Court were to confirm the judgment of the
local courts, then the objectionable articles of the law would
have been declared unconstitutional by the highest legal
authority in Mexico itself.

In his first interview with President Calles on November 2,
1927, Morrow had carefully refrained from raising any controversial question. A second private interview had been
fixed for November 8th and before it took place the Presi-

dent intimated to the Ambassador that he was perfectly ready to discuss the oil question. He in fact opened the conversation by himself asking Morrow whether he could suggest any solution of this long-outstanding diplomatic controversy. "Diplomatic?" Morrow answered, "I am a lawyer, Mr. President, and not a diplomatist. The problem suggests itself to me as a legal problem, not as either a political or a diplomatic problem." Plutarco Calles, at this, pricked up his ears. He remained silent for a moment, allowing his heavy brown cheek to droop sideways, turning slowly upon his brown but freckled finger a huge silver ring enriched with a large turquoise. He then begged the Ambassador to develop this wholly unexpected thesis. Morrow at that launched out into a learned disquisition, citing in particular the rulings of the Mexican Supreme Court in the Texas Oil Company cases which involved the application of one of the Carranza decrees to oil rights acquired before 1917. The Ambassador intimated that if a similar ruling could be given in the present juncture the ground might be cleared for a satisfactory adjustment of the whole matter.

"The President," recorded Morrow, "then asked me if I thought that a decision of the Supreme Court following the Texas case would settle the main controversy in the oil dispute. I told him that I thought such a decision would remove the main difficulty. He then rather startled me by saying that such a decision could be expected in two months."

President Calles was even better than his word. On November 17, 1927, the Supreme Court of Mexico handed down a decision to the effect that Articles 14 and 15 of the Petroleum Law were unconstitutional. On December 26, 1927, President Calles sent a message to the Mexican

Congress asking them to amend these articles accordingly. A bill providing that pre-constitutional rights should be confirmed by the issuance of confirmatory concessions without limitation of time was obediently passed by the Chamber and Senate of Mexico on December 28th and was ratified by the President on January 3, 1928. On January 11th it entered into force. It still remained to bring the Regulations of the Department of Industry, Commerce, and Labor into harmony with this amended legislation. A difficult situation at this stage arose. The oil companies prepared a draft of these Regulations which Luis Morones, the Minister of Commerce, flatly refused to accept.[5] A new draft was therefore prepared by Morrow and Reuben Clark which was tactfully based, not upon what the oil companies wanted, but upon statements made at different periods by successive Mexican Ministers. This draft was eventually accepted both by the companies and by Luis Morones. On March 28, 1928, the State Department issued an announcement that "the steps voluntarily taken by the Mexican Government would appear to bring to a practical conclusion discussions which began ten years ago. . . . The Department feels, as does Ambassador Morrow, that such questions, if any, as may hereafter arise, can be settled through the due operation of the Mexican administrative departments and the Mexican Courts."

What, in fact, was the essence of the agreement so ingeniously reached? The Mexican Government, while maintaining the principle that the sub-soil was the property of

---

[5] The local executives and lawyers of the oil companies were not to blame for this obstruction. It was from their principals in the United States that the main opposition came. "They take the position," wrote Morrow to Parker Gilbert, "that they must make an example of Mexico in order to make their properties safe in other countries." And in fact the Morrow settlement with the Mexican Government constituted an inconvenient precedent.

the nation, explicitly withdrew their claim to limit enjoyment of oil rights obtained prior to 1917 to a period of fifty years, and implicitly abandoned the Calvo Clause. The United States Government, in return for the express recognition that holders of oil lands retained all rights acquired previous to 1917, abandoned their objection to the issuance of confirmatory concessions by the Mexican Government. They also went far to meet the Mexican interpretation of the meaning of "positive acts." In other words, the United States had maintained the principle of vested property rights; the Mexican Government had maintained the principle of the nationalization of the sub-soil. Both were content.

The rapidity with which this agreement had been reached burst upon an astonished world. Morrow was hailed by the United States press as a diplomatic magician. This was both to underestimate and to overestimate his achievement. "Public feeling," wrote Walter Lippmann to Morrow in April 1928, "is tremendously enthusiastic about this settlement. There is a disposition in some quarters to ascribe it to some private magic which you have at your disposal and not to realize the enormous amount of brain-work and careful negotiation which it has involved."

Morrow's own conception of his achievement was as usual realistic. He was a little shocked, however, by the summary manner in which Calles had treated his Legislature and his Judiciary. In addressing the Royal Institute of Foreign Affairs in London on March 3, 1930, Morrow summarized the negotiation in very modest terms:

"As for oil, I think this was more or less an artificial issue. The oil companies were probably much more hurt by taxation than by the laws to which all our Governments objected so much. We had no difficulty in getting the President to arrange to have the law of 1917 declared unconstitutional and to have a new law passed providing that people who had rights prior to 1917 were to continue to enjoy them in spite of the Constitution."

From that moment large sections of American opinion came to regard Dwight Morrow as the greatest diplomatist which the United States had yet produced. They were not incorrect in this assumption; but it was based upon intuitive feelings rather than upon informed thinking.

4

In January 1928 Morrow left Mexico for Havana to attend the Sixth International Conference of American States. Although this conference was one of great importance, he played but small part in its deliberations. His object in going was to resume contact with President Coolidge and Secretary Kellogg. Fortified by their warm approval and encouragement he returned, on January 29th, to his post.

Having settled the oil controversy he turned his attention to the other outstanding problems of land, claims, and debts. Of these, the debt question came to a head after his return from the London Conference in July 1930, and will therefore be examined in the last chapter. With the problem of claims he was himself little concerned. Two conventions had been signed in September 1923, the one providing for the settlement of general claims arising after July 1868 and the other providing for the adjudication of special claims for losses incurred by United States citizens during the "Revolutionary Period," November 1910 to May 1920. The adjudication of these claims had been entrusted to two mixed commissions which, in an atmosphere of some asperity and much delay, continued their discussion throughout the period of Morrow's mission. It was not until after his departure that the Embassy was called upon to intervene in this dispute.

The agrarian question in its effect upon United States citizens owning land in Mexico, caused him constant preoccupation. His method of dealing with it furnishes a good illustration of what might be called his tactics of multiple approach. It has already been mentioned that the revolution of 1910 assumed in some cases the character of an agrarian rising and that, under the guise of executing the Land Law of 1925 and the Agrarian Regulations of 1926, the local committees proceeded to acts of spoilation and outrage. The United States Government did not question the right of the Mexican Government to alter by legislation the system of land tenure in its own country. All they contended was that this legislation should not discriminate against foreigners and that fair compensation should be paid for all expropriated lands. They claimed further that discrimination was being exercised against United States citizens by forbidding them to own property 100 kilometres from the frontier and 50 kilometres from the sea-coast, that the Calvo Clause was a violation of established international practice, and that the paper bonds offered as compensation were worthless in themselves and based on an unfair assessment of actual values.

The Mexican Government paid little attention to these arguments. At the time of Morrow's arrival some 250 cases had occurred in which American-owned properties had been seized. He at once decided that it would be useless to question the principles involved; he therefore concentrated upon modifying the practice. For this purpose he adopted several different methods.

His first method was that of personal pressure in the third degree. He would force the Mexican officials concerned to accompany him or his Staff on exhausting and inconvenient journeys to visit the scenes of such expropriations on the spot. By this method he was able in many cases to obtain the reversal of confiscations decreed by local agrarian commissions. His second method was to stimulate President Calles' personal interest in scientific agriculture and to suggest to him that his high aims could better be achieved by instituting agricultural banks and colleges and by large scale irrigation schemes, than by handing over to the uneducated peons vast tracts of land which they were unable, and indeed unwilling, to cultivate. His third method was to insist that sums promised, in the form of bonds, as compensation, should be debited to the Mexican budget and that no confiscations should be undertaken in any one year beyond the capacity of that budget. His fourth method was to encourage United States claimants to bring actions, in all cases of flagrant outrage, in the Mexican courts. And his fifth method was to play for time.

"The whole agrarian question," he wrote to the Secretary of State in November 1927, "seems so complex that I had hoped, if the Department approves, I might be able to persuade President Calles that Mexico has already taken more land than was needed for peons available to go upon it and that the Mexican Government without definitively changing its policy could now stop taking new lands and devote its energy to improving the land already taken and to other reforms."

By such methods the agrarian problem was postponed and mitigated; it remained unsolved.

Meanwhile Morrow concentrated his efforts on improving

his personal relations with President Calles, with the members of his Cabinet, and with the several sections of Mexican opinion. The Foreign Minister, Genaro Estrada, was a man of culture and intelligence; he wrote poetry, he collected Chinese jade, his bed was a reproduction of the tomb of Lorenzo il Magnifico. Señor Estrada had a sense of humor; with him Morrow was soon upon intimate and cheerful terms. With the Minister of Finance, Montes de Oca, Morrow was also able to establish coöperation; he was careful, before raising matters of finance, to compliment the Minister upon his general education, as also upon his command of the English language; Montes de Oca responded readily to this method of approach. Nor was it with Cabinet circles only that Morrow entered into personal contact. He studied with care and not without sympathy the interesting, and in fact experimental, program of the Mexican Labor movement and especially the theories and action of the important Confederación Regiónal Obrera Mexicana, generally known as the C.R.O.M., and of its leader, Luis Morones, who was at that date still a factor of affluent importance. He even accepted an invitation to luncheon with the leaders of the Mexican communist party. And he lost no opportunity of getting into touch with the Mexican people themselves.

Dwight Morrow was never a linguist. In spite of his intense interest in France, his knowledge of the French language scarcely advanced beyond the Allegheny standard. "Bon accent," he would explain to M. Briand, "pas de vocabulaire." During his first months in Mexico he took lessons in Spanish from a professor of botany; these lessons never passed from the analytical to the synthetic stage; to the end of his days he would refer to the State of Sonora as "Señora" and his communications with Sabino, the Embassy butler, with Miguel, his devoted valet, were confined to gesticulation interspersed with a few unrelated Castilian sounds.

His love of Mexico, his appreciation of all things Mexican, was none the less apparent in everything he did. He would walk every morning in Chapultepec Park, directing his rapid little footsteps along the Calzada de los Filosofos, along the Calzada de los Artistos, to where, under the huge shade of Montezuma's cypresses the little Cervantes fountain splashes among the periwinkles and the yellow tiles.

And then, in his second Mexican year, came Cuernavaca.

Some fifty miles from Mexico City—halfway between the central plateau and the tropical regions of the coast—lies the small town of Cuernavaca, huddling its roofs below the Cathedral and around the pink municipal building which was the last palace of Hernando Cortes. It is a place of water and sunshine, of fruit and flowers, of songs and silence. Morrow had first fallen in love with Cuernavaca when he lunched with the British Minister, Mr. Esmond Ovey,[6] who possessed a little house and garden in the alley known as Calle Arteaga. The house next to Mr. Ovey belonged to an American resident, Mr. Fred Davis. He consented to sell it to Dwight Morrow and after an infinity of legal complications the purchase was completed. The house at first was no more than a single-storied adobe building opening upon a small court. Morrow was able to acquire three, and then four, adjoining plots of land. The house was extended: the garden developed six tiny terraces flanked by oleander, heliotrope, banana trees, plumbago, and datura; a bathing pool was constructed on one of the terraces, and a small tower or *mirador* was built, from where a view extended northwards

[6] Now Sir Esmond Ovey, British Ambassador in Brussels.

to the pine-clad heights of the Tres Marias, southwards to where the Cathedral tower showed solemn bells against an amber, or a purple, sweep of plain and mountain; eastwards, past the little pink church with the two cypresses, beyond the Aztec pyramid to the high white cone of Popocatepetl and the recumbent snow masses of Ixtaccihuatl.

Morrow came to love this house and garden more than he had ever loved a house before. He would spend hours selecting objects of Mexican handicraft to decorate the rooms, or in placing Indian jars and water-pots at fitting distances upon the steps and terraces. Three different fountains spoke with three different notes of cheerfulness. It was here that, after the tension of the city, he would find happiness and repose. He would come down there on Friday evenings and remain till late on Sunday. He would climb up to the *mirador* and watch the sunset melt into green behind the mountains while the two volcanoes still glowed pink and violet in the east. The night, with tropic suddenness, would spread its blankets patined with white stars. From the lane below would come the padding of Aztec sandals, and as the night deepened the sound of singing, the reedy throb of xylophones, would rise in flights and bursts of muffled laughter among the palm trees and the humble roofs.

The house at Cuernavaca, the Casa Mañana of his fantasy, remains today the property of Mrs. Morrow and his children.

5

"The happy effect," writes Arnold Toynbee, "upon the relations between the two countries which Mr. Morrow's presence in Mexico City instantly produced . . . became one of the main features in the situation as between Mexico and the United States. Yet the greatest diplomatic triumph which Mr. Morrow achieved was the contribution which he made, by his good offices, to the settlement of the conflict between the Mexican State and the Catholic Church—an extraordinarily delicate enterprise for a citizen of the United States, who did not happen to be a Catholic himself, to undertake in a country where he was his own Government's official representative." [7]

Dwight Morrow was under no illusions regarding the delicacy of any intervention on his part in the conflict between the Mexican Church and State. He was well aware that the Mexican Revolutionary Government, and President Calles in particular, had deeply resented the support given by the Church to Victoriano Huerta, and the propaganda conducted both inside and outside Mexico by Catholic organizations whether native or foreign. And he was conscious that it would be inconsistent in one who had so loudly proclaimed his respect for Mexican sovereignty to intervene in a quarrel which was regarded as of an essentially domestic nature. Yet he was drawn towards this controversy by every strand in his being. He had for many years been interested in the history of the struggle between Church and State, and the works of Bishops Stubbs and Creighton, of Lord Acton and Professor Maitland, had for long constituted his favorite study. The temptation to regard the Mexican controversy as a problem in applied history was almost irresistible. It pained him moreover to observe that 90 per cent of the population were suffering acutely, even though superstitiously, from the denial of a religion for which they yearned. And he felt convinced that the Mexican Govern-

[7] Professor Arnold Toynbee in "Survey of International Affairs: 1930," pp. 384-5.

339

ment would never establish internal order, or obtain abroad the credit of representing a civilized and progressive system, until the poison of this controversy and the endemic condition of civil strife which resulted were removed from the Mexican body politic. And behind all this was his persistent passion for solving the insoluble.

The struggle between Church and State in Mexico dates from the time of the Conquest; for three centuries battle had waged between the secular and the ecclesiastical authority, between the Viceroys and the Archbishops. Drastic anti-clerical legislation had during the nineteenth century been passed by Juárez and his successors; the Church had been deprived of its special courts, its enormous properties, and its monastic orders. During the Díaz régime some of these privileges had been recovered but with the coming of the socialist revolution of 1910 it became inevitable that the old legislation would be enforced with greater vigor and that new legislation would be introduced curbing the political and educational influence which the priests exercised and enjoyed. The Government contended, with some justice, that the Mexican priesthood was as degraded, as corrupt, and as obscurantist as that of Abyssinia, and that the moral and material hold which it had obtained over the Indian population rendered it impossible to improve the ethical or educational standards of the peons, or to introduce into the Republic the beneficent influence of universal suffrage. The Church argued, with equal justice, that the fact that isolated abuses had occurred did not justify the Government in depriving nine-tenths of the population of that religious consolation which they unquestionably desired and that the policy of President Calles and his associates was confiscatory, atheistical, and undemocratic.

340

The Constitution of 1917 laid it down that the Church could not claim a corporate existence, could own no property, not even its own churches, could conduct no primary education and must regard itself merely as a "profession" completely under the orders of the civil authority. It was also provided that the several State Legislatures could fix the number of priests required in each State. Priests were to be of Mexican birth, were not to hold public office, had no vote, and must refrain from expressing political opinions. These provisions were not enforced very drastically until early in 1926 when certain ecclesiastics, including the Archbishop of Guadalajara, were accused of having fomented a rising in the State of Jalisco. Regulations were issued obliging all priests to swear allegiance to the Republic and to enroll themselves on a national register. The Mexican bishops, not without encouragement from the Vatican, forbade priests to comply with this decree under the threat of excommunication, issued pastoral letters urging the political and economic boycott of the Government, and ordered as from July 31, 1926, the suspension of all religious services. "The League for the Defense of Religious Liberty" was at the same time organized among the faithful, and armed bands of "Cristeros" took to the mountains from where they endeavored to terrorize the Government into surrender. By July 1927 the Cristeros had been practically suppressed. Even at the height of the rising their number did not exceed 6,000; they were never a serious military menace, but they created a general atmosphere of disaffection and insecurity highly damaging to the credit of the Calles Government. Such was the position when Morrow arrived.

In October 1927, before his departure for Mexico, he had been induced by Cardinal Hayes and Judge Morgan O'Brien to receive Father John J. Burke, General Secretary of the National Catholic Welfare Conference. Father Burke asked whether it would be possible for him to visit President Calles and to discuss confidentially some basis of mediation or compromise. Morrow returned an evasive answer, but in January 1928 Father Burke managed to catch him during the Havana Conference. He repeated his former suggestion. Morrow at first replied that any intervention would be resented but later promised to sound Calles. On his return to Mexico, Morrow inquired of the President whether he would be prepared to receive an American citizen, an ecclesiastic, who was anxious to discuss with him the controversy between Church and State. Calles assented; Father Burke was notified; but at that moment a rumor of the interview appeared in the American press and Calles at once withdrew his promise. Morrow waited until April before resuming his request. He then induced President Calles to receive Father Burke in the island fortress of San Juan de Ulloa at Vera Cruz. This meeting took place in circumstances of the greatest secrecy on April 4, 1928. Morrow was present at the meeting, at which an agreement was drafted according to which the Mexican Church would allow the reopening of the churches (or in other words call off their religious strike) if the Government would declare that it was not their intention "to destroy the identity of the Church" and would be willing to confer with the authorized heads of the Church in Mexico regarding the application of the recent laws and regulations. This draft agreement was submitted by Father Burke to the Apostolic Delegate in Washington, who stated that he would postpone sending it to the Vatican pending the results of a Conference then taking place between the Mexican Bishops at San Antonio, Texas. The Bishops in their turn demanded that President Calles should receive their own senior prelate, Monsignor Leopoldo Ruíz y Flores, and confirm to him the promises made to Father Burke. It was with the very greatest difficulty that Morrow induced President Calles to receive this mild and conciliatory priest. A meeting was eventually arranged on May 17, 1928; the previous arrangement, which was in the form of an interchange of letters, was confirmed; and Monsignor Ruíz left for Rome to obtain the approval of the Vatican.

6

In passing through Paris, Monsignor Ruíz committed the imprudence of giving an interview to the press. The result was unfortunate. On the one hand it encouraged reactionary circles to urge on Rome that the draft agreement represented surrender on the part of the Church and would strengthen the bolshevik system of Plutarco Calles. On the other hand Calles himself was seriously embarrassed, and threatened to publish the whole correspondence. It was at this stage that the negotiations were interrupted by a serious internal crisis in Mexico.

President Calles' term of office was due to expire on November 30, 1928. He had pledged himself not to stand for reëlection, but it had been arranged, in order that the system might be safeguarded, that his ally and partner, General Obregón, should be elected in his place. On July 17, 1928, General Obregón was murdered by a young Catholic fanatic while attending a banquet in the suburb of San Angel. Not only did this incident render impossible any armistice between Church and State, but it raised the problem whether

President Calles should violate his own pledge not to stand again or whether he should risk the collapse of the whole system by entrusting the helm to weaker hands. Morrow was much perplexed by this situation. On the one hand his democratic conscience wished to see the principle of "no reëlection" established; on the other hand he dreaded what might happen were Calles to retire into private life. He suggested to the latter in August that he might remain as "temporary President" (or *"Presidente Interino"*) until the situation was secure. Calles answered that he would never become a Dictator, that he was determined to abide by his pledges, that he would retire into private life, remaining but "a citizen and soldier of the Republic." The latter reservation was of some importance. When, in the following March, a military revolution broke out under General Escobar, Calles was obliged to emerge from his retirement, became Minister of War, and suppressed the revolution after an arduous but successful campaign. He thereafter remained the soldier of the Republic to whom subsequent Presidents deferred obedience.

In the end, Morrow's democratic conscience triumphed over his sense of expediency. When, at the opening of the Mexican Congress in September 1928, Calles announced that institutions were more important than individuals and that he would not accept reëlection, Morrow leaned forward in the diplomatic box and applauded with overt hands. "I suppose," he murmured to the British Minister on regaining his seat after this dramatic demonstration, "I suppose I ought *not* to have done that?" "No," Mr. Ovey answered. "You ought *not.*"

Meanwhile, however, the Church negotiations were indefinitely postponed. Morrow was disheartened. Not only did the situation in Mexico City appear devoid of any hope, but the Vatican had stiffened to an uncompromising attitude as a result of the reprisals taken against the Catholics in revenge for the murder of Obregón. The *Osservatore Romano* fulminated against the whole Mexican Republic. There was nothing to be done. Morrow waited patiently for a period of ten months. Yet he was not inactive. Again and again did he urge on President Calles and upon his successor, President Portes Gil, the necessity of resuming negotiations. Again and again did he endeavor, through various channels, to modify the uncompromising attitude of the Vatican. In April 1929, with the collapse of the Escobar revolution, and with the revival of Cristero warfare, he felt that a favorable moment had arrived for more intensive pressure. President Portes Gil was not unreceptive. On May 2, 1929, the latter gave an interview to a New York newspaper in which he indicated his readiness to compromise, and on May 3rd this olive branch was answered from Washington by Monsignor Ruíz in an equally conciliatory spirit. A fortnight later Monsignor Ruíz was appointed apostolic delegate to Mexico and asked whether he would be received by the President. Morrow at that moment was absent in Englewood for the marriage of his second daughter to Colonel Lindbergh. He left for Washington at the conclusion of the ceremony and on June 10th he arrived back in Mexico City, bringing with him in his private car not only the Apostolic Delegate, but Archbishop Díaz. He housed these prelates secretly in the apartment of his Naval Attaché and proceeded thereafter to submit the President to persistent persuasion. By June 19th a draft agreement had been reached and on June 21st the approval of the Vatican was obtained. Under this agreement the Church promised to call off the strike and to resume religious services, and the Government declared that it was not their intention to destroy the Church. It was also agreed that although priests would still be obliged to register themselves according to the Constitution, yet they might be appointed by their own hierarchy and might give religious instruction in their churches though not in schools. It was also provided that Catholics, including members of the League for the Defense of Religious Liberty, might petition Congress for a modification of the Constitution.

Morrow never claimed that this agreement was more than a temporary armistice. "The problem," he would say, "cannot be solved. But it can be stated." He did not solve the Catholic question in Mexico. All he did was to ease the deadlock, to lay down a basis for future coöperation and negotiation, to enable the Church without loss of face to resume religious services, and to rid the Government of the dangers of the Cristeros and the Defense League, while diminishing the odium with which they were regarded in the United States and Europe. The Morrow armistice has not, since the agreement of June 21, 1929, worked so well as he anticipated; the politicians claim that the priests still interfere in politics; the priests claim that the politicians still persecute the Church. In certain States the exercise of religion is, it is true, severely hampered, only one priest being allowed to 25,000 inhabitants. Other States are more tolerant. But to Morrow it is due that today many millions of Mexicans can still enjoy the rights of the Church in birth and death and marriage, that the bells still echo in the mountains and that in the cool of many thousand churches the little lights still flicker before the sacred shrines.

It had been a hard and thankless struggle. It had en-

THOUGHT AND PERSUASION

dangered his relations with Calles and the revolutionary Government. It had exposed him to abuse and even peril from both sides.[8] He had been accused in the press, both Catholic and secular, of meddling in affairs which were not his own. His final success, exaggerated though it was, increased his reputation in his own country and beyond. It brought him some sentimental compensations. On Sunday, June 30th, the churches were reopened throughout Mexico and in a thousand thanksgiving services prayers were invoked "for that good man who helped the Church find the way to peace."

He had escaped, the night before, to Cuernavaca. He was awakened at dawn by the crash of the Cathedral bells, by the clangor of all the other bells released suddenly after three sad years of silence. "Betty," he called across to his wife, "do you hear that? I have opened the churches in Mexico." The noise continued unabated and was increased by the explosion of fireworks and maroons. "Would you," Morrow asked after half an hour of this inferno, "now like me to close the churches in Mexico?"

[8] His life was continually being threatened throughout the negotiations and menacing broadsheets were posted in the town and thrown over the wall of the Embassy garden. The following is typical of these incitements:

"Mister Morrow! A few days after your arrival, in the center of the city there were executed with a shamelessness which stunned the civilized world, the priest Pro Juarez and his three companions. Before that torrent of blood you observed silence. You went on a pleasure trip with Calles. On that trip you trailed your own dignity in the mud and mire and challenged the anguished soul of the Mexican Nation, joining in abominable cohabitation with the assassin. Mister Morrow! You are going too far! Take care! Take great care! An infuriated people is a terrible thing. Fear the wrath of a people! Fear the wrath of God! Mister Morrow! Do not forget that ideas are dynamite. Know that people have learnt of the infamous rôle you are playing. Be warned that ideas resolve themselves into action!"

XVII. The London Conference
1930—January 21 to April 22

IT may appear strange that a man of such ability and reputation should not already have been chosen for Cabinet office.
True it is that Calvin Coolidge, on relinquishing his responsibilities, warmly recommended Dwight Morrow to Herbert
Hoover as the ideal Secretary of State. The President-elect
was not enthusiastic regarding this almost posthumous suggestion. On the one hand his own acquaintance with Morrow had not, as yet, been favorable; there had been that
incident after the Armistice, that incident respecting Cuban
sugar; he remembered also how one evening in 1920 Morrow had thrust a little booklet into his hand entitled "Have
Faith in Massachusetts." "Calvin Coolidge," Morrow had
said, "is the man best fitted to be President of the United
States."

It was convenient and beautiful, of course, that Dwight Morrow should remain a detached and solitary example of political disinterestedness. "The historic achievement," wrote Walter Lippmann, "was that he broke through these conventions of insincerity in public life and raised a standard of intrinsic worth to which men could repair. Like the greatest teachers, he taught by example." [1] Yet supposing that Dwight Morrow were to leave his show-case in the Republican Museum and cease to serve as an inheritor of unfulfilled renown? That would be equally beautiful but far less convenient. His chairmanship of the Aircraft Board, the Lindbergh connection, and the whole Mexican drama had given him great popular glamor. So long as it was only the intellectuals who admired him, the politicians would feel secure. Yet already the name of Dwight Morrow was being canvassed upon electoral lips, already there had been those who had suggested him as the ideal successor to Calvin Coolidge. This was most disquieting. The moment had arrived when Dwight Morrow might cease to be a public servant and might become a public figure. It was far safer to keep him down in Mexico. His work there was so profitable, so high-minded, so humane, and above all so distant. One cannot blame Mr. Hoover for the skill with which he rendered a formidable rival the most repaying of all his assistants.

Mr. Hoover, none the less, was a conscientious man. He did not ignore the recommendation made to him by Calvin Coolidge. In January 1929 he telegraphed to Morrow summoning him to Miami. Morrow arrived at the Flamingo Hotel on January 22nd. The news of this visit caused excited speculation; the newspapers, both in the United States and

[1] Walter Lippmann, New York *Herald Tribune*, October 7, 1931.

Mexico, carried headlines to the effect that the President-elect was already forming his Cabinet and that Dwight Morrow was to receive the post of Secretary of State. Much alarm was caused in Mexico City by this pronouncement. The Minister of Foreign Affairs sent an urgent cable to Morrow begging him not to abandon Mexico until the position of the Portes Gil administration had become more stable. Morrow was much touched by this appeal. Mexico still needed him. His protective instincts were aroused.

On January 24th he had his interview with Herbert Hoover. The President-elect admitted that he had been exposed to strong pressure to nominate Morrow as his new Secretary of State. Yet Mexico at the moment was the most important post in the public service. Did Morrow really feel that he could abandon his responsibilities towards America's disordered neighbor in the south? Morrow answered that he felt that his duty demanded that he should complete his Mexican task. The President-elect was overjoyed by this exhibition of public spirit. He complimented Morrow in the warmest terms. Five days later Morrow returned to Mexico City. And Henry L. Stimson was eventually appointed Secretary of State.

In November 1929, however, two successive opportunities were offered to him. On November 12th, Secretary Stimson telephoned from Washington inquiring whether he would agree to serve on the United States Delegation to the impending Naval Conference in London. He replied in the affirmative. On November 26th, an even stranger message reached him from Trenton, New Jersey.

On the afternoon of that day, Mr. Daniel Pomeroy, member for New Jersey of the Republican National Committee, telephoned to say that Governor Larson was in some diffi-

culty regarding the appointment of a Senator to fill the
unexpired term of Walter E. Edge, who had been appointed
by President Hoover as United States Ambassador in Paris.
The name of David Baird had been suggested, but it was
hoped that Morrow himself would agree to accept the post.
Morrow was well aware that Mr. Pomeroy was speaking
with the knowledge, if not at the instigation, of Mr. Charles
D. Hilles [2]—a man whose political wisdom always com-
manded his respect. He thus replied that he must consult
the State Department before committing himself to a decision. The confusion of the following days echoes in Mrs.
Morrow's diary:

November 27. The day has been full of excitement about the
Senator appointment. I think Dwight is not going to accept it.
He was anxious this morning as we talked about it. We said our
prayers together. This noon Joe Cotton telephoned me. He is all
in favor of it. Tonight he talked to Dwight. The President will
not commit himself on it at all. George Rublee is very anxious
for Dwight to take it. Captain McBride is not for it. I am really
only afraid that after the chance is gone Dwight will regret it.
It would be a fine dignified life—and we would leave here
before Dwight's prestige wanes.

November 28. Cuernavaca. Dwight has decided after talking
with Governor Larson that Baird is to be appointed Senator.
If after Dwight returns from London the Governor and Baird
still feel the same, Baird is to resign and Dwight will run for
the Senate in the fall. I have felt all day that we shall not see
this lovely place again.

November 29. Cuernavaca. Elisabeth and I are here alone tonight. I wonder if it is our last night at Cuernavaca! I went

[2] Charles D. Hilles, b. Ohio, 1867; Assistant Secretary of the Treasury 1909-11;
secretary to President Taft 1911-13; influential member of the Republican National Committee; director Guggenheim Foundation.

up to the *mirador* before breakfast—Popo and Ixte were clear and beautiful—sheer white against the sky. I looked hard for memory's sake.

November 30. Elisabeth and I had a lovely morning at Cuernavaca. We arranged the little Mexican kitchen with our pots and pitchers and then we said good-by to everything. We took a swim just before we left. The sun was so hot and the pool was so blue. As I swam across in the sun I looked slowly at all the loveliness. I said, "I will remember it all—the blue sky, the gardener trimming the yellow mimosa tree above our wall in his big sombrero and white clothes, the blue plumbago and the sprays of heliotrope, the gay awning, the big pots with geraniums, the pink arch, the Cathedral spire—everything." I find Dwight terribly upset. The Senator plan is coming out in the papers. He feels his hand has been forced.

December 3. Last night was terrible! Dwight hardly slept at all. He talked and talked about the Senatorship. He feels very unhappy over it. He thinks he has been tricked into apparently making a decision. He feels that he should not hurry away from Mexico and that above all he should not have his hand forced into making a decision of such importance in a hurry and at a long distance. I have been miserable about it. Diego Rivera here this afternoon to arrange about the Cortés Palace frescoes at Cuernavaca.

What actually happened was that Morrow, while not finally rejecting the proposal, had asked for full time to consider his decision and had urged that in any case he was committed to serve on the Delegation to the London Conference and to finish off his work in Mexico. Mr. Pomeroy, on behalf of Governor Larson, had replied that in that case David Baird would accept the appointment on the understanding that he would resign it in favor of Dwight Morrow so soon as the latter was ready to step into his place.

Morrow, on the long distance telephone, had answered that this seemed to him a very generous attitude for David Baird to adopt. The whole arrangement was then published in the New York papers. Morrow was justifiably indignant. On the one hand he had been committed to a decision which required the most careful consideration. On the other hand he had been publicly represented as participating in an arrangement which might seem more expedient than democratic. He was to regret this misunderstanding even more bitterly in the months that followed.

He left Mexico on December 5th, for Washington. In the hall of the Vanderbilt Hotel in New York he encountered his old classmate, Calvin Coolidge. The latter greeted him almost warmly. He invited him to share his bedroom. Morrow had already engaged an apartment of his own but he sat upon the spare bed while Coolidge retired to rest. The ex-President approved of his candidature for the Senate. He was ready even to furnish advice. "Talk as little as you can," he urged him, "but if you have to talk, talk about patriotism. They seem to like it."

On January 9, 1930, Morrow sailed with the other delegates for London. He was accompanied by Mrs. Morrow and by his eldest daughter Elisabeth, then in the flower of her loveliness and charm. On January 17th they arrived at Plymouth. They stayed with the rest of the delegation at the Ritz Hotel.

2

The problem before the London Conference on Naval Disarmament can, in its simplest terms, be stated as follows. Great Britain, having for three centuries maintained her sovereignty over the seas, was now prepared to share that sovereignty with the United States.[3] The British Government had, before the Conference met, committed itself to the principle of "parity" with the United States, or in other words had agreed that it would not construct a fleet larger or more powerful than that of America. Only a few cruiser details remained to be settled in so far as the Anglo-American problem was concerned. On the other hand, the necessity of safeguarding communications with India and Australasia rendered it essential for the British Government to maintain what was practically a two-power standard

[3] Before the London Conference, the problem of Naval Disarmament had passed through three stages, namely: (1) *The Washington Conference* (November 1921-February 1922) reached an agreement only on capital ships, i.e., on ships over 10,000 tons or with guns above 8-inch calibre. The agreed ratio in this respect between Great Britain, the United States, Japan, France, and Italy was 5: 5: 3: 1.67: 1.67, the whole problem to be again reviewed not later than 1931. (2) *The Coolidge Conference* held in Geneva in June 1927. France and Italy do not attend. Purpose of this Conference was to apply the Washington ratios to ships other than capital ships. It at once became apparent that the combative capacity of cruisers and other auxiliaries could not be estimated on a flat tonnage basis as with battleships. The United States wanted a few 10,000-ton cruisers with 8-inch guns, whereas Great Britain wanted a great many 6,000-ton cruisers with 6-inch guns. The Conference therefore failed to reach agreement. The unfortunate effect of this failure was much increased by the stupidity of the British Government in thereafter opening separate negotiations with the French. American opinion was much incensed by this manoeuvre and an enormous naval construction program was passed by Congress. (3) *The Rapidan Conversations,* October 1929. Ramsay MacDonald became Prime Minister in June 1929 and at once set about easing the situation. The "splendid dramatics" of his visit to New York were followed by a private conversation with President Hoover upon a log beside the Rapidan River. The differences between Great Britain and the United States were thereby narrowed down to the single question whether the latter should have 21 or only 18 cruisers with 8-inch guns. At the time when the London Conference opened it may be said, therefore, that there was no substantial disagreement between Great Britain and the United States. It is important to recollect also that the old doctrine of the Freedom of the Seas, which for more than a century had been the main point of naval controversy between Great Britain and the United States, was beginning to lose its validity. America, during the war, had herself abandoned the doctrine. Great Britain was beginning to feel that the defensive protection of the doctrine might become more valuable to her than the offensive powers of the opposite.

354

in the Mediterranean, that is, to possess a fleet larger than the combined fleets of France and Italy. The latter country, while asserting her readiness to effect substantial reductions in her naval program, insisted that she must have "parity" with France; Italy did not mind how small a fleet she possessed, provided that the French fleet was reduced to an exactly similar size. The French, while not overtly rejecting the Italian demand for parity, were determined to build a fleet which would in practice be larger than any fleet which Italy could, given her smaller financial resources, afford to build. Thus the Italian claim for parity forced up the French naval construction program; the French *statut naval* in its turn obliged Great Britain to budget for a large fleet; and the British program consequently increased the American program and rendered it impossible for the Hoover Administration to effect those naval economies to which it was pledged. It was obvious from the first that Italy would never abandon her claim for parity. It thus became the main object of the American Delegation to induce France to modify her *statut naval* and thus enable the British, and therefore the Americans themselves, to scale down their own construction programs. It was for this reason that Morrow's constant negotiation with the French was of such central importance.

The French people, at the moment, were in an intractable mood. After an overwhelming victory over Germany they had been forced by Anglo-American pressure to surrender the complete security which would have been given them by the Rhine frontier, in return for a Guarantee Treaty which Great Britain and the United States had almost immediately repudiated. Having hoped to restore their own finances by a huge indemnity, they had been cheated of that indemnity, partly by German inflation and partly by the persistent pressure of the two Anglo-Saxon countries. A new enemy had now arisen on their flank in the shape of fascist Italy. Although France had to defend herself on two seas, she was now being asked to reduce her navy to the level of a purely Mediterranean Power, and to expose her position in Tunis and her vital communications with her other African dependencies to the menace of an Italian fleet of equal magnitude with her own.[4] The French objected moreover to this piecemeal treatment of the disarmament problem. They foresaw that Great Britain and America, having agreed to reductions in their respective navies, would then turn upon France in a mood of unctuous self-righteousness and demand analogous reductions in the French Army. And they were well aware that no Anglo-Saxon would appreciate the difference between British naval disarmament in deference to the United States and French military disarmament in the face of Germany. It is not surprising that the French Delegation arrived in London with the obstinate determination to wreck the whole Conference.

Neither in Great Britain nor in the United States did public opinion appreciate the very real and justifiable grievance of the French people. In England the impression had been conveyed, largely by Lord Snowden, that French recalcitrance was impeding the reëstablishment of peace and purchasing power on the Continent. The American people, being immune from external menace, could not comprehend that to the French people the word "security" represented the most central of all their aspirations; only if Japan were

---

[4] In order to prove to Italy that parity with France would be beyond her financial resources, the French Government had in December 1924 presented a *statut naval* to the Chamber which provided for the construction by 1942 of a fleet of 850,000 tons.

situated in Mexico could they have formed any conception of how deep and constant a preoccupation territorial insecurity can become. To them "disarmament" came to represent not merely immediate budgetary economy but an obvious ethical ideal; being both profitable and righteous, it became just the sort of gospel which most appeals to their missionary spirit; and they were inclined to regard those who hesitated to accept this gospel as possessing darkened and even wicked minds.

This superficial, and therefore unfair, estimate of French policy was reflected in the attitude both of the American and of the British Delegations. It was Dwight Morrow who, with his deep knowledge of French conditions and his instinctive sympathy for the misunderstood, was able to modify such prejudices and to coax the French Delegation into a less destructive frame of mind. "Without him," wrote Paul Scott Mowrer, "the Naval Conference of 1930 could not have reached an agreement." "Had it not been for Morrow," records Sir Arthur Salter, "there would never have been an agreement. He was the most important of all the Delegates." It remains to examine, in terms of Morrow's actual contribution to the Conference, how far these eulogies are justified.

3

The United States Delegation to the London Conference was composed of seven Delegates, of nine Advisers, and of twelve naval technicians. Secretary Henry L. Stimson presided over the Delegation. Ambassador Dawes flitted in and out of the limelight with truculent aggressiveness. Mr. Charles Francis Adams, Secretary of the Navy, occupied what was mainly a representative function. Senator Joseph T. Robinson of Arkansas was present in the invaluable capacity of democratic observer. The three most active of the Delegates were Dwight Morrow, who concentrated on the Franco-Italian problem, Senator David A. Reed, who dealt with great ability with the Japanese problem, and Ambassador Hugh Gibson, whose long and embittered experience of international conferences and of naval disarmament in particular was of the greatest value to his delegation. Prominent among the Advisers were Admiral William V. Pratt and (for a short period) Rear Admiral Hilary P. Jones, who, with a large staff of technical assistants, represented the naval point of view. Mr. Arthur Wilson Page endeavored to cope with the gifted but all too independent correspondents present in London on behalf of the United States press. Mr. George Rublee was invaluable as the friend and assistant of Dwight Morrow. And Mr. Ray Atherton, the able and popular Counselor of the United States Embassy in London, was there to help his delegation with his deep understanding of British conditions and personalities. "Not since the Conference of Ghent," writes Benjamin Williams, "had a delegation of such all-round strength and prestige gone abroad to represent the American Government in an international negotiation." [5]

The French Delegation, in its first phase, was headed by André Tardieu, a man who combined the opportunism inevitable in a French politician of that date with a bewildering capacity for assimilating facts. M. Tardieu was backed by Aristide Briand, veteran of a hundred conferences, by M. Leygues, his Minister of Marine, and by M. de Fleuriau, the French Ambassador in London. He was accompanied

[5] Benjamin Williams, in "The United States and Disarmament," page 189.

by two of the most gifted officials of the Quai D'Orsay, M. Massigli and M. Léger. The Japanese Delegation was headed by a former Prime Minister, Reijiro Wakatsuki, and the Italian Delegation by Dino Grandi, Mussolini's young and ardent Minister of Foreign Affairs. The British Delegation was presided over by J. Ramsay MacDonald, Prime Minister, who had as his main assistants Mr. Arthur Henderson, the Foreign Secretary, and Mr. A. V. Alexander, the First Lord of the Admiralty. Sir Maurice Hankey acted as Secretary General to the Conference.

In the negotiations which followed, the wood became rapidly obscured by trees. The Washington Conference had found it comparatively simple to assess the relative strengths of each country in terms of capital ships. The moment, however, one came to discuss relative strengths of cruisers and other auxiliaries the problem arose as to the meaning of the two words "strength" and "relative." Such confusing elements as size, gun-calibre, speed, cruising capacity, age, and armor came to blur the simple distinctions of tonnage displacement. There was also the problem of "needs." The British Empire "needed" a large number of small cruisers to protect its lines of communication; the United States "needed" large cruisers in view of the vast distances between its naval bases; the French and Italians "needed" submarines as being the most economical defensive weapon for a small-navy Power. It thus became impossible to assess actual "strength" in simple terms of "size" or even "number." To meet this difficulty several methods of assessment had been devised. There was the method of allotting to each country a maximum figure of "global tonnage" and allowing each Government to distribute that tonnage according to its "needs." There was the method of dividing the several branches of naval construction into "categories" and thereby limiting the allotment to each country under such headings as capital ships, large cruisers, small cruisers, destroyers, and submarines. There was Ambassador Gibson's "yardstick" under which some estimate of relative strengths could be reached by a system of value-awards and discounts based on a comparison of needs, cruising capacity, armament, and gun-calibre. The worst of Mr. Gibson's yardstick was that it so rapidly became a sliding rule. And there was the Paul Boncour compromise plan, under which, within limits, a Government might transfer a proportion of the tonnage allotted to it in one category to a higher category. To the technical intricacies of such assessments must be added the time factor, namely, the rate at which older ships became "obsolescent" and the time within which such ships would be "replaced."

To examine the London Conference in such technical terms would lead only to confusion. It should be realized, however, that underlying the main negotiation was this tangle of intricate detail in regard to which the civilian delegates were largely at the mercy of their naval advisers. Thus if Admiral Hilary Jones assured Mr. Stimson that the United States required a minimum of twenty-one 10,000-ton cruisers armed with 8-inch guns, there was little that Mr. Stimson could say to rebut this argument. The main delegates tended, therefore, to avoid the more technical details, feeling rightly that in that direction lay confusion. Morrow did not avoid them. He mastered the figures in all their intricacy and would carry in his pocket a little black and crumpled notebook with which he would floor astonished Admirals when they presumed too much on the ignorance of the layman. He was thus able, on one important occasion, to convince

Mr. Briand that the figures with which the French naval advisers had provided him were misleading, not to say inaccurate. The point is of importance in what followed. Morrow's purely diplomatic handling of the discussions was enormously strengthened by the fact that he was the only civilian delegate who had really mastered the technical details. The immense authority which he acquired over the Conference is largely to be explained by this circumstance. Not only was he able to see the wood for the trees, but he knew more about the trees and undergrowth than any of those with whom he negotiated.

It is not proposed, in the sections that follow, to examine Morrow's treatment of the technical details. His diplomatic ingenuity and persistence are of far greater interest. Nor is it proposed to describe the overt course of the Conference, since that again was of less importance than the negotiations which took place in confidence. Some general idea of the public procedure of the London Conference must however be conveyed.

The Conference was opened by King George at 11.00 A.M. on Tuesday, January 21st, in the fog-dimmed atmosphere of the House of Lords. Subsequent meetings were held in St. James's Palace. Rooms adjoining the Conference Chamber had been prepared for the accommodation and solace of the Press. There were little dryad chairs disposed conveniently around white tables bearing ash trays and innumerable match boxes. There was an adjoining writing room with many tables, telephone booths, and telegraph instruments. There was a canteen where English coffee was served by bright brisk waitresses. And there were amplifiers attached through which the 'cello tones of Aristide Briand and the superb rutilations of Ramsay MacDonald could be heard above the throb of the Morse code, the click of typewriters, and the tinkle of cups.

Four plenary sessions were held between January 21st and February 11th. At the first session Ramsay MacDonald, as chairman of the Conference, spoke of the need of disarmament both on land and sea. "For the British Empire," he said, "a navy is no superfluity. It *is* us." M. Tardieu replied by stating that for France security was more important than any formulas: "L'étreinte de la vie brise les formules." On January 23rd a second plenary session was held. The British spoke of the need of protecting imperial communications; the French and the Japanese spoke of the requirements of security; the Italians claimed parity with France. At the third session, on January 30th, a somewhat artificial discussion was staged regarding alternative methods of assessment, whether according to "global" tonnage, or according to categories, or according to the French compromise scheme, known as the "Paul Boncour Plan," under which a percentage of tonnage could be transferred from one category to another. The fourth plenary meeting, held on February 11th, disclosed that, whereas Great Britain and the United States were anxious to abolish the submarine, this view was not shared by France, Italy, or Japan. At that stage the plenary sessions of the Conference were interrupted by the fall on February 17th of M. Tardieu.

During the same period the First Committee of the Conference, which was a more technical body and one less exposed to publicity, had held many sessions under the chairmanship of Mr. A. V. Alexander. By February 17th this Committee could show some positive results. Unanimous agreement had been reached in respect of a five-year holiday for battleships and in regard to regulations, which represented a new version of the former resolutions of Elihu Root, for the "humanizing" of submarine warfare. No agreement had, however, been reached regarding Franco-Italian parity, nor had Senator Reed yet been able to induce the Japanese to abate their demand for a 10: 10: 7 ratio in respect of large cruisers.[6]

Yet the real work of the Conference was not done either in the plenary sessions or in the meetings of the First Committee. The real discussions, as is inevitable in all delicate negotiation, were conducted in confidential conversations between the leading delegates. It was in these conversations that Dwight Morrow played so brilliant a part.

4

Those who have had the patience to follow this narrative throughout its course will already be familiar with the methods of negotiation which Morrow had evolved. The essence of that method was that he always assumed his opponent to be in the right until a careful examination of the facts had incontestably demonstrated that he was in the wrong. It was in this spirit that he approached the Franco-Italian controversy.

To most of the Delegates at the London Conference, the

---

[6] This difficulty was eventually surmounted by an agreement negotiated between Senator Reed and M. Matsudaira, Japanese Ambassador in London. Japan's claim for a 70% ratio was reduced to a 60% ratio, but in compensation the United States agreed not to build up to the limit of her own allotment so as to give Japan a 72% ratio until 1936. Japan was accorded parity in respect of submarines and 70% in respect of light cruisers. Great difficulty was experienced in obtaining approval of this arrangement from Tokyo. It was not till April 9th—twelve days before the Three Power Treaty was signed—that Tokyo consented. Great praise is due to Senator Reed and Ambassador Matsudaira for their admirable work in this connection.

Italian demand for parity with France appeared but as a gesture of nationalist vanity, all the more irritating since Italy's concurrent offer to reduce her navy if France would do the same, might appear to ignorant people as both generous and pacific. Dwight Morrow approached the Italian contention from a different angle. He studied the actual facts of the Italian security and food problems and was able to convince Dino Grandi that he at least among the Anglo-Saxons viewed Italian claims under this heading as largely justified by their needs. He then turned his sympathetic attention to the element of national prestige inextricably involved in the Italian claim. He did not, as did the others, envisage this element as a symptom of fascist vanity; he approached it from the angle of the effect of proclaimed disparity upon ordinary national dignity. He thereby evolved a proposal by which he hoped to separate the facts of disparity from the galling implications inherent in the principle.

With this in mind he had recourse to two of his favorite methods of approach—first to his "inductive" method which worked upwards from a basis of fact towards a principle; and secondly to his "gradual" method, on the "and then inquire again" principle, under which something short and definite was attained in preference to something long and vague. In a written memorandum which he addressed to Mr. Stimson he pointed out that the Washington Conference had, by the ratio system, placed certain countries in a position of inferiority and therefore of humiliation. Could not this difficulty be met by substituting for a "ratio contract" imposed by other Powers a "building program" adopted of its own volition by each nation and denounceable only after due notice to other interested parties? Such a program should run for a period "short enough to pre-clude the fear of an undue change in relative needs" yet long enough to represent a real interlude in competitive naval construction. "This method," he contended, "would avoid the imposition of permanent inferiority or supe-riority."

"To the sober people of the world," he continued, "who have struggled so long with Treaties of perpetual Peace, it would seem to be a very practical step for President Hoover not to deal with the question as though he had the wisdom to settle it for all time, but to deal with it effectively and economically during the next seven years. This has the merit of dealing with conditions which we understand and of assuming obligations to be kept by individuals of our own time whom we know, without involving posterity whose action would have to be taken in circumstances we can know nothing about."

At a later stage of the Conference Morrow pushed this line of reasoning even further. He contended that the Dele-gates should cease arguing about each other's "rights" and should concentrate on "feasibility"; or, in other words, that they should cease discussing what each country "might" build and begin to examine what each country "could" build. He hoped by this method to eliminate, if only for the mo-ment, the emotional mists occasioned by national prestige, and to remind the Conference that unrestricted naval com-petition would in terms of budgets not be "feasible" and that the only alternative was an all-round self-denying ordinance. This line of argument was extremely valuable in reminding the Conference from time to time that they were there for coöperative and not for competitive purposes.

Having by such gestures of sympathy and understanding

convinced the Italians that he fully appreciated their point of view, Morrow concentrated his attention on the French. Already Aristide Briand, that expert judge of men, had singled Morrow out from the other members of the United States Delegation. "Do you—" he had said to M. Léger, when driving away from the second plenary session—"do you know the little American with the untidy hair?" M. Léger told him that he had already met Dwight Morrow. "Il est dégourdi," mumbled the French statesman, "comme une pocheté de souris"—as sharp as a nest of mice. In the weeks that followed, M. Briand was to learn that Morrow was something more than merely astute.

Morrow realized very early in the Conference that there was little hope of the French agreeing to parity with Italy. He therefore concentrated on getting M. Briand to agree, firstly to a substantial reduction of the French *statut naval* which would release Great Britain and therefore the United States from the necessity of increasing their own programs; and secondly to his own plan for dropping all mention of parity in principle and reaching an agreement upon a five-year program based upon what each Power considered to be its needs. To this second proposal M. Briand showed himself sympathetic. The first suggestion, in view of the feeling in the French Chamber, was more difficult of acceptance.

On Sunday, February 9th, Briand indicated to Morrow that it might be possible to effect some reduction in the French naval program if France could be guaranteed security in the Mediterranean. This idea was expanded further by M. Massigli when he dined with Morrow on February 14th. This wise diplomatist explained that the French Government and Chamber were disturbed by the growth of isolationist feeling in Great Britain; neither the League of Nations Covenant nor the Treaties of Locarno provided any real sense of security for France since it was questionable whether, if a crisis arose, Great Britain would execute the obligations deriving upon her under these engagements. What France desired was a definite Mediterranean Pact. These conversations were interrupted by the fall of the Tardieu Cabinet on February 17th.

During the ensuing interval Morrow pursued the Pact question with cautious persistence. He had repeated interviews with the French Ambassador and with those of the French Delegation, such as M. Aubert, who had remained in London. Certain definite facts emerged from these conversations. The French would not reduce their naval estimates unless they received from Great Britain a security guarantee in the Mediterranean. The British were unwilling to give such a guarantee in view of the then existing isolationist feeling in the country and in the House of Commons. Morrow then suggested that the British Government, while not entering into any new engagements, might reaffirm its old commitments under the League Covenant and the Locarno Treaties in such form as to give the French the assurance they desired. Here again the British showed some hesitation. Were they to commit themselves in all circumstances to execute Article XVI of the Covenant they might easily become involved in a serious controversy with the United States regarding neutral rights as affected by a blockade decreed by the League of Nations. There was, for example, that awkward gap between the Covenant, which in the last resort provided for "a League war," and the Kellogg Pact, under which war, in any form, had been outlawed. It was in order to meet these British apprehensions that Morrow cautiously evolved the theory of a "Consultative Pact" into which the United States might enter.

Mr. Stimson was at first horrified by any such suggestion. Morrow pointed out to him that the United States was not being asked to enter into any entangling alliances in Europe, but merely to assure Great Britain that America "would not impede her in the performance of her continental obligations." Meanwhile the report of the Morrow proposal brought M. Briand back to London. On March 7th Morrow and Rublee dined alone with M. Léger. On March 8th Morrow thrust M. Briand into an automobile and dragged him down to Stanmore to interview Mr. Stimson. As a result of this interview a "Special Committee" was created for the purpose of examining how far the French *statut naval* could be scaled down. The French stated bluntly that they had no confidence in Great Britain's willingness to fulfill her continental obligations under either the Covenant or Locarno. Morrow explained that the idea had already been mooted that in order to meet British apprehension the United States might agree to some codicil to the Kellogg Pact providing for "joint consultation" in the event of any menace to peace in the Mediterranean. At that moment a serious hitch occurred. Owing to an indiscretion in the American Delegation exaggerated accounts of the proposal reached the United States and provoked the inevitable reaction. On March 11th Mr. Stimson repudiated publicly any idea that he would sign a consultative pact. M. Briand, at that, announced that he would return, a second time, to Paris. Morrow, almost by physical force, prevented him from carrying out this intention. From 11.45 P.M. till 1.30 A.M. he remained closeted in M. Briand's room at the Carlton, representing to him the bad effect upon American opinion of a

sudden French withdrawal, urging him as the leading statesman of Europe to have patience for a little longer. "This
Conference," urged Morrow, "may be very ill, but you
have saved many a Conference, M. Briand, that was far
more sick than this." The old man smiled wearily. But he
consented to stay.

Meanwhile the conclusion of the Reed-Matsudaira agreement rendered it conceivable that a Three Power Treaty
might after all be signed. M. Tardieu himself crossed to
London and on March 16th offered to reduce the French
naval estimates if they could be assured of a permanent
200,000-ton superiority over Italy. The bright hopes aroused
by this overture were dashed three days later when the
Fascist Grand Council reaffirmed that parity alone would
satisfy Italian demands. A deadlock had again been reached
and M. Briand returned for the second time to Paris.

5

The London Conference, by this stage, seemed doomed
to failure. The Italians had refused to abate their demand
for parity with France; the French had refused to scale down
their *statut naval* except in return for a British guarantee of
their maritime security; the British had refused, not only to
enter into any form of Mediterranean Pact, but even to reaffirm their existing commitments in such a manner as
might satisfy the French. And Mr. Stimson had publicly
announced that the United States would enter into no form
of Consultative Agreement. It was taken for granted that,
although the Conference might still achieve a Three Power
Treaty as between the United States, Great Britain, and

Japan, there was no hope of persuading France or Italy to be even indirectly associated with such a consummation. This deadlock aroused the bull-dog quality in Dwight Morrow. He realized that behind all these conflicts of interest there was a basic misunderstanding of purpose. He realized that the French suspected the United States of wishing to detach Great Britain from her solidarity with Europe, whereas the British had gained the impression that America was opposed to Great Britain's entering into any new guarantees of French security. Morrow was able, with the loyal and in fact courageous assistance of Secretary Stimson, to dispel these illusions. Had the Stimson declaration come earlier, a Five Power Treaty might well have been secured. Even as it was, Morrow succeeded in locating and sterilizing this double centre of infection. It was with this in mind that he was determined by some means or other to get the French back to St. James's Palace.

On March 21st he had a long conversation with Aubert and Massigli. He asked them whether France had in fact "abandoned" the Conference. Supposing that after all the United States Government would agree to a consultative agreement, would there then be no possibility of M. Briand's return? M. Massigli assured him that if "a new situation arose" the French Delegation would resume official contact with the Conference. They might even go further. They might agree to leave the principle of parity open for later discussion and they might offer to lay down no more than 35,000 tons a year for the six years 1931-1936, provided that Italy agreed not to lay down more than 25,000 tons a year during the same period.

Armed with this assurance, Dwight Morrow, with the full approval of his Delegation, decided that Mr. Hoover must be approached again. He spent the whole of that Sunday at Stanmore drafting a detailed cable to the President. Mr. Hoover consented. On March 25th Mr. Stimson notified Mr. Ramsay MacDonald that in spite of his disclaimer of March 11th the United States was prepared to consider a consultative pact provided that it were made clear that any such pact would entail no military commitments in Europe. The Prime Minister contended that his own public opinion would not allow him to enter, even with explicit American approval, into any obligations upon the European continent. It seemed as if the American gesture had been made in vain.

Morrow was not discouraged. With the help of Lord Robert Cecil and Mr. Noel Baker he unearthed a document in which the British Government had already "defined" in comparatively precise terms their obligations under the Covenant. This document was Annex F of the Locarno Treaties by which Sir Austen Chamberlain had explained to Dr. Stresemann the nature of British commitments under Article XVI. He suggested that if the British Government were to reaffirm this previous explanation, the resultant assurance, coupled with the moral support of Mr. Stimson, might induce the French to agree to the modifications of the *statut naval* which M. Massigli had suggested. A committee was appointed to examine this new aspect and to go further into the question of the gap between the Kellogg Pact and Article XVI of the Covenant. This Committee did not, it is true, achieve any formula such as Ramsay MacDonald could accept. But it brought M. Briand back to London. As a result, although the London Naval Treaty was essentially a Three Power Treaty, yet the French and Italians subscribed to the subsidiary instruments and pledged themselves to a further conference between themselves. Thus the Conference culminated in a unity of intention, if not of achievement, between the Five Powers. And the fact that the French were present at the final sessions was due entirely to Morrow's resourcefulness and persistence.

By what means did he accomplish this result?

6

The efficacy of American diplomacy in its relation with European Powers is hampered by circumstances. Some of these circumstances are remediable and some are not. America can never give, and Europe should never expect, that degree of coöperation which would render continuously effective her influence as the greatest Power in the world. Owing to the isolationist tradition of the American people, to say nothing of the right of veto possessed and jealously upheld by the Senate, American action in Europe must always remain tentative, intermittent, and uncertain. At the same time, the missionary spirit of the American people creates in them from time to time a sense of responsibility towards the human race. Both these instincts are admirable and, if properly apprehended, should form a perfectly dependable basis of coöperation between the Old and the New Worlds. The instinct for isolation provides humanity with a whole hemisphere of external quiet. The missionary instinct provides humanity with a wide reservoir of detached idealism. The misfortune is that neither of these two instincts is correctly apprehended by European or American opinion.

In Europe there is an ignorant and indeed foolish tendency to regard the isolationist instinct as selfish and the missionary instinct as self-righteous. In America the tension between the two instincts produces, quite unnecessarily, a mood of self-distrust, expressing itself, sometimes in an unreasoned contempt for all things European, and sometimes in an endeavor to interpret political and even frontier problems in terms of ethical theory. Being conscious of this confusion in popular thought, American negotiators become diffident and as such suspicious. It is a curious fact that, whereas an American business man will with the utmost gullibility invest in the bonds of some small German municipality, even an experienced American statesman is convinced, when he lands in Europe, that he is as a lamb among wolves.

The explanation of the unprecedented influence which Morrow acquired over the diplomatists of Europe was that here at last they found an American who, while remaining wholly representative of his own country, did not proceed from the assumption that the main purpose of British, French, German, and Italian statesmen was to deceive. Morrow was devoid of all feelings of ethical superiority, even as he was devoid of all feelings of intellectual inferiority. Not for one moment did he feel that he was either holier or more ignorant than Briand or Ramsay MacDonald. He understood their point of view as well as they did; he knew the facts of their problems far better than they did; he became for them a work of reference, a powerful assistant, a suggestive companion, a worker of infinite ingenuity, of astounding persistence, and of absolute trustworthiness. "He was," wrote Lord Cecil to Arthur Springer in October 1931, "one of those we looked to for a sound judgment on all international affairs, with the courage and ability to carry that judgment into effect." Only from this angle can one appreciate the pang of despair with which the statesmen and diplomatists of Europe learned that he was dead.

During the rush and clatter of the London Conference Morrow retained his equanimity undisturbed. It was soon realized that the central problem was not one of Anglo-American parity, not even one of Japanese ratios, but whether France could be morally identified with naval disarmament or whether she would leave the Conference in a mood of resentment. It was also realized that the solution of this problem lay in Morrow's hands. All others stepped aside. And the fact that by his persistence he rendered the final sessions of the Conference a demonstration of unity gave him, among those who knew, a reputation such as few Americans have achieved. He was himself wholly unaffected by this prominence. He remained the Dwight Morrow of the Amherst days. He would seize Prime Ministers by their coat lapels and tug at their attention; he would dig Ambassadors in the ribs; he would stand upon the curb of his fireplace, puffing at an unlit pipe, fumbling for matches, losing his eyeglasses, losing his papers, losing his every possession except his possession of the argument. He would interview irate admirals, curling up on the sofa, nursing his little foot, twisting paper spills into his ear, twinkling with brilliance and benignity. None of those who were present at that Conference will ever forget the combination of driving power and lubricant which he supplied.

It was Morrow who, when the Treaty had to be cast in final shape, was appointed chairman of the drafting committee. The material which reached them from the main Conference and the several committees was confused and contradictory. Morrow kept his collaborators working incessantly. Easter Sunday and Easter Monday passed in a flash. When they murmured for luncheon, he would send out for soda and crackers. Sir William Malkin, the British representative on the drafting committee, kept him supplied with box after box of cigarettes. "You see," Morrow explained, "I never carry cigarettes myself. I have promised my wife not to smoke." The draft was completed by the afternoon of Monday, April 21st. It was signed on Tuesday, April 22nd, at 10.30 A.M.

The London Naval Treaty did not achieve all that had at one time been expected. Yet it did exclude, and for ever, the danger of Anglo-American naval rivalry. It did achieve a temporary solution of the Japanese problem. It contained many useful stipulations regarding the humanization of submarine warfare. It did much to clarify confused thinking on such subjects as global tonnage and categories. And it did create a naval holiday in respect of capital ships. It saved Great Britain an expenditure of some £60,000,000, it saved the United States some $500,000,000, and Japan some £13,500,000.

After a difficult negotiation, in which Senator Robinson played a valuable part, the Treaty was ratified by the United States Senate on July 21st; by Great Britain on August 1st; and by Japan on October 2nd. It entered into force on January 1, 1931.

The Treaty also provided for subsequent Franco-Italian negotiations. These negotiations continued throughout the autumn and winter of 1930 and culminated in a basis of agreement in March 1931. The British Government questioned this agreement on the ground that it enabled the French to lay down replacement tonnage in 1935 and 1936 to an extent which, under the Three Power Treaty, was not accorded to Great Britain. Dwight Morrow, who at the time was on his way to Europe, broke his journey in London and was able to explain to Washington the exact nature of the misunderstanding. He was not, however, actually concerned with the subsequent developments of this long-drawn controversy. His essential connection with Naval Disarmament ended when the Three Power Treaty was signed.

XVIII. The Last Year
April 1930–October 1931

ON April 29, 1930, Dwight Morrow returned to Englewood, triumphant but exhausted. He was at once plunged
into his election campaign for the New Jersey primary. His
opponents for the Republican nomination were Senator Frelinghuysen and, two weeks later, Congressman Franklin
Fort. The latter had the support of the Anti-Saloon League
and was known as a personal friend of President Hoover.
It was obvious that the election would be fought mainly
upon the issue of Prohibition.

During Morrow's absence in London his manager, Mr.
Douglas Thomson of Englewood, and his other supporters
(prominent among whom was his young, his brilliant, and
his devoted nephew Richard Scandrett) had been anything
but inactive. They had held many meetings on his behalf;
they had prepared a very flattering biography of the candidate, which was graced with an introduction by ex-Presi-

dent Coolidge; a vast amount of election literature and
photographs had been distributed throughout New Jersey;
and an active organization had been established, with headquarters at Newark.

So abrupt a transition from the intellectual contests of a
world conference to the emotional unrealities of a popular
election filled him with despair. He felt for a moment as
if he had exchanged a hive of bees for a nest of wasps. A
cloud of voluntary supporters buzzed around him tendering
encouragement and advice. Some assured him that it was
essential that he should take a firm stand for the repeal of
Prohibition. Others, and General Charles Dawes among
them, urged that although New Jersey was regarded as a
wet State, the New Jersey Republicans were predominantly
dry; a wet platform would lose him the election and ruin
his future prospects as a public man. He felt harassed, uncertain, and strained.

Within a week he had recovered his composure, although
not his usual high spirits. As always in such predicaments
he cut through the tangle of conflicting expediencies to the
central core of his own convictions. He was not himself a
total abstainer. How could he preach a doctrine which he
had never practiced, which he was not then practicing and
which he would be most unwilling to practice in the future?
During those weeks he worked hard at the problem with
the assistance of George Rublee, Dean Acheson, and others.
"I do not care," he said to them, "whether I am elected or
not. But I do care if I take up a position of which I may be
ashamed in ten years from now." He was then urged to
choose a middle course; if he were determined, against all
advice, to adopt a wet platform, then let him at least refrain
from hazardous extremes; let him stand for the modification

of the Volstead Act, and not incur certain defeat by insisting on repeal of the Eighteenth Amendment. Morrow resisted all such blandishments; he had formed his own conviction as to the principle involved; he refused to hedge.

These struggles between expediency and conviction left him exhausted and discouraged; his spiritual depression during those days is reflected in Mrs. Morrow's diary:

May 13. Dwight is so tired; so discouraged; so *wild* that he has been trapped into this Senatorial campaign. He is exhausted, does not want it, would be glad to lose.

May 14. Dwight is sick with regret that he has ever gone into this thing.

On the following day, Thursday, May 15th, he opened his formal campaign in the Krueger Hall at Newark. His speech was relayed by amplifiers to the seething crowds who struggled for admittance.[1] He began by stating that the whole Prohibition controversy must be approached not in such imprecise terms as "wet" or "dry" but as a problem in government. What had been the experience of the last ten years? Prohibition had worked well in those States in which it corresponded to the feelings of the people. In those States where it was opposed to the feelings of the people, it had not only worked badly, but it had exposed the Federal Government and its agents to demoralization and contempt. Such a situation was obviously an unhealthy situation. How could it be remedied? Not by any modification of the Volstead Act, but by a complete repeal of the Eighteenth Amendment and the substitution of legislation which would restore to the States their power to determine their own

---

[1] A vivid and very critical account of this scene is furnished in Edmund Wilson's admirable work, "American Jitters."

policy in regard to the sale, transport, and consumption of liquor within their borders.

The effect of this pronouncement was startling. Morrow's suggested solution may seem today a very mild proposal for the temporary easement of a situation which had obviously become intolerable. At the time it appeared apocalyptic. And in fact Morrow was the first Federal Government official who had dared openly to condemn the Eighteenth Amendment as unworkable; unequivocally to advocate its repeal; and calmly to suggest a solution which, in the then state of public opinion, appeared both feasible and wise. The speech was greeted with tumultuous applause. Under the heading "Leadership in a Time of Hesitation," the New York *Times* burst into an editorial of almost hysterical eulogy. It spoke of the speech as being "in the highest tradition of political leadership"; it hailed Morrow as "a public man of clear vision and calm courage." "People everywhere," it wrote, "will feel that at last a real leader has come to the front. The honors and distinctions which have already come to him he is willing to use as a sort of elevated position from which to speak words of truth and soberness to all Americans. . . . The watchword has been given. It will be taken up by a vast army happy to follow an inspiring leader."

It must not be supposed that the rapid growth from then onward of Morrow's national importance was due solely to this oration, any more than it was due to the publicity accorded to the early stages of his Mexican mission. It was due to an increasing consciousness in the minds of millions of men and women that here was a man who possessed disinterested qualities of character and intelligence. The nature of the admiration he evoked was defined, after his death, by Walter Lippmann:

380

"Morrow did nothing to promote his popularity; it gathered about him from all quarters and from every station in a kind of deep murmur of implicit confidence and deeply felt need. . . . For by a kind of deep instinct, which is the saving grace of popular government, it was known in this country that in Dwight W. Morrow the American nation had once again bred a public figure of the first magnitude."[2]

On June 7th Morrow was elected as Republican candidate with a plurality over Franklin Fort of more than 300,000 votes. He then returned to Mexico, anxious to complete his task.

2

He reached the Embassy on July 3rd. Mrs. Morrow did not accompany him, having been detained for a few weeks at Englewood by the birth of her first grandchild, Charles A. Lindbergh, Jr., on June 22nd. He was thus deprived, during the distressing weeks that followed, of that love and intelligence, of that high standard of wisdom and fortitude, which for twenty-seven years had formed the inspiration of his genius and the buttress of his strength.

He was lonely and unwell. Since his departure eight months ago a change had come over the Mexican atmosphere. President Portes Gil, the direct inheritor of the Calles tradition, had been succeeded by Señor Ortiz Rubio, who had not experienced the magnetic attraction which Morrow had exercised during those winter months of 1927. The politicians of Mexico City were becoming a little tired of the Morrow legend. True it was that he had been helpful and sympathetic in the early days of his mission, but that period

2 Walter Lippmann in the New York *Herald Tribune,* October 6 and 7, 1931.

was now past. Morrow might well have become an outstanding figure in his own country and in Europe; to the Mexican
ministers he was now no more than a delightful little gentleman who was about to leave. Morrow had returned to his
Cephalonia; the Cephalonian politicians wished him a warm
farewell.

This reaction against him had been increased by an unfortunate incident. On April 23rd, Colonel Alexander Macnab, formerly Military Attaché in Mexico City, was allowed
by organizers of the Morrow campaign to say a few chosen
words to a Newark audience. In his desire to assist his former
chief he spoke of his Mexican achievements in terms which,
although not ill-intentioned, were indiscreet. He described
him as "having put Mexico on her feet and given her a strong
Government." "There is," said Colonel Macnab, "no department of government in Mexico which he has not advised
and directed. He took the Secretary of Finance under his
wing and taught him finance."

A full report of this speech appeared in the Mexican
papers. President Ortiz Rubio and the members of his Cabinet were, in spite of the disclaimers issued by Colonel Macnab, deeply wounded; they determined that on Morrow's
return they would demonstrate their displeasure and their
independence. It happened also that Plutarco Calles, who
might have stemmed the reaction, was at the moment feeling
ruffled owing to an interview published in the American
press by a well-known journalist of the name of Isaac Mar-
cosson. Morrow, in loyalty to Colonel Macnab, deliberately
underestimated the strength of the feeling aroused by the
Colonel's indiscretion. He applied himself to the ungrateful
task of advising the Mexican Cabinet on the eternal but delicate subject of their foreign debt.

It is not necessary, for an understanding of the unhappy controversy which then reached its culmination, to examine the dealings of the Mexican Government with their creditors since 1914,[3] other than to note that there had been a succession of separate agreements with various classes of creditors, foreign and domestic, which it had proved impossible to perform. All that need be borne in mind is that when, on July 3rd, Morrow returned to Mexico, Señor Montes de Oca, who had during two years shown in word and action his accord with Morrow's ideas on the rehabilitation of Mexican finances, was in New York, negotiating still another agreement with Lamont representing only the foreign holders of Mexican bonds; and that between Morrow on the one hand, and Lamont, his former partner, on the other, there existed a profound difference of opinion as to the basic principles of any such exclusive agreement—exclusive, that is, of other classes of Mexican creditors, most important among whom, so far as Morrow's mission to Mexico was concerned, were the individual Americans whose claims had been espoused by the State Department.

[3] Under Díaz and Limantour the Mexican debt, external and internal, which had been accumulating since 1822, was reorganized on a much-reduced scale and gradually refunded. This operation restored Mexican credit to a point which permitted the government to borrow in the world markets at 4¼% (1904 and 1910). After the fall of Díaz, the service of the foreign debt was continued till January 1, 1914, when the Mexican Government defaulted. In 1919 the International Committee of Bankers on Mexico was constituted, under the chairmanship of Thomas W. Lamont of J. P. Morgan & Co., "for the purpose of protecting the holders of securities of the Mexican Republic, and of the various railway systems of Mexico, and, generally, of such other enterprises as have their field of action in Mexico." These securities were held to the extent of about 35% in England, 23% in France, 20% in the United States, and the remainder largely in other European countries. In 1922 Mr. Lamont negotiated with de la Huerta an agreement for partial resumption of the service on the bonded debt of the government and of the railways (which in 1925 was revised by the Lamont-Pani agreement, under which full service was to be resumed in 1928). It was owing to the impossibility of this resumption that Mr. Montes de Oca, in 1927, 1928, and finally in June and July 1930, carried on negotiations with the Committee with a view to arranging modification of the previous agreements.

In Morrow's view, the Mexican Government, after sixteen years of complete or partial defaults on its debts, ought to consider itself insolvent "and should impose on itself the same obligations with reference to its creditors as a court would impose upon an insolvent corporation. . . . I think it in the interest of all creditors (including the bondholders) that Mexico should divide the available surplus on some equitable principle rather than in some wholly haphazard way." The equitable principle which he advocated was that current revenues must first be used to meet current obligations—salaries current or in arrears, bills for services and supplies—and not be earmarked in the interests of any single class of creditors, internal or external, for such a course in regard to old debts while new debts were still being created could not result to the advantage of Mexico, in the restoration of her credit, or in the long run to that of the temporarily favored class of creditors. "I regret," he wrote to Vernon Munroe, "that the International Committee still feels it desirable to have a *contract* rather than to use its great influence with the Mexican Government in the formation of a *program*. In this, however, the International Committee is merely following the same course that is followed by the other creditors. The result is that none of the contracts can be relied upon as effective. . . . The International Committee must realize that its contract can only be kept by the Government's breaking other contracts made by the same authorities to be performed during the same period."

These views were not shared either by the Committee, whose first duty lay to the bondholders, or by Montes de Oca, who was now determined to show that he was independent of Morrow's tutelage. In their opinion, an opinion that could not well be shared by the American Ambassador or the

American State Department, the external bonded debt was the most important of all Mexico's obligations, both in amount and character. It had been secured, in part, by the solemn pledge of certain public revenues, and these revenues were now being collected in substantial excess of the required debt service. Were the International Committee to throw away this opportunity of making another agreement, which might at least result in some temporary payments, they might very well be repudiated by the foreign bondholders whose interests they were supposed to represent. It was obviously impossible for Thomas Lamont to be more Mexican than the Mexicans themselves.

On the afternoon of July 25th an agreement was signed at 23 Wall Street between Thomas Lamont and Montes de Oca, under which the Mexican external debt was scaled down by 763,000,000 pesos, and a new consolidated debt was created secured on the customs revenues. Full service on this debt was not to begin till 1936.

Morrow continued to regard this agreement as inequitable and unwise. He felt that it was unfair to discriminate in favor of foreign bondholders, who were backed by a strong organization, to the disadvantage of the unorganized creditors, internal and external. He also felt that this course might very well result in placing the American State Department, on behalf of American claimants, in the position of a rival creditor to the detriment of the improved diplomatic relations which he had striven so hard to accomplish. He preferred friendly and orderly collaboration by all those at interest, including the Mexican Government, to the system of pressure and favoritism which had characterized the past fifteen years and which had failed to restore stability and credit to Mexican finance. He had never accepted defeat with any readiness; the fact that he had but a few weeks in front of him wherein to remedy the mistakes which had been committed, rendered him less cautious, less tolerant, than was his wont. Painful as it was for him to disagree with so devoted a friend as Thomas Lamont, he determined to continue his efforts to persuade the Mexican Government to delay its ratification of this latest agreement with the bondholders until it could conclude similar agreements with other classes of creditors in order to insure that all would be within the possibilities of the Mexican budget. He had been reading Cromer's "Egypt" with great assiduity; yet whereas Lord Cromer took twenty years to achieve a sound adjustment of Egyptian finances, Dwight Morrow had at his disposal scarcely twenty days.

On August 20th, after oral conferences with Señor Estrada, Minister of Foreign Affairs, and President Ortiz Rubio, he addressed to the latter at his own request a letter enclosing a memorandum prepared by his Naval Attaché, Captain McBride. The memorandum explored the possibilities of a general reorganization of the entire Mexican debt. The letter summed up Morrow's position: "I feel that the policy of dealing with the debt as a whole is the only one which conserves both the interests of Mexico itself and the interests of all her creditors." [4] The view was expressed that the conclusion of the agreement would represent a "repetition of previous errors."

Following the return of Señor Montes de Oca, President Ortiz Rubio found this letter "improper" ("inconveniente"). The Ambassador at once withdrew the letter; the memo-

---

[4] The Lamont-Montes de Oca agreement has not yet been ratified by the Mexican Congress.

MR. AND MRS. DWIGHT MORROW AT CAERNAVACA

randum was not returned. Fifteen days later Dwight Morrow left Mexico City for ever.

This unhappy incident threw a cloud over his last days in the country which he had loved so deeply and for which he had done so much. It did not, however, detract from the value of his achievement. He had shown the Mexican people that an American Ambassador could understand their desires and could assist their aspirations. To this day the name of Morrow is remembered with trust and with affection by the people of Mexico, and even so late as 1935, the street in which he had lived at Cuernavaca has been christened with his name. He had shown the State Department that with tolerance and sympathy something, even in Mexico, could be secured. He had taught professional diplomatists of every country how, by tact and sincerity, knowledge and persistence, even the most vainglorious nationalism can be conciliated. And he had proved to himself that his own system of regarding facts as more important than theories, of preferring credulity to suspicion, was a system which could be justified by concrete results.

Nor did the excitements of the debt controversy leave behind them any personal rancor. Even with Montes de Oca he effected a reconciliation. He left Mexico by the western route and at Mazatlán he stopped his train for an hour and swam out to sea. On returning to shallower waters he was accosted by a little figure in a striped bathing suit. Being without his eyeglasses Morrow did not at first recognize his fellow bather. It was Montes de Oca. There, amid the brown waves of the Pacific Ocean, they made their peace.

On September 30th he reached Washington, where he formally resigned his office as Ambassador. He then returned to Englewood and for a whole week he kept to his bed surrounded by a library of detective novels. By October 8th he felt sufficiently recovered to embark upon his second election campaign. An arduous four weeks ensued. The result was practically a foregone conclusion. On November 4th he was elected by a majority of 200,000 votes. He took the oath as Senator on December 3rd.

3

Dwight Morrow entered the United States Senate on what might be called a double mandate. In the first place he had been elected to fill what remained of the unexpired term of Ambassador Edge, that is, for the short period from December 3, 1930, to March 3, 1931. In the second place he had been elected on a six-year mandate for the term beginning March 4, 1931.

It has already been noticed how sensitive he was to all unfamiliar environments. "I feel," he wrote to Robert de Forest, "like a student setting out to attend a new school." This new-boy feeling was increased, that December term, by the fact that he was the only new boy to arrive. He was conscious also that the enormous publicity which had been aroused by his campaign would not predispose his fellow Senators in his favor. The newspapers had proclaimed with unwelcome reiteration that now at last a man of intelligence, knowledge, and integrity had been elected to the Senate. Morrow realized that in such circumstances it was incumbent on him to display the greatest modesty. "A baby Senator," he would say, "should be seen and not heard."

He occupied an inconspicuous seat, namely, the right-hand seat in the last row; he remained ensconced in that seat

throughout the session, and refrained from parading on the
floor of the House. He refused an invitation to serve upon the
Banking and Currency Committee. His manner throughout
was studious, unassertive, and respectful.

He was confident that in the six years which opened in
front of him he would have time enough to win the sympathy of his fellow Senators and to impose upon them the
precision of his intellect, the force of his knowledge and
experience, the illumination of his vision. For the moment,
he would concentrate upon the task of mastering the initial
problem. He therefore applied himself to an intensive study
of Parliamentary practice in general; and in particular of the
complicated rules which govern the procedure of the United
States Senate. He was determined to rival Joseph G. Cannon
and George W. Norris in his mastery of Congressional rules.
Then and then only would he feel himself at his ease and be
fitted to take an authoritative part in the debates:

"It was," records his chief senatorial secretary, Mr. George
Dye, "a long tedious job for us in the office. He never got
through asking questions. He would follow every rabbit
track. . . . Most men would go to some acknowledged authority
and ask him for advice. Mr. Morrow would not do this. He
would study it until he became an authority and had to ask
nobody. I thought he would never get done with his study of
the rules. He began by wanting to know the present rules. Then
we had to get him all the old rules. Then he wanted a comparison of the previous rules with the old rules. He wanted every
change noted and why it had been made."

No less original was his treatment of patronage. He refused to concern himself with minor patronage, leaving all
post office appointments to his colleague, Senator Kean. He

insisted, however, on being consulted in regard to judicial appointments and took especial pains over the nomination of cadets to West Point and Annapolis. He was particularly scrupulous, moreover, in his handling of correspondence with his constituents. His secretaries would draft replies in the conventional form, "I shall be glad to do all I possibly can for you. . . ." These letters would be returned with the word "properly" substituted for the word "possibly." On one occasion, in reply to a demand for a subscription, Mr. Dye had replied, in the prescribed manner: "I do not feel that I can make a further contribution. . . ." "George," exclaimed Morrow, when the letter was submitted for his signature, "this is wrong, anyway. I *do* feel that I can give them the money they ask for. But I don't want to. Just bear that in mind when you redraft the letter."

Those first months in the Senate were not an enlivening experience either for Morrow or his wife. For her they entailed exile from all she prized most dearly and imposed those social obligations which render Washington a nightmare to all Senatorial wives. In him they created a mood of democratic pessimism. Was this, in fact, the Areopagus of democratic institutions? Were these his colleagues really representative of all that was best in the American idea? With his usual tolerance he refused to criticize; yet the unaccustomed sharpness with which he would suppress any domestic levity on the subject of Senators proved in itself that he was ill at ease. "I find," he wrote to Reuben Clark whom he had suggested be named to succeed him in Mexico, "I find the work in the Senate somewhat puzzling for me. It is very hard for one who has never had any legislative experience to be required to cast several votes a day on subjects which he feels he has not had a chance to study, and as to which debates throw very little light. I wish I might have someone like yourself here with whom to counsel. I am not enjoying it very much. . . ."

The cynical superficiality of Parliamentary work filled him with a profound depression. In a moment of expansion he confided his disillusion to Stanley King. "The life," he said to him, "which you and I have led thus far has completely unfitted us for service in the United States Senate." During those initial months he recorded his vote almost automatically according to party convention. He voted against a motion to curb the privileges of the Power Trusts; he voted against Senator Robinson's proposed dole of $25,000,000 for food relief; he voted against the Soldiers' Bonus bill; he voted in support of the motion for more modern battleships, and he voted against the Frazier amendment providing that no money should be given from War Department funds for military training in schools. In some cases these votes were recorded from a real conviction that the proposed measures were demagogic and therefore unwise. On other cases he was voting mechanically, being confident that once he had mastered the procedure his intrinsic liberalism could speak with more authority. His purpose was to make his first speech in the Senate upon the problem of the unemployment dole—a subject which he had studied for years and to which he then devoted renewed research. He well knew that, by some dramatic gesture, he could revive the almost passionate public interest which had been aroused by his election. He felt, however, that this interest had been artificial and unreal. He had six years in front of him: he was perfectly prepared to lose this artificial reputation, knowing that in the years that followed a more solid and authentic influence could be erected in its place.

For the moment, however, much criticism was aroused. He was attacked by certain journalists for having "spent a lifetime getting a reputation as a great Liberal only to spend three months in the Senate blasting it."

Morrow was not disturbed by such criticisms. He had suffered so much recently from journalistic eulogy that he almost welcomed a little journalistic abuse. He knew very well that he was neither a reactionary nor a radical, but a man who, while believing in the machinery of party government, also believed that correct theory can only be based upon a patient and scholarly appreciation of the facts. He regarded that first lame-duck session of the Senate as a purely formal initiation. He was confident that during the six long years which opened before him he would be able to impose his personality upon the Senate, even as he had imposed it on Amherst, on Columbia Law School, on the New York Bar, on J. P. Morgan & Co., on the A.M.T.C., on General Pershing, on Cuba, on Mexico, and upon the leading statesmen of Europe. He had no desire for any sudden or dramatic Senatorial triumph. He had already mastered the rules of procedure to an extent equaled by only one or two of his colleagues; before the next session he would complete his profound study of unemployment relief; from the intrenched fortress of accurate knowledge he would deploy the mobile cavalry of his mind. Even his domestic surroundings would be solidified; he had selected a pleasant house in Georgetown; his wife would render that house a simple but important centre of social life; that also would be more durable than a transitory sojourn at the Shoreham Hotel.

4

On March 11, 1931, Dwight Morrow, accompanied by his wife and their devoted friend Miss Amey Aldrich, embarked on the *Leviathan* for a holiday in Sicily. A wireless message from Secretary Stimson begged him to break his journey in London and to assist in straightening out a hitch in the Franco-Italian naval conversations which were then being conducted as supplementary to the Naval Treaty.[5] He only remained there five days, renewing contacts with old friends and familiar statistics. By March 23rd he was in Naples and from there they continued their journey to Sicily. While his wife and Miss Aldrich visited Greek temples, Morrow read Thucydides. He was immensely refreshed. On April 15th they were back in Rome. Morrow had paid a short and rather formal visit to Mussolini. "The interview," wrote Mrs. Morrow to her daughter Constance, "did not reach the point where Daddy offered any suggestions as to how to govern Italy!" On April 25th he had a longer and

---

[5] Italy, immediately after the London Conference, embarked upon an increased naval program. The French countered by putting into force their *statut naval*. A six months' naval holiday was arranged and on the expiration of this armistice Ambassador Gibson, and subsequently Mr. Arthur Henderson, endeavored to negotiate a Franco-Italian settlement. Under this arrangement the word "parity" was dropped and the phrase "building programs" substituted. France was to reduce her big cruiser program to the Italian level and in return was allowed two more battleships. A difficulty arose, however, owing to the French claim to replace 66,000 tons of obsolescent battleships before 1936. It was on this point that Morrow was asked to assist. He arrived in London on March 16th and on March 18th was able to telephone to Mr. Stimson to the effect that he had achieved a compromise under which the French had agreed to reduce their replacement program to a figure acceptable to the Italians. He then left for Naples. It was there that he learned that the sudden negotiation of a customs union between Germany and Austria had destroyed all hope of further French concessions to Italy.

more interesting conversation with M. Briand in Paris. By May 5th they had returned to the United States.

By that date the cloud of economic depression had blotted all sunshine from the American sky. Morrow, who had foreseen it all as long ago as 1917, was none the less distressed by the havoc which it created in the fortunes of his friends and neighbors. He tried to steer a middle course between vapid optimism and dispiriting despair. While condemning all those who spoke of "prosperity around the corner," he would cheer his anxious friends by assuring them that the depression would be over "six months before any of you realize it." He well knew that the crisis was inevitable and he believed that it would furnish a fine test of American capacity and character. "The years 1928 and 1929," he said, "were years for caution; the years 1930 and 1931 are years for courage." He was afraid lest the national suffering might lead to hysterical or unscientific legislation:

"I think," he wrote to Charles Burnett on May 7, 1931, "the best way to get rid of business cycles would be to prove that they are inevitable. The easiest way to exaggerate them is to teach that we are in a new economic era, in which a magic formula has been produced which enables men to avoid responsibility for their mistakes."

He dreaded inflation, not so much for its effect upon the banking world as for its demoralizing social consequences. "Bankers," he wrote, "are trained to cope with that sort of thing. It is the social effect which is so dangerous. It transfers the habit of spending from those who have had long experience of spending to those who have had no experience." He was equally suspicious of the extravagant expenditure of national funds: "The State and Municipal Governments," he said, "cannot of themselves bring back prosperity. . . . There is no cure for hard times in the waste of public funds. Waste does not make wealth."

"Most of my friends," he said to Stanley King, "think the world is coming to an end, that is, the world as we know it. I don't think it is. But if it is, there is nothing I can do, so I am not worrying."

Yet he *was* worrying. He would lie awake at night revolving miraculous remedies, picturing the anxieties of his friends, the distress and suffering of one hundred million people. It was no consolation to him that his own private fortune had survived the hurricane almost intact. The whole coast was strewn with the wrecks of what had once been happy little ships. "Charles," he said to his son-in-law during those sombre months, "never let yourself worry. It is bad for the mind."

Nor were these his only preoccupations. Throughout that summer he was summoned incessantly to the White House to confer with President Hoover upon the imminent danger of a collapse of German credit and the disastrous effect of such a calamity upon the $2,500,000,000 which American investors had recklessly poured into Germany since 1924. Morrow was one of the few financial experts of the time who had realized from the first that debts and reparation did not represent "money," whether hired or unhired, but represented goods and services. During the war Europe had been delighted to receive goods from the United States in the shape of war material; after the war, the United States was not in the least inclined to receive goods from Europe; yet it was only in the shape of goods that debts and reparations could eventually be paid. Morrow was aware also of the vicious and artificial circle which had been created, within the orbit of which the American banker lent money to Germany, Germany used that money to pay reparation to the Allies, and the Allies used that reparation to pay their interest on the war debts. He was quick to point out that such a situation meant that in the long run the American investor was paying the American tax-payer and that when once the former ceased to have confidence in German credit, the latter would cease to be paid. Mr. Hoover, being neither a financial expert nor a trained economist, thought only in terms of "money." Moreover, his mind was darkened by an obstinate prejudice against France. Thus although Morrow fully approved of the Hoover moratorium of June 1931, and would in fact have increased it to three or even four years, he did not approve of the announcement of that moratorium without prior consultation with France. He was unable, however, wholly to convince Mr. Hoover of these necessities. As a result, an opportunity for constructive statesmanship was allowed to pass.

So soon, moreover, as it became clear that the Hoover moratorium—largely owing to the fact that French co-operation had not been secured from the outset—was not going to save the situation, Morrow was instrumental in inducing the New York bankers to accept the "Stand-still Agreement" whereby some $600,000,000 of American short-term credits were left frozen in Germany. Morrow was at no time very optimistic regarding this agreement. And in fact it proved a palliative which delayed merely, and did not prevent, the complete, and perhaps salutary, disaster which followed. The abscess, he contended, had developed beyond the help of unguents; the wise doctor should wait until it burst.

from a drawing by Cartotto

DWIGHT MORROW, 1931

5

On July 4, 1931, the whole family gathered at Englewood. It had been their custom, in the days of the old home on Palisade Avenue, to record on a panel in the dining room the dates of such reunions. This panel had been preserved when the house was demolished and was inserted in the new dining room at Next Day Hill. "All the family and only the family," records Mrs. Morrow in her diary. "I wonder when that will happen again?" Underneath this entry the word "Never" has been inserted.

Three days later they moved to their island farm at North Haven, Maine. On July 29th their daughter and son-in-law left on their flight to the Far East. During the next three months Morrow was summoned four times to Washington. He returned to North Haven "in high spirits" on August 28th.

He would sit on the little terrace at Deacon Brown's Point looking across that island-studded sea to the blue outlines of the Camden Hills, but it was impossible to make him rest. He was deep in the study of unemployment relief, buried in statistics, overwhelmed with the official publications of England, Germany, and France. Nor were these his only occupations. His nephew, Richard Scandrett, arrived at Deacon Brown's Point to find him in anxious discussion with the members of the local council advising them how to balance their next year's budget. To such small matters he would devote the full energy of his mind. He would approach them with what his children called his "Oh-let-us-be-thorough" manner.

On September 10th Mr. Roy Howard anchored in his

yacht off North Haven. He invited the Morrows to luncheon. During the course of that luncheon Dwight Morrow had a slight seizure and for some two minutes he remained paralyzed in the right arm and leg. The doctors were summoned and diagnosed a vascular spasm. On the next day he seemed to be completely recovered.

On September 19th they returned to Englewood. On September 30th he gave a farewell dinner to Arthur Schoenfeld, his former Counselor at the Embassy in Mexico, who had just been appointed Minister to Santo Domingo. Speeches were exchanged and for an hour or so his memory was gladdened by the sunshine and triumphs of his happiest Mexican days. On Thursday, October 1st, he left for Washington. For the next twenty-four hours he was in constant consultation with Secretary Stimson regarding the approaching negotiations with the Laval Mission. He telephoned to Paris, inquiring what experts would accompany M. Laval and was delighted to hear that his old friend, M. Aubert, would be coming. Secretary Stimson asked whether he would be willing to head the United States Delegation to the Disarmament Conference of 1932. Morrow accepted this invitation with small enthusiasm. He agreed with Hugh Gibson that Europe was not ready for any such experiment. On Friday, October 2nd, he dined with Secretary Stimson and then took the night train back to New York. He shared a drawing room with Mr. John Marshall. The latter has left a record of that last journey:

"He seemed rather tired, but pleased with what Secretary Stimson had said to him, namely, that he wanted him to head the American Delegation to the Disarmament Conference at Geneva and that the Secretary wished to make an immediate announcement 'since it would have a beneficial effect on the rest of the world.' He seemed to find satisfaction in the thought that his appointment would give reassurance on the other side of the water. He said more than once, 'John, that was a compliment, wasn't it?' I asked him if he would like to go and he said, 'No! I had hoped they would send Borah.' He had also been discussing the impending negotiations with the Laval Mission. He was glad to learn that two of his own friends were coming with the French Prime Minister. He said to me, 'You know, John, there are always people who do the work and what ought to be found out in a matter of this sort is who they are.'

"In the morning I said to him, 'Mr. Morrow, did you sleep?' He said, 'Not very well; I kept waking up thinking what a hell of a mess the world is in.' Getting off the train that morning he was in high spirits and a bit annoyed at having dressed in his Tuxedo rather than in his business suit, but he joked with the train employees and when we were almost out of the train he wanted to go back and show me the new type of passenger coach being used by people who travel by rail but are unable to afford Pullman accommodations. He explained to me how much more comfortable they are than the old type. I assumed he was recalling his own experience."

From New York he drove out to Englewood. That afternoon he held a reception at his house in honor of Senator Baird. He stood for several hours shaking hands with six thousand people. In the evening he dined with the Bergen County Committee and was accorded an enthusiastic ovation. The morning of Sunday, October 4th, was spent in interviewing callers and in the afternoon he and Mrs. Morrow drove to the White Stadium and reviewed F Company of the 104th Engineers. That night he had consented to speak at a dinner given at the Commodore Hotel, New York, in support of Jewish philanthropic societies. He dressed early and bade a gay good night to his wife and eldest daughter.

They listened afterwards to his speech on the radio. He spoke on the nature of human charity.

When he returned to Englewood the house was in darkness. During the early morning he had a cerebral hemorrhage. He died, without recovering consciousness, in the afternoon of Monday, October 5th.

INDEX

Abbott, Lawrence, 114
Acheson, Dean, 378
Adams, Charles F., 357
Aguinaldo, Emilio, 65
Aircraft Inquiry, 280-286
Aldrich, Amey, 293, 393
Aldrich, Chester, 290
Alexander, A. V., 359, 362
Allardyce, Sir William, 187, 259
Allied Maritime Transport Council, 204-220
Allegheny, 9
Alvarez, General, 313
American Gas and Electric Company, 96
American Locomotive Company, 96
Amherst College:
    D. W. M. enters, 20
    Description of, 21, 22
    D. W. M.'s devotion to, 22-25
    As an influence in D. W. M.'s life, 49, 51
    Backus controversy, 113-115
    D. W. M. Life Trustee, 248
    Meiklejohn controversy, 248-257
Anderson, Arthur M., 168, 169
Andrews, Charles, 41
Anglo-French Loan, 1915, 173
Armistice, The, 222, 223
Asquith, H. H., 164
Atherton, Ray, 358
Attolico, Professor B. D., 206, 211, 215
Aubert, Louis, 367, 370, 398

Backus, Grosvenor, 108, 112, 114, 115
Baird, David, 351, 352, 353, 399
Baker, George F., 153, 155
Baker, Newton D., 217
Baker, Philip Noel, 371
Bankers Association Speech, 191
Banking System in U. S. A., 140-141
Banks, Septimus, 54
Barker, Professor Ernest, 249
Barnes, Harry Elmer, 196
Barnes, Henry B., 63, 64
Barton, Bruce, 270
Baruch, Bernard, 216
Bayne, Colonel, 16, 17
Beaverbrook, Lord, 247
Belgian Stabilization Loan, 1926, 279
Bérenger, Henry, 279
Beveridge, Senator, 65
Bingham, Senator Hiram, 282

Birch, Stephen, 102, 149, 315
Blackett, Sir Basil, 179, 201
Blockade, British War, 184, 185
Bliss, Cornelius N., 57, 112
Bliss, Mrs. Cornelius N., 112
Bogart, Professor E. L., 179 note
Boncour, Paul, 360, 362
Borah, Senator, 399
Brady Will Case, 278 note
Brandeis, Justice, 216
Briand, Aristide, 228, 336, 358, 361, 362, 366, 368, 369, 370, 371, 373, 394
Bryan, William J., 47, 64, 65, 193
Burke, Alfred, 313
Burke, Father John J., 342
Burnett, Charles T., 33, 44, 45, 48, 49, 67, 73, 76; letters to, 43, 44, 45, 46, 47, 68, 81, 90, 119, 132, 394
Butler, Anthony, 300
Byington, Margaret, 113

Caillaux, Joseph, 279
Calles, Plutarco Elias, 304, 308, 309, 312, 313-318, 319, 320, 329, 330, 332, 335, 339, 340, 342, 343, 344, 345, 347, 381, 382
"Calvo Clause," the, 327, 332, 334
Cannon, Henry W., 96
Cannon, Joseph G., 389
Carranza, President, 302, 303
Case, George, 128
Cecil, Viscount, 215, 231, 371, 373
Central Colorado Power Company, 96
Cephalonia, the roads of, 138, 382
Chamberlain, Sir Austen, 371
Chicago Convention, 233, 234
Clark, J. Reuben, 322, 326 note, 390
Claudel, Paul, 279
Clémentel, Étienne, 205, 215, 220
Clews, Henry, Jr., 27
Cochran, Thomas, 153, 154, 156, 229, 232, 233
Coffin, C. A., 96
Coffin, Howard E., 282
Columbia Law School, 53-58, 94, 292
Comert, Pierre, 223
Coolidge, Calvin:
    D. W. M.'s first meeting with, 28
    As a classmate, 33, 34
    His early opinion of D. W. M., 34, 35

Coolidge, Calvin (*cont.*)
His theory of ambition, 87
On D. W. M. joining Morgan's, 131
His loyalty to D. W. M., 135, 267-269, 287, 348
D. W. M.'s support of, 229-234
D. W. M.'s attempts to educate, 230, 231
D. W. M.'s views on, 232, 233, 269, 270, 349
Letter to, on Meiklejohn controversy, 255
Becomes President, 267
Appoints D. W. M. to Aircraft Board, 280-281
Offers him Mexican Embassy, 289
Views on public service, 291
Views on Mexican policy, 306, 313, 314
At Havana Conference, 333
On public speaking, 353
His introduction to D. W. M.'s biography, 378
"Coolidge Conference" on disarmament, 354 note
Cotton, Joseph P., 69, 213 note, 216, 228, 324, 351
Cowans, Sir John, 218
Cravath, Paul D., 188, 218, 219
Crespi, Silvio, 215
Cromer, Lord, 386
Crowder, General Enoch H., 264
Cuba, D. W. M.'s connection with, 260-266
Cuernavaca, 337-338, 347
Curtis, George William, 193
Curtis, Lionel, 294 note
Curzon, Lord, 273
Cutter, Miss Annie Spencer, 72
Cutter, Miss Edith (Mrs. Sheldon Yates), 72
Cutter, Elizabeth Reeve, see Morrow, Mrs. Dwight W.

Davis, Fred, 337
Davis, Professor Joseph S., 244
Davis, Peter, 32
Davison, Henry P., 110, 111, 125, 130, 138, 149, 165, 166, 168, 169, 170, 172, 173, 176, 188, 227
Dawes, General Charles G., 175, 218, 273, 357, 378
Dawes Loan, the, 276, 277
Dawes Report, the, 273
Dawson, Allan, 322 note

Debt settlements, D. W. M.'s views on, 280
de Forest, Johnston, 56, 57
de Forest, Robert W., 56, 58, 77, 132, 388
Denison, Judge Arthur C., 282
Díaz, Archbishop, 345
Díaz, Porfirio, 300 and note, 301, 302, 313, 315, 340, 383
Dickinson, Elijah, 22
Dickinson, Emily, 22
Dickson, William B., 195, 196
Drummond, Sir Eric, 246
du Pont, General T. Coleman, 96, 97, 98, 154, 155
du Pont, Pierre, 156, 157
Durand, William F., 282
Durant, William C., 151, 156, 157
Dye, George, 389, 390

Edge, Walter E., 196, 199, 351, 388
Electric Bond and Share Co., 96, 99, 122
Electrical Securities Co., 96
Ellershaw, General Wilfrid, 179 and note
Englewood, N. J., 79, 80, 81, 82, 83, 110, 111, 112, 113, 227, 397, 398
Equitable Life Assurance Society, 151-155
Equitable Office Building Corporation, 96, 97, 98
Erie Railroad, 148
Escobar, General, 344
Estrada, Genaro, 336, 386

Fay, Charles J., 62, 63, 64, 68, 69, 70, 139, 288
Field, Henry P., 116
Fitschen, Mrs., 112
Fletcher, Rear Admiral Frank F., 282
Fleuriau, Aimé de, 358, 367
Foley, George, 105
Fort, Franklin, 377, 381
Foster, Dr., 122
Frelinghuysen, Senator, 377
Frost, Robert, 34 note, 267

Garman, Professor Charles E., 36, 37, 76, 117
Gelabert, Secretary, 264
General Electric, 99, 125
George, David Lloyd, 172, 173, 176, 204, 236
Germany and U. S. opinion, 185, 186
Gibbons, Professor Henry, 20, 26

INDEX

Morrow, Dwight Whitney—*Biography*
(*cont.*)
Early years in college, 25-35
Record of college achievement, 29, 30
Friendship with Charles Burnett, 33
Influence of Professors Olds, Garman and Morse, 37, 38
Class orator, 40, 41
Return to Pittsburgh, 42-48
Homesickness for the East, 43-45
Columbia Law School, 42-58
Reed, Simpson, Thacher and Barnum, 58
Rises in salary, 62
Studies income tax problem, 66, 67
Engagement and marriage, 69-83
Honeymoon, 76-77
Settles in Englewood, 79-83
As a corporation lawyer, 87, 91, 92, 93, 94, 97, 99, 100, 101, 102
Becomes partner in Simpson, Thacher and Bartlett, 95
His increasing income, 83, 105, 258
Visits Europe, 106-109
Englewood friends and activities, 110-113
Involved in Backus controversy, 113-115
Early interest in politics, 117-121
Attack of pneumonia, 122
Invited to join J. P. Morgan and Co., 125
Hesitation to do so, 126-136
Enters 23 Wall Street, 136
Initial depression, 137-139
As a banker, 140-144
Odd jobs at 23 Wall Street, 145-157
Domestic atmosphere, 158-163
Outbreak of war, 164-171
New Jersey penal system, 194-199
Director of National War Savings, N. J., 199-202
Employed on A. M. T. C., 204-220
At American headquarters, 217, 218
Awarded D. S. M., 218
Prophecies at time of armistice, 223
Charitable work and donations, 225, 258
Honorary degrees, 226
Coolidge campaign, 229-234
Chicago Convention, 233
Interested in League of Nations, 238-241
Work on European reconstruction, 241-245

Morrow, Dwight Whitney—*Biography*
(*cont.*)
Statistical survey of France, 244, 245
Offered presidency of Yale, 246-248
Deals with Meiklejohn controversy, 248-257
Deals with Cuban reconstruction, 260-266
Relations with Coolidge, 267-273
Candidate for post of Agent General, 274, 275
Contacts with foreign statesmen, 279
Chairman of Aircraft Board, 281-287
Suggested as Secretary of the Treasury, 287
Offered and accepts Mexican Embassy, 288-293
Mexico: First stage, 294-320; second stage, 321-347; third stage, 381-388
Significance of his work in Mexico, 294-296, 297
Relations with Calles, 315-318, 336
Presents letters of credence, 316
Accompanies Calles on northern tour, 318-320
Deals with oil problem, 325-333
At Havana Conference, 333, 342
Deals with agrarian problem, 334, 335
Discovers and falls in love with Cuernavaca, 337, 338
Deals with Church problem, 338-347
His views on Calles' reëlection, 344
His life threatened, 347 note
Relations with Herbert Hoover, 348-350
Suggested as Secretary of State, 350
Nominated as Senator, 353
At London Naval Conference, 353-376
His influence on Europeans, 373
New Jersey primary campaign, 377
Prohibition issue and Newark speech, 378-391
Return to Mexico, 381, 382
Deals with debt question, 383-388
Leaves Mexico, 387
Elected Senator, 388
In the Senate, 388-392
Sicilian journey, 393
Assists President Hoover in Reparation problem, 396, 397
Lasts days and death, 397-400

INDEX

Thacher, Thomas, 94
Thacher, Thomas D., 93, 94, 135, 288
Thomson, Douglas, 377
Toynbee, Arnold, 294 note, 338

United States:
  And Cuba, 260-262
  Foreign policy of, 185-193, 260-261,
    296-299, 372-373
  And Latin America, 296-299
  And Mexico, 304-309
  And the shipping crisis of 1917, 209,
    210
  Trade balances, 1914-1916, 171,
    172
United States, *public opinion regard-
ing:*
  Corporation lawyers, 88
  Cuba, 260-262
  Imperialism, 65
  Mexico, 304-309
  Naval disarmament, 356, 357
  Neutrality and intervention, 185-193
  Wall Street, 134
  War, outbreak of, 164, 165
Utah Power and Light Company, 99-
  102, 123

Van Horne, Dr., 80
Villa, Francisco, 303

Vinson, Carl, 282
Viviani, René, 244

Wakatsuki, Reijiro, 359
Walker, Miss Fanny, 14
War, outbreak of, 164-165
War Savings Committee, New Jersey,
  199-202
Washington Conference, 354 note, 359,
  364
Weddell, Alexander, 322 note
Weddell, Mrs. Alexander, 313
"White Horse," ballad of the, 292
White, William Allen, 64
Whitman, Judge, 114
Whitney, George, 156
Williams, Benjamin, 358
Wilson, Edmund, 379 note
Wilson, Henry Lane, 300
Wilson, Woodrow, 118, 185, 192, 204,
  205, 229, 237, 238, 240, 298, 305
Winslow, Alan F., 322 note
Woodbridge, Professor F. J. E., 253
Wright, Orville, 283

Yale, presidency of, 246
Young, Owen D., 52, 273, 275 note

Zapata, 302, 303
Zayas, President, 262, 263

Nicolson, *Hon.* **Harold George,** 1886–1968.
  Dwight Morrow, by Harold Nicolson ...   New York,
Harcourt, Brace and comapny [ᶜ1935]

  xvi p., 2 l., 3–409 p.   front., ports., facsim.   22 cm.

  "First edition."

  1. Morrow, Dwight Whitney, 1873–1931.